A History of the Toledo Jewish Community 1895 - 2006

A Rich Tapestry of Historical Information

David M. Noel

A project of the Toledo Jewish Historical Society
of Jewish Federation of Greater Toledo

"IT IS NOT INCUMBENT UPON YOU TO COMPLETE THE WORK, BUT NEITHER ARE YOU AT LIBERTY TO DESIST FROM IT."

Pirkei Avot [Ethics of the Fathers, from the Talmud]

"Be careful what you wish for!" Ask Marvin Jacobs, Erwin Katz and Stanford Odesky the meaning of this simple admonition. Nearly fifteen years ago, all three independently had an epiphany. Proud — and prominent — lifelong residents of Toledo, each envisioned compiling a permanent history of the strong Jewish community in Toledo that goes back nearly 200 years!

Beginning with their collective memories, they formed a Toledo Jewish Historical Society, ("TJHS") composed of over 30 prominent Jewish citizens to help them turn dream into reality. In this age of exploding digital technology, VHS tapes had recently become available in the public marketplace. How wonderful to be able to capture the actual faces as well as voices of local Jews whose entire lives documented the history of Jewish life in a midwestern American mid-size city (c. 300,000). They conducted 50 plus oral histories over a five year period, 2001-2006.

Having discovered an earlier Ph.D. dissertation at The University of Toledo, submitted by Elaine S. Anderson, entitled "The Jews of Toledo 1845-1895," the TJHS was inspired to hire a professional author to continue that history from 1895 to the present. The end result was "A History of the Toledo Jewish Community, 1895-2006."

With a grant from the Jewish Federation of Greater Toledo, well-known local author and director of local history at the Toledo-Lucas County Public Library, David Noel, accepted the challenge of producing a comprehensive book utilizing all available resources, including both documentation and interviews with leaders of Jewish community organizations and synagogues. In 2008, Noel completed his manuscript. The Federation reproduced it in newspaper form and distributed it widely.

Now for the "rest of the story." Regarding completion of the gargantuan undertaking, as stated in *Introductory Message to the Toledo Jewish Community* by Odesky, Jacobs and Katz, "Little did any of us or those we recruited anticipate the time involved ... In addition, copies will also be hardbound and made available to libraries and history groups."

So it is for us to "complete the work." The 2008 newsprint edition of Noel's history is herein reproduced without any substantive change. Only those typos and misspellings of which we are aware have been corrected.

Those persons absolutely indispensable for the completion of our project include:

Arleen Levine (my months long motivator and helpmate): Arleen, you even donned jeans on a particularly sultry summer's day to search the Federation's hot, dusty attic in search of the oral history tapes, which had been missing for nearly 8 years! When you excitedly called to tell me you had found a box full of VHS tapes and cassettes in the attic, I knew this project was "beshert!"

Paul Causman: Your amazing technical and graphic design skills were indispensable in converting the newsprint version to publication-ready digital form.

Mark Jacobs (son of Marvin): for his assistance with the transformation of the digitized version of David Noel's book into a more permanent form.

Joel Marcovitch and the Federation staff: Thanks for your willingness to cooperate in any way possible, despite any personal inconvenience.

Most importantly, **Marvin Jacobs, Erwin Katz, and Stanford Odesky**: Your foresight, flawless sense of timing, and years of hard, dedicated primary research through priceless preserved testimony of over 50 individuals, many of them no longer with us, are what created a true, multi-generational history of Toledo's Jewish community. Your contributions have been incalculable. We hope the production of a hardbound edition of "The History of the Toledo Jewish Community 1895-2006" gives you the satisfaction you so richly deserve.

Thank you for the honor and privilege of spearheading this important preservation effort, from which none of us is "at liberty to desist."

L'Dor V'ador!
Lynn Balshone Jacobs

November 2015

A History of the Toledo Jewish Community 1895 - 2006 was generously funded by a grant from the Toledo Jewish Community Foundation.

Contents

Author's Preface

Introduction

This history hopes to do two things: First, it wishes to interest and inform the reader, preferably as a pleasant experience. Second, it seeks to preserve and present the history of the Toledo Jewish community for current and future generations. It does not try to be exhaustively inclusive and it is not. Rather, it attempts to be one place where a reader can go to gain an overview, to complement some personal memories in readers and to suggest other sources for further learning.

People like history because it is usually interesting, frequently instructive and sometimes even inspiring. It is also selective. Random circumstances and premeditated actions jointly select what materials are preserved. Pure chance and a wide variety of conditions affect what is later reviewed. Personal interests and human decisions influence the final version of a new historical account. All those factors played a role in this history. For my own errors of commission and omission in this whole process, I apologize. Ultimately, I am grateful to have been allowed to add to the region's local history resources and to learn more about Toledo's Jewish community.

This is the third substantial history of the local Jewish community. Elaine Anderson wrote The Jews of Toledo, 1845 - 1895 in 1974 as her doctoral dissertation at the University of Toledo. Susan Hughes wrote The Growth and Development of the Jewish Community Center in Toledo, Ohio 1906 – 1976 in 1987 as a graduate project at Bowling Green State University. Both have been invaluable resources for this current history.

Acknowledgments

While I was a child, my parents reminded me to say "thank you" when someone gave me something. I remember that training and I sincerely wish to say "thank you" to many people who gave me so much in one way or another regarding this project.

To Elaine Anderson and Susan Hughes, authors of the two

previous histories of the local Jewish community, thank you for the historical background and context you provided.

To all the members of the steering committee for this project, who showed commendable commitment during some six years, donated hours to the review of earlier drafts and individually offered many useful suggestions, thank you so much.

To the three co-chairs of the steering committee, Marvin Jacobs, Erwin Katz and Stanford Odesky, for your countless occasions of individual and collective counsel and support, my deepest personal thanks for the opportunity to be involved in this project.

To all other members of the Toledo Jewish community, who assisted with interview, artifacts, responses to questions and general interest and support, thank you for making it clear that this history deserved to be written and for making it better because of your personal involvement.

To those individuals at the United Jewish Council who played important roles at critical times in the project, thus helping it proceed from concept to finished publication, Joel Beren, Paul Causman, Robin Estrin, Arleen Levine and Chris Ullom, thank you for your professional assistance and personal thoughtfulness.

To James Marshall and Michael Lora, managers of the Local History and Genealogy Department of the Toledo-Lucas County Public Library during my period of research, and to each of the department reference staff members, each of whom tirelessly provided a wide variety of resource materials and so ably exemplified the indispensable benefit of a community's local history collection, thank you so much from one of your former colleagues.

Last in order but not in importance, to my wife Adrienne, who has lived with this project nearly as much as I have, and who has given unrelenting encouragement, and to all my family and close friends who have also expressed interest and listened to me talk about this project over the years, thank you for sticking it out and doing so with genuine friendship.

Bibliographic note

One of the real values of this history, I hope, is that it can serve as a beginning point for others to do additional research. Just as I greatly benefited from the earlier work of others, I wish to be as helpful as possible for future researchers. Thus, I have used footnotes extensively to identify sources. The footnotes also serve as a bibliography by including a full citation of the source the first time it is used. Subsequent citations are in briefer form. Many of the newspaper citations include the notation "clipping, n. p. [no page number]." The vast majority of these clippings are located in the history scrapbooks of the Local History and Genealogy Department, Toledo-Lucas County Public Library. The remaining clippings came from a variety of helpful sources and will be deposited in the United Jewish Council archives. All other primary and secondary source items will be returned to the persons who loaned them for the project or deposited in the U. J. C. archives. This project has produced a very valuable collateral benefit: a collection of several dozen videotaped interviews with members of the local Jewish community. The tapes were very helpful to this history and remain yet to be more fully tapped by future researchers who can mine the rich memories recorded on those tapes. They are in the U. J. C. archives as well.

David M. Noel
May 2008

Toledo Jewish Historical Society Members

Chairmen
Marvin K. Jacobs
Erwin D. Katz
Stanford H. Odesky

Committee

Eli C. Abramson	David Perlman
Alice Applebaum	Sharon Rainwasser
Albert Brookenthal	Lawrence Rayman
Melvin Conn	Arnold and Marlene Remer
James L. Eppstein	William Rosenberg
Eden Feldstein	Seymour D. Rothman
Irwin and Carol Friedman	Alfred H. Samborn
Philip Gaines	Marikay Schwartz
George M. Glasser	Donald L. Solomon
Jay S. Glassman	Donald Steinberg
Harry Goldman	Bernard Treuhaft
Marcia Hess	Roy Treuhaft
Marshall Isenberg	Nemo Wexler
Bob Lubell	Nadalynne Weisberg
Harry I. Nistel	Leon M. Williams

Cover Photo: standing left to right, Minnie Remer, Henry Remer, Bertha Leibovich;
sitting left to right, Gittel Leibovich, Jake Leibovich, Bertha's friend.

Toledo Jewish Community Members,

Over a decade ago, three of us independently had the idea of making sure an updated history of Toledo's Jewish community was completed. The three of us met and planned an approach covering the identification and recruitment of individuals who had knowledge and interest in assisting in the project, possible funding sources and potential authors to write the text. Little did any of us or those we recruited anticipate the time involved.

The initial ideas were modified and revised over the years to design this document, "A History of the Toledo Jewish Community 1895-2006" and to make it available to everyone on the UJC mailing list. In addition, copies will also be hard bound and made available to libraries and history groups.

Our author, David Noel, in his introduction and acknowledgements correctly thanks those who deserve to be recognized. David's efforts deserve our special recognition and thanks for his tremendous effort in pulling together the breadth of detail and presenting in such an interesting manner the enormous amount of information, research and personal stories that make this history so interesting.

Please take special recognition of the community members who provided information, research, direction and input over the many years of developing this history.

Finally our thanks go to the UJC personnel who have provided counsel, funding, design assistance and distribution for this task.

Some items may need enhancing and or inclusion in future updates. Please forward any thoughts and/or details you have along those lines c/o Toledo Historical Society at UJC.

Read and enjoy!
Stan Odesky
Erwin Katz
Marvin Jacobs

Chapter One
Neighborhoods

Introduction

This chapter tries to provide a foundation for a history of the Toledo Jewish community by tracing immigration waves coming here, the demographic characteristics of the community and its settlement patterns. It also gives examples of the business activities that supported daily life, provided the resources for the community's various religious, social, cultural and philanthropic activities and helped connect the Jewish community to the greater Toledo society.

Immigration

The history of Jews in Toledo, Ohio begins elsewhere. The original threads of the Toledo Jewish tapestry lead back to Europe and need to be traced from the Old World so that the New World experience can be more fully appreciated. Immigration from various European regions is one of several commonalities that members of the first generation of Toledo Jews shared with each other; they shared it with the later waves of immigrants also. Virtually every Jewish family in Toledo has some awareness of "where they came from" in a geographic sense. Dr. Elaine Anderson's research and anecdotal evidence gained through interviews for this history show a strong and direct relationship between the national immigration patterns and the Toledo Jewish experience.[1]

The Jewish migration to what would become the United States began in 1654 with the arrival of twenty-three Jews in New Amsterdam (later New York City), refugees from Portuguese hostility in colonial Brazil. By 1775 the Jewish population in the American colonies numbered between 1,000 and 2,500.[2]

To truly appreciate the wave of humanity that flowed westward from Europe, consider these numbers: The story of Jewish immigration from Europe to the United States in the 19th century had one strong and simple trend: once begun, the stream of migrants continuously grew larger for about a century. In 1820, an (inexact) estimate placed Jewish numbers at 3,000. Twenty years later the total grew to 15,000. By 1860, the growth was tenfold, to 150,000. The first "official" census of American Jews in 1877 cited a total of 250,000. By 1897 the total Jewish population in the United States numbered 940,000, nearly a four-fold increase from the 230,000 recorded just seventeen years earlier. This growth rate was nearly fifteen times larger than the nation's growth rate overall and four times higher than the non-Jewish immigration rate to America.[3]

Furthermore, this massive tide came from many areas of the Jewish Diaspora. As early as the 1830 U. S. Census, Jews gave England, Holland, Germany, Poland, France, the West Indies, Ireland, Hungary, Bohemia and Morocco as the places of their respective births.

However, the numbers of émigrés from each of these areas varied greatly in totals. Most Jews who came to the United States from the mid-1820s to the mid-1870s were from Central Europe. These groups, predominantly from what is now western Germany (then called Bavaria and West Prussia) and the region of Posnan in eastern Germany (then Prussian territory) numbered in the scores of thousands. In contrast, only about 7,000 Jews from Eastern Europe had settled in America by 1870.[4]

Generally, these Jewish settlers in the New World were "young, single and poor." About 30 percent of them, however, came with their wives and children. A more recent study has shown many of them not to be "poorest of the poor," but rather "lower middle class" Jews.[5]

With some concept of the numbers of this immigration, what accounted for such a movement? There were two inter-related sets of factors. One set pushed the Jews from Europe and some of these forces applied to both Jews and gentiles. Periodic regional famines due to weather, crop diseases and poor agricultural practices were a major pressure to seek more food elsewhere. Discontent with political conditions, especially after widespread anti-government revolts in 1848 and subsequent official repression, was a second factor. Villages, home to generations of Jews and gentiles alike, were being depopulated and sometimes dislocated due to growing urbanization. Industrialization and its characteristic of mass production negated the need for some skills and trades (albeit also offering opportunities for persons willing to learn new ones). In addition to these conditions that affected Jews and gentiles, Jews also faced official restrictions on where they could live, trades they could practice and, in some lands, even whether they could marry.[6]

A second set of factors pulled the migrants to the New World, most strongly to the United States. Perhaps economic opportunity, largely free of government restrictions, exerted the strongest force to stimulate migration. Closely related to economic potential was the nation's growing need for many of the trades and skills the immigrants possessed or were willing to acquire.

Not to be discounted, of course, was the relatively greater toleration towards Jews; though not totally absent to be sure, anti-Semitism was less in the U. S. and not largely based on government fiat.[7] European anti-Semitism played an even greater role in the later decades of the 19th century and was especially harsh in Eastern Europe due to governmental sponsorship there, which helps explain the sharp increase in immigration from those regions in that period.[8]

Immigration to America involved two opposite beliefs within the Jewish community. On the positive side, centuries of past Jewish migration clearly proved that "Judaism was portable," capable of being moved from its historical home and taking root elsewhere. Migration to the United States was only the most recent example of such geographic adaptability.

The second, more negative, concern about Jewish immigration to America was the fear in the mind of some, especially leaders of Jewish communities in Europe, that the less-restricted and more opportunistic-laden environment of the United States would seduce Jews from practicing their faith or even preserving their cultural identity. To combat this potential threat, Jews remaining in Europe would prepare special blessings and admonitions for those Jews relocating to the New World, especially if an entire family household was moving.

One interesting example comes from Cleveland, and it is easy to imagine a similar instance for Toledo-bound Jews: Moses and Yetta Alsbacher came to Cleveland from Germany in 1839. Their religious teacher, Lazarus Kohn, presented them with an "ethical testament" that included a Hebrew blessing: "May God send His angel before you / May no ill befall you / In all your ways know Him / And he [sic] will make your paths straight." The document also included the names of all the Jews from the couple's hometown with the "fervent wish" that future generations be read these names so that the couple's Old World roots would be remembered.[9]

Toledo's own Rabbi Leon Feuer clearly identified with this concern. One hundred and thirty years after the Albachers settled in Ohio, Rabbi Feuer wrote in his autobiography, "Jews being particularly sensitive to social change, Jewish life has been profoundly affected. In the United States, the danger of attrition through assimilation is very real. Yet, it would seem to me that the rabbi's primary task is to struggle against that eventuality."[10]

A fitting conclusion to this view of Jewish immigration comes in the form of a letter from Jewish immigrant Aaron Phillips to his parents still living in Bavaria: "How on earth is it possible to live under a government, where you can not even enjoy the simple privileges that correspond to a human being. . . . Here [in America] we are all the same, all the religions are honored and respected and have the same rights. An Israelite with talent who does well, can like many others achieve the highest honors . . . . America the promised land, the free and glad America has all my heart's desire. . . . Dear parents, if only the Israelites knew how well you can live in this country, no one really would live in Germany any longer."[11]

His parents were probably grateful to hear such a positive report. Such letters had a further impact as well. Family members and friends circulated them and sometimes newspapers in the migrants' respective hometowns printed them, thus enabling the praise for America to influence an even wider audience[12].

Immigration to Toledo

Jewish movement edged closer to Toledo with the arrival of one Joseph Jonas, an English Jew and watchmaker, in Cincinnati, Ohio in 1817. In 1824 the eleven Jews then living in Cincinnati formed the first Jewish congregation in what was regarded as the nation's "West" at the time. A second Ohio congregation appeared at Cleveland in 1839 and by the time of the Civil War, formal congregations existed in Akron, Circleville, Columbus, Dayton, Elyria, Hamilton, Piqua and Portsmouth.[13]

The first Jews most probably reached Toledo in the late 1850s, coming either north from Cincinnati along the Miami and Erie Canal or from Cleveland via Lake Erie. Confirming this probability is a reporter's reference in an 1857 issue of *The Occident and American Jewish Advocate* magazine: "Though there are Israelites [in Toledo], no attempt had been made . . . to organize a congregation." The journalist had been sent throughout the Midwest to determine the presence and size of Jewish settlements. [14]

His observation supports two points. First, there were Jews living in Toledo at the time, not just passing through to other destinations. Second, they were concentrating on making a living and caring for a family (which might have been in Toledo also or still living at a former resident city), not forming a congregation as yet. Since their numbers were so vague, but undoubtedly few, perhaps they lacked the required quorum of ten males to form a *minyan*, the nucleus of a congregation.

By 1870 one estimate put Toledo's Jewish population at seventy families.[15] Four years earlier, the first local congregation, B'nai Israel, had been formally incorporated in 1866. Dr. Elaine Anderson found mention in an issue of *The Israelite* for 1874 that some Toledo Jews were trying to form the city's second congregation, one based on Reform doctrine.

Toledo's Jewish population experienced great relative growth in the next two decades. By 1895 the predominantly German immigration (both Jewish and gentile) was virtually over and an Eastern European migration (both Jewish and gentile) was well underway. One of the early Polish Jews who heralded the later great influx was Alies S. Cohen, born in Warsaw in 1842 and living in Toledo by 1866, active in the clothing trades. More Eastern European Jews came in the 1870s and 1880s and settled in the north side Jewish neighborhood.[16] The first Russian Jews (either from Russia or from then-Russian controlled Polish territory) in Toledo arrived in the early 1880s.[17]

Toledo Jewish Community Demographics in 1895

Historian Anderson provided an excellent demographic description of Toledo's Jewish community in 1895. Based on a detailed analysis of the city directory for that year, she estimated "The Jewish population of Toledo in 1895 probably exceeded 1500 people, between 1 and 2 per cent of the total population of the city and environs. This figure is based on 575 Jewish names in the city directory for 1895 and using the multiplier of 2 1/2 which the directory compilers employed in that year to arrive at a city-wide population of 122,760." The total of 575 names included 453 males and 122 females.[18]

She included many noteworthy statistics about the males. Examples included the following: Only thirty-five were listed as unemployed, which would have included retired males. Nine men were identified as students, including two currently at the University of Michigan. Of the employed men, fifty-one were peddlers, forty-four were clerks, fifteen were tailors, twenty-six made cigars, thirty-two were listed as 'traveling agent,' four worked as 'cutters' in a garment factory, five were barbers, three were shoemakers and sixteen were classed as 'laborers.' Overall, 266 men (64.5%) worked for others while the remaining 35.5% were self-employed or members of firms. Of the self-employed, most were in the fields of clothing (manufacturers, wholesalers, retailers), wines and liquors, or the production and sale of cigars. There was the beginning of a professional class as well: three rabbis, one school principal, one teacher, five physicians and three attorneys were listed in the 1895 city directory.

Dr. Anderson also detailed statistics about the women. Seventy-one of the 122 females were listed as unemployed, with twenty-two identified as widows. "The remaining forty-nine were undoubtedly unmarried daughters or sisters living at home. Married women's names did not appear in the directory if their husbands were living. Five women were listed as students with no indication of whether they were in college, in a business school, or what kind of training they were taking." Among the forty-nine who worked outside the home, seventeen (the largest single category) worked as clerks or 'shop girls' for such firms as Lasalle and Koch, Lamsons, The Lion Store, Toledo Laundry, W. L. Milner, Eaton and Co. and others. The next largest group worked in the garment trade: four as dressmakers, two as milliners and one as a finisher. Four were educators (one principal – Adele Dallet at Junction School – and three teachers). Three were bookkeepers and two were packers for Woolson Spice. Individuals worked as stenographer, cashier, boxmaker, cook, domestic and the society editor of a local newspaper. Seven owned and/or managed businesses, sometimes having taken over from their husbands: a cigar store, a dry goods store, a music store, a news depot and three clothing stores.

Neighborhoods – Late 19th Century to WW II

The story of Toledo's Jewish neighborhoods from the 1890s to the present shows an evolutionary process, with households moving gradually from one district to another over time. Yet, the inhabitants were well aware of the process as it occurred and, in fact, adjusted to it as a community. *(Photo 1 J.E.L. Building 1912-1953, page 89)*

Once Jews arrived in Toledo in the late 19th century or early 20th century, where did they settle? Following the pattern of virtually all other immigrant groups, they sought to live with others who shared their beliefs, culture and, in some cases, geographic background. In Toledo, that meant they primarily settled from Summit Street to Seventeenth Street, with the core being the Canton Avenue – Woodruff Avenue area just north of the downtown business district.[19]

The initial Jewish neighborhood was pretty clearly defined. Its residents included many, but by no means all, Toledo Jews who had arrived earlier. Bakeries, delicatessens, kosher butcher and poultry shops, the *shokhet* (ritual slaughterer) and other businesses, many of them Jewish-owned and/or operated, catering to Jewish preferences or requirements were concentrated in the district. *(Photo 2 Sam Davis, Co., page 89)*

At the turn of the century, Jews operated a number of small businesses that helped form the retail infrastructure of the local Jewish community, especially its neighborhood. Among those businesses were ". . . a shoe store, two crockery stores, two furniture stores, a hotel, a notion[s] business, a preparer of toiletries, a hide business, a retail wallpaper store, a dry cleaner, four jewelry stores, five meat markets, two drug stores, a fruit market, a milk distributorship, six saloons, six grocery stores, one real estate office and two pawnbroker-loan establishments."[20]

This inclusion of businesses within the neighborhood was practical and common among immigrant groups. As Jewish historian Jonathan Sarna summarized it, ". . . Jews tended to hire and patronize other Jews, thereby transforming the faith and ancestry that anti-Semites considered a liability into a productive asset. The result may be characterized as a Jewish 'sub-economy,' linking employments, employees, consumers, and suppliers in one commercial web. Through their purchases of goods and services, Jews helped to sustain one another."[21]

"As the prosperity of the First World War and then of the twenties affected Jews throughout the United States, they moved from their area of first settlement to new city districts. . ."[22] The local manifestation of that national trend meant that the initial Jewish quarter expanded west (beyond Franklin Avenue, crossing Collingwood and into the Old West End) and north (past E. Bancroft, passing Winthrop and Machen, and lapping over Central Avenue), with some growth northeast of Cherry Street, overlapping a Polish neighborhood also. (figs. 3, 4 & 5, page 90)

This neighborhood expansion can be traced through its major buildings. B'nai Israel congregation had built its first real home at 1902 Union Street, now North 12th Street in 1889. The group worshipped there as the community grew until it built a new and much larger synagogue at North 12th and E. Bancroft streets in 1913. A B'nai Jacob shul joined the neighborhood in 1902 at 936 North 12th Street (corner of Union, now State, Street).[23] The building of the new Sharei Zedeck synagogue at 2102 Mulberry Street (corner of Moore Street) in 1925 indicated the expansion of the Jewish population to the northeast. The last Orthodox congregation for the district was Anshai Sfard, which began worship in the early 20th century at Canton and Woodruff and in 1915 moved to a new shul at Canton and Scott streets.

Another unmistakable sign that the surrounding quarter included many Jews was the 1912 opening of the Jewish Educational League building, the first Jewish Community Center, at the northeast corner of Southard Street and Linwood Avenue. Placement in the heart of the Jewish neighborhood was logical and essential if the Center's many activities were to be easily accessible to adults and youngsters.

In contrast, and as a reminder that not all Toledo Jews lived in just one area, in 1889 local Reform Jews built their Temple on Tenth Street, corner of Washington Street. Congregation Shomer Emunim remained there until 1907, when it relocated to Scottwood Avenue (which reflected the Jewish move into the Old West End).

Neighborhoods – Post-WW II into the 21st Century

For the latter half of the 20th century, ". . . the Jewish communities of America were made up rapidly emptying areas of first settlement (inner cities), rapidly growing areas of second settlement (middle-class apartment houses, two-family and single-family houses) and areas of third settlement (expensive apartment houses-area or suburban developments of single-family houses."[24] This is an accurate summary of Toledo's situation, which is detailed below.

Confirming the migration process of the preceding twenty-five years, a 1944 population census estimated 6,100 Jews in Toledo, divided among slightly more than 2,000 households.[25] Some 1,238 of these households (62%) were located in a triangle formed by Cherry Street, Detroit Avenue and Woodruff Avenue.[26] That is, an area encompassing the original settlement district on the north edge of the downtown plus its early 20th century spread west and north.

As with the development of the older Jewish quarter, the movement of synagogues tracked the demographic action. The Reform Temple of Congregation Shomer Emunim moved into the Old West End on Scottwood Avenue in 1907 and ten years later moved a short distance to Collingwood Boulevard (and larger quarters). B'nai Jacob moved from the old neighborhood to Parkwood Avenue in 1950.

Also following a precedent from four decades earlier, the Jewish Community Center also relocated from Linwood and Southard to Collingwood. A study began in 1949 subsequently concluded that a new site farther to the west would attract more support from the Jewish community, in part due to its location vis-à-vis where most Toledo Jews were then living. The new J. C. C. building opened in 1953.[27]

The second aspect of Jewish settlement in this period involved a smaller percentage of Jews who moved even further west, ranging widely over the suburbs of Old Orchard, Ottawa Hills and adjacent developments. Within just five years of the 1944 population study mentioned above, the number of Jewish households in the Detroit-Cherry-Woodruff triangle declined by 149 (12%). For the same time period, the number of Jewish households in Old Orchard increased by 86 (59%) and households in Ottawa Hills increased by sixty (41%). Neatly, the 149 households lost from the older district were virtually matched by 146 households gained in the other two districts.[28]

As noted in the earlier section, businesses, especially small retail operations, were a vital and integral part of the Jewish neighborhood. Given the rich resources available in city directories and the many videotaped interviews collected as research for this history project, it seemed useful to revisit several of the residential neighborhoods, especially as seen through their businesses.

Neighborhood Businesses: Canton Avenue – E. Bancroft Street

Canton Avenue had developed as the original neighborhood's business corridor. It remained the site of many Jewish businesses until well after World War II. Two members of Toledo's Jewish community, Marvin Jacobs and Erwin Katz, recalled that scene, so familiar to them and many others, in a joint video interview in 2003.[29] With supplementary information from other community members and Toledo city directories of the period, a part of a neighborhood familiar to many can be recalled.[30] *(Photo 6, page 91, 1937 Canton Ave)*

This hypothetical neighborhood "journey" can begin at Samuel and Eva Malkin's poultry store at 2053 Canton Avenue. "They sold live chickens," Marvin said in the interview. Erwin added that women would take a live chicken from one of the coops in front of the store, turn it over on its back and blow on its feathers to separate them in order to see if the bird was plump enough. "If it had lots of *schmaltz* [fat], that was a good bird," he recalled. Once a buyer had made a choice, the bird would be taken to 2047 Canton, the "Kosher Chicken Slaughter House" (according to the 1951 city directory) where the *shokhet* (ritual slaughterer) would kill the animal with one stroke across its neck, thus making the bird kosher and edible. The carcass was then placed in one of several cone-shaped devices so the blood could drain out and be properly disposed of, as the Torah commands. Women in the rear of the store then removed the feathers, including using a large gas flame to burn off the pin feathers. Once the homemaker had taken the chicken home, the organs would be removed according to ritual. But, if one of the organs appeared to be abnormal, the bird would have to be taken to Rabbi Nehemiah Katz's house. The rabbi would inspect it and decide if the chicken was still kosher. If it was not, it could not be eaten in a Jewish household. Such buying trips were usually on Thursday, in preparation for Friday.

Around the corner of Canton, going along Beacon Street to 12th, Joseph and Dorothy Stark Applebaum operated Joe's Food Center and Joe's Bar through the decades of the 1930s, 1940s and 1950s.[31] *(Photo 7, page 91, Kosher market on Canton Avenue)*

Proceeding further down the street, there was a small shop that sold Judaica, such as *kippot* (or *yarmulkes* in Yiddish) or *yartzeit* candles (which were lighted to honor the deceased on the anniversary of the death).

Siegel's Kosher Market was at 2029 Canton, near to the corner of Scott Street. On the northeast corner of Canton and Scott was Anshai Sfard synagogue. *(Photo 8, page 91, Siegle's)*

Abraham Goodman's Bakery stood at 2013. "Their rye bread was wonderful," recalled Marvin. They also had a branch store on E. Bancroft Street. Charles Cannon's print shop was close by at 2007-2009. He also operated a Gulf gas station on the corner of Canton and E. Woodruff. Erwin remembered being told that that was "where the Licavoli gang kept their cars." At 1950 Canton, corner of E. Woodruff, stood Samuel and Frieda Schuster's delicatessen, the grandparents of E. J. Leizerman.[32]

Further south at 1905 Canton, closer to Southard, was Feldman's Bakeries, Inc., Samuel Swartzberg, manager, which sold directly to retail customers and also wholesale to many local restaurants. The bakery featured a distinct "Pullman loaf," quite long and square in shape, and used a horse-drawn wagon for home delivery. After 7 p.m. on Sundays, one could get a fresh loaf of bread at the store. There was also a store on E. Bancroft Street.

Nearing the intersection of State, the Ideal Laundry & Dry Cleaning Company stood at 1930 – 1940 Canton, Leslie Thal, president, and Preston Thal, vice president.

Solomon and Pauline Flaum's Market was at 1927 Canton. It was later Sid Bauer's grocery and subsequently was razed for a Child Study Institute parking lot.

Then, following WW I, as the Jewish population grew and expanded west and north, so did the neighborhood businesses, primarily along E. Bancroft and into the Franklin-Ashland area.

Neighborhood Businesses: E. Bancroft Street -- Franklin Avenue

The Whirligig Nite Club at 222 E. Bancroft, corner of N. 14th Street, was part-way between the Canton Avenue corridor and the E. Bancroft venue.

Walking west on E. Bancroft from Linwood Avenue, one would encounter Harry Kupperman's butcher shop at 118 E. Bancroft, the first of several kosher meat markets that served the neighborhood. Like all the other neighborhood butcher shops, it had a distinctive aroma, due in part to the fresh sawdust spread daily on the floor. At the corner of E. Bancroft and Vermont (102 E. Bancroft) was the Bell Drug store, operated by Tip Klein. Crossing Vermont and continuing west, at 22 was the M & R 5¢ to $1, also known as Marcel's (after owner Marcel Kaufman). Next door at 18 was Frederick Villhauer's Meat Market, notable for being not a Jewish-owned business.

At 16 E. Bancroft was a branch of Goodman's Bakery. Rye bread sold for 15 cents a loaf and when it was sliced for the customer, kids could grab the newly sliced heels to eat. Erwin Katz tried to save a nickel whenever he could so that he could buy an éclair there.

In the next block at 8 E. Bancroft was George and Jennie Etigson's beauty shop, Jews who had moved from Canada. A Kroger storefront at number 6 came next. When Kroger's later moved out, the Schwartz brothers moved in from across the street and operated a grocery in the same building called S & S Food Market No. 1. On the corner of Bancroft and Franklin was Abe Newmark's Sohio gas station.

A neighborhood fire station stood on the south-west corner. Its doors used to open on Bancroft, though now the doors open on Franklin. During the Great Depression, it was a distribution point for relief coupons and food. Moving west on Bancroft, one came to Siegel's Market, which moved here from Canton Avenue in the 1950s.

Nathan Levey's bar was on the northeast corner, 1 – 3 E. Bancroft. Neighborhood residents played cards and shuffleboard upstairs. A place of treats of another sort was at 2216 Franklin Avenue a few doors from Levey's: Franklin Ice Cream. It left pleasant memories. Marvin Jacobs recalled malts there, always served with a wrapped package of two small cookies, "really nice." Erwin remembered that customers could buy ice cream scoops in glasses and his family then used those glasses for juice glasses at home. With that supply and with the *yartzeit* glasses (glasses which could hold candles that were lighted on the anniversary date of a loved one's death) at home, his mother didn't have to buy other glasses for a long time.

Philip Kaminsky's Fish Market was at 9 E. Bancroft. It was the place for neighborhood Jewish women to shop for fish to make *gefiltefisch*. Marvin recalled seeing clerks slice the lox right off the fresh salmon. "It was a wonderful place, always kept clean and neat. It was where everyone shopped for fish,"

Feldman's bakery had a branch outlet next door. Ed Warren had his plumbing shop next and then came Ted's barber shop, about a four or five chair operation. Another kosher meat market, Harry Yaffee's, was at 15 E. Bancroft. The city directory listed the Fong Lee Chinese laundry at 23. The Paul Adams (actually "Adamides") barber shop at 25 completed the line up as Vermont Avenue intersected.

Across Vermont at 101 – 103 was Oscar Budrow's deli and above the deli was the office of Dr. Siegel and Dr. Phil Katz, who subsequently specialized in anesthesiology. By 1951 Hyman Posner's deli was operating in the building. Mrs. Claire Simons' Beauty Shop was next to Budrow's at number 105.

Virtually nothing except a very few buildings dating from this period still exist. Government-funded urban renewal programs leveled nearly all of these blocks for new housing complexes. Two of the largest are Beacon Place along Canton and Woodruff Village along E. Woodruff.

Neighborhood Businesses: Ashland Avenue – Fulton Street

Three groceries in this neighborhood did a big home delivery business: William Weinstein and Samuel Weinstein ran the Prescott Quality Market at 2119 Ashland, at Prescott, and then at Bancroft and Franklin. They also had stores at 2119 Dorr and 1840 W. Bancroft. Herbert and Esther Felker's Market was on Ashland, between Bancroft and Floyd. Abraham Greenberg and his brother Nathan operated the Ashland Market at 2107-2109. Ashland.

Rose Naftalin's Rose Food Shop at 2204 Ashland was a well-known establishment. Marvin Jacobs remembered that Rose's ". . . had elegant [items], the best baked goods of anyone. She had mousse cakes, strawberry cakes [as a specialty]." She later relocated to Portland, Oregon and wrote several recipe books.

Harry Maza had Maza Drugs at 2553 Cherry, almost across from Central Catholic. The same Maza had a partnership in M & M Drugs at Madison and Michigan downtown. Also on Cherry, at 2222, Irving and Marian Odesky opened Odesky's Sweet Shop in 1945 and it soon became popular for neighborhood residents as well as convenient for people calling on patients at St. Vincent's Hospital across the street or who worked at the medical center.

At 2484 Fulton, corner of Delaware, Harry Gottesman and Max Jaffe operated the Modern Kosher Butcher Shop. Close by at 2482 Fulton, Nate "Red" Goodman operated a grocery store. Daniel Steingroot, who had clerked at Prescott Quality Foods in 1936, later bought and operated the former Goodman store with his wife Ruth.

Gustave Wexler ran the Wexler Sports Center & Grill at 1301 Yates; by the 1960s it became Wexler's Grill and Carry Out. Joseph Nemo Wexler was the proprietor of the Collingwood Bowl-O-Drome, 2525 Collingwood, between Delaware and Melrose.

Neighborhood Businesses:

Near South End

Just as all Jews did not live within the precincts described above, neither did all Jewish businesses operate there. Small stores, sometimes called "mom and pop" stores, were also south of downtown. Erwin Katz, whose parents, Harry and Dora, operated "Harry's Market" at Norwood and Wells, explained that the small markets were a relatively easy business to get into, in part because limited initial capital investment was needed. If the couple worked well together, "they could make a nice living."

Sol Jacobs began as a clerk at Miller's Butcher Shop and after saving his money for a while, he and his wife Mollie opened a shop on City Park, later on John R at 15th (with Harry Walensky) and then moved the "Busy Bee Market" to 239 Pinewood and 15th (where the Expressway interchange is now). During the Depression, he accepted City of Toledo-issued script from his customers, but later had to sue the city to get cash reimbursement for the script.

Down John R from the Jacobs market was Nathan Berenson's store at 239 Avondale. Sol Bauer and his wife Esther ran a store at 399 Nebraska, at Division; later he had a wholesale meat and poultry business on Superior Street. His son, Sid, bought Flaum's on Canton and his brother Frank had a store on City Park and Belmont. Abraham, Frank and Harold Bauer had the B & B grocery at 397 Nebraska.

Molly Kagan and her husband David bought Long's Market on Washington, about a block from the Jacobs store. The Shamy family also had a market on Washington, just a few doors down, the same family that later operated a furniture and antiques store and one son went into the heating-ventilation-air conditioning business. Charles Perlman, father of Jose Perlman and Dave Perlman's brother, operated Tripp's Market at 302 Avondale. Up at 2511 Collingwood, Milton and Rose Kalniz had the Market Basket. Morris Greenberg operated the G & W Market at 2231 Monroe Street, where Monroe, Oakwood and Collingwood intersected.

Then there was the Judis family store. Thelma, the mother, was a widow and lived with her family in the back of the store at 735 Oakwood, where Glenwood dead ends into Oakwood. Gustave and Edith Wexler (another Gustave not associated with Gustave Wexler's Sports Center & Grill) lived on Islington and operated the Star Food Market at 1602 Lawrence, by Norwood.

Downtown Businesses

The Jewish neighborhoods enjoyed a great range of retail businesses for local residents, but Jews did not do all their shopping there, anymore than residents of other Toledo neighborhoods did all theirs within walking distance of their homes. Until the rise of suburban shopping centers and later malls, all Toledoans did some of their shopping "downtown," and spent many of their entertainment dollars there as well. Government buildings and many lawyers' chambers were also in the central business district. It was everyone's shared neighborhood. It included a number of Jewish owned and operated business also, selling to both Jews and gentiles, and Erwin Katz and Marvin Jacobs' joint recollections also help recall that aspect of Jewish Toledo. *Photo 9, page 92, Gross Electric*

A downtown anchor store, and one anchored in the memories of many Toledoans in the first half of the 20th century, was Tiedtke's on Summit Street. Gentile brothers Charles and Ernest Tiedtke started it in the late 19th century. The store occupied several different downtown sites before ending up at its most famous location, the east side of Summit Street, at the foot of Adams Street. The Kobacker family of Columbus bought the store in the 1920s and the father and son team of Jerome and Marvin moved to Toledo to manage the store and several other businesses. Right across from Tiedtke's was the Fair Store, which the Kobackers operated as well, selling mainly home furnishings.

Another major downtown department store was Lasalle and Koch The partnership of Jacob Lasalle and Joseph Koch started in the 19th century when the two German immigrants combined their dry goods expertise gained with other Jewish merchants in Toledo and elsewhere. In 1917 they built their third and most impressive store at the corner of Adams and Huron. Marvin Jacobs, whose law office was next door in the Spitzer Building for thirty years, recalled it as "very elegant," and its convenient connection to the Spitzer Arcade enabled pedestrians to walk, and shop, from Madison to Adams entirely indoors.

There were a couple of smaller clothing stores. Morris Palman had his ladies apparel shop in the Spitzer Building Arcade. Webber's Clothing House was at 401 - 411 Monroe, corner of St. Clair. The 1951 city directory listed Bernard Lempert as president and Julius Yeager as vice president. Erwin Katz remembered buying his Bar Mitzah suit there in the 1940s, when the selection was sparse due to the war.

On one corner of Michigan and Madison was Samuel Shwartz' Pharmacy, one of several he operated. On another corner of that intersection Harry Sherman and Harry Maza ran M & M Drug, 901 Madison, which was open 24 hours a day.

The Valentine Theatre at 409 St. Clair had become part of the Loew's nationwide chain by mid-century and Abe Ludacer was the manager, usually dressed in a tuxedo for show times, a familiar sight to the thousands of Toledoans attending the first-run films there.

Readers seeking out-of-town newspapers visited the sidewalk news stand of Joseph Hirsch, which opened in 1911. The following year it moved outside the Boody House hotel at St. Clair and Madison and his sons Morris and William joined the business as they came of age. Late in 1941 it occupied a storefront at 319 St. Clair, with Morris' son Gordon making it a three-generation operation. In 1959 it relocated to 614 Adams Street and in the late 1960s shifted emphasis from newspapers/magazines to books. The store closed when Morris retired in 1981.[33]

In 1967 Leo's Book and Wine Shop filled the out-of-town newspaper and magazine niche when Leo Yourist opened his small store in the 300 block of Superior Street. Six years later he moved into a 5,000 square feet site in the same block and it now occupies its third site across the street and operates under the ownership of Leo's son, Daryl, and his grandson, Brian, works in the store. To fill another niche, Daryl launched Academi-Text at the store as well, which sells medical, scientific computer and business materials to a nationwide clientele.[34]

Several prominent jewelry stores fit into the story. Leo and Mollie Marks' was at 508 Adams across from the Morrow Nut Shop (509 ½ Adams). In 1948 Dan Silverblatt and Chester Yaney operated their jewelry firm, called "Dan-Chester," at 235 St. Clair Street. Aaron Dolgin's store was originally at 707 Adams, a few doors from Erie Street. Much later it relocated to Monroe Street, just west of Talmadge Road. Originally Lewis Osterman and Ruby Levy operated their store at 404 Summit and later Osterman's was at the corner of Adams and St. Clair before being sold to the Zales chain.

Restaurants and delicatessens were a well-known category. Harry, Emanuel, Sidney and Lilly Levison originally opened Eppes Essen at 416 Superior Street, behind B. R. Baker's clothing store. During WW II, soldiers wearing their uniforms received free meals.

In this time period, Hy Posner moved his deli from near the University of Toledo to Adams Street, between Erie and Huron streets. Zimmerman's Restaurant at 436 Huron was run by Isabel Greunke and Wanda Mitchell according to the 1951 city directory. Pictures of show business celebrities who had played in Toledo and had eaten at Zimmerman's lined the walls. Kable's Restaurant, on Madison, was a favorite memory of Erwin Katz, whose father took him there for breakfast after they bought produce at the Farmers' Market for his father's grocery.

There were some specialty stores as well. Harry Himmelhoch had Harry's Auto Store at 713 Adams, between Erie and Ontario, as well as six other sites in 1948. Max and Sarah Tavel's gift shop at 420 - 422 Superior, between Adams and Jackson, sold upscale lamps and others accessories. Ferdinand Roth's fur store was at 232 N. Erie Street and son Philip still operates at that location. Irving and Selma Shore owned and operated the Beauticians Products Company and the Academy of Beauty Culture at 333 St. Clair Street.

The legal profession is represented elsewhere in this history, but one downtown firm which supported the work of lawyers and others participating in the court system was the Phil Gaines Reporting Service. He moved to Toledo from Cleveland to manage a court reporting office his Cleveland employer had acquired in the early 1960s. Then about 1972 he opened his own reporting firm and since has specialized in taking depositions and, more recently, has added video recording to the process in lieu of live testimony, especially when medical doctors are involved.

Local and Regional Businesses

While most of the preceding section has covered retail businesses, it is also reasonable to include a brief review of several other business sectors that exhibited a major Jewish presence during some or all of the period covered and some of whom had operations that reached beyond Toledo.

(Photo 10, page 92, Toledo Window Cleaning Company)

Local and Regional Businesses: Building Maintenance

The bulk of Jewish immigrants had the good fortune to come to Toledo during the city's most prolonged boom period, from the Civil War to the Great Depression. Many commercial and institutional buildings were erected during this period and they provided a market for building maintenance services. In about 1908 or 1909 Leopold Rendely, believed to be Jewish, founded Toledo Window Cleaning Company. Then in 1935 brothers Joseph and Samuel Friedman, immigrants originally from Kharastkov in the Ukraine, bought a half interest in the Toledo firm from Aetna Window Cleaning of Cleveland. The brothers were already owners of a similar firm in Grand Rapids, Michigan, but Joseph subsequently relocated to Toledo to operate the local business. Hyman Gloger of Toledo owned the other half of the firm until the Friedmans soon bought his interest. Eventually Joseph and Sam traded their interests in their two businesses, leaving Joseph sole owner of the Toledo operation. Joseph's son Joel followed his father in the business and expanded it and his sons Larry and Bruce are now making it a third generation firm.[35]

Local and Regional Businesses: Electrical Contracting

Jack and Max Romanoff (coincidently not brothers, just friends with identical surnames) were immigrants from Russia to Cleveland, Ohio, where they worked as electricians before relocating to Toledo in 1926 and 1927, respectively. They established Romanoff Electric Company in 1927 and began to compile an impressive record of contracting work on many of the community's commercial and industrial buildings, as well as the Anthony Wayne bridge. Alvin Lobert, cousin of Jack Romanoff and son-in-law to Max Romanoff, led the company in the 1960s and into the 1970s. In 1969 Noel Romanoff, son of Max, joined the management team, following the family tradition of first gaining field experience as a journeyman electrician, foreman and superintendent. He became president and CEO in 1977 upon Alvin Lobert's retirement, withdrew from active company involvement in 2000 and died in 2001. At the time of the firm's 60th anniversary celebration, two of Noel's children – Matthew and Cyndi- were working for the company, making it a third generation firm. In 1981, Honda awarded Romanoff a $10 million-plus contract for the entire electrical infrastructure in its new auto assembly plant in Marysville, Ohio, besting fourteen other competing firms. The company later received other Honda contracts, which helped make it the 19th largest electrical contractor in the country in the late 1980s and by 2002 it had $38 million in annual sales. The company was sold to Encompass Services Corporation of Houston, Texas in 1998. Encompass sold the firm in 2002 and it still operates in the Toledo market.[36]

Local and Regional Businesses: Produce

Metzger Produce was the largest wholesale produce dealer in the city for several decades. Richard Metzger recalled that in 1914 his father, Siegfried, stopped in Toledo to visit a cousin as part of a longer journey to California to see another cousin. Instead of traveling on, he stayed and worked for the Toledo relative until he began a produce partnership, Crane and Metzger, in 1923. In 1936 the S. Metzger Company was organized, with its original store on Main Street. By the time Richard joined the firm in 1949 following graduation from The Ohio State University, the company had moved to its downtown location. As a wholesale-only operation, Metzger's primarily provided produce that could not be grown locally, shipments coming mostly from California. At one time, fourteen trucks distributed Metzger produce, while some other operators of the 525 grocery outlets in the greater Toledo community came to the store. Customers included "mom and pop" neighborhood stores, independent grocers and Kroger and A&P warehouses. Richard Metzger closed the firm in 1995 and retired.[37]

The Sam Okun Produce Company illustrates the evolution of a business. The story began in 1917 when Sam and Rose Okun lived on Canton Avenue, next to Congregation Anshai Sfard. (Sam, four sisters and their parents had moved to Toledo after his sister Fanny had already settled here and wrote to the rest of the family then in New York City that Toledo was "a nice place to do business and raise a family.") Just across Scott Street they operated a wholesale and retail store selling smoked fish, herring, dairy products, pickles in the barrel and other assorted food items. Before long, Sam along with son Max, entered the trucking business, with a single vehicle. One of his largest customers came to be the Gendron Wheel Company, a national manufacturer of bicycles and other wheeled machines. As his trips for Gendron took him west to Chicago and east to New York, he sought cargo for his return journey. As the most profitable commodities were seasonal fruits and vegetables, the Sam Okun Produce Company was born in 1920. Once the produce was back in the city, he sold to small independent grocery stores, initially from a market stall on Cherry near Summit, moving to12 N. Huron in the 1920s and then across the street to 33 N. Huron in 1946, the firm's present location.[38] Max's sons, Donald, Fred and Larry, followed their father into the business, each serving as president in turn. Members of the family's fourth generation are now working in the company's operation.[39]

Local and Regional Businesses: Scrap Recycling and Steel

The Jewish scrap business is an ancient trade. A Jewish website in San Francisco credits a Jew from Syria winning the contract to remove the iron skeleton and bronze outer covering of the Colossus of Rhodes, one of the Seven Wonders of the Ancient World, following its collapse after an earthquake in 226 B. C.. According to legend, the fallen debris had laid about for some 800 years since its collapse, still amazing people who came to see the pieces of the statue, which had towered two-thirds the height of the Statue of Liberty. When Arabs conquered the island of Rhodes in 654 A. D. they hired a Jewish scrap dealer to remove the estimated 18,000 pounds of iron and 30,000 pounds of bronze. He used camels (one account says 90 beasts and another says 900).[40]

More locally, the scrap industry became a clearly identifiable business sector from around the turn of the 19th into the 20th century. Circumstances in Toledo and other U. S. urban areas favored the growth of the scrap business then. The evolving industrial age, especially iron and steel production, called for more and more scrap to add to raw commodities for smelting. This increasing demand raised the value of combing both rural and metropolitan areas for suitable scrap metals. The increased manufacture of metal products fed the cycle as well for previously built items were discarded and thus became prime material for gathering into the expanding scrap collecting network. Eventually, re-sold and discarded automobiles became a major percentage of all scrap.

At the same time, increasing numbers of immigrants, including many Jews, were settling in urban areas, looking for work. The scrap business needed very little investment – a push cart would do initially, later a horse and wagon, and eventually a small truck – and each dealer could be his own entrepreneur, thus avoiding some of the discrimination and drawbacks that came with working in gentile establishments. Toledo Jewish peddlers moved throughout both the city itself and the surrounding rural areas, exchanging or selling a wide variety of merchandise their customers wanted for an equally varied assortment of scrap items. This pattern was duplicated in a number of urban areas around the nation and thus created networks centered on major cities that collected metallic scrap and funneled it to central collection points for processing and re-sale. By 1936 a *Fortune* magazine article estimated that nationally 90% of scrap industry owners were Jewish. A Cleveland scrap dealer joked that "Attending a trade organization conference was like going to B'nai B'rith."[41]

Among Toledo's early scrap dealers was Joseph Kasle, who passed away in 2000, age 107. Born in the then Russian-controlled portion of modern Poland, he left his family in 1910 to escape conscription into the Russian army and immigrated to the United States, joining his older brother Sam. By 1912 the brothers were in Toledo and they organized Kasle Iron & Metal Company, on Elm Street near Champlain. In 1920 the firm moved to Lagrange Street and today the site is below the Buckeye Basin Greenbelt Parkway. In 1945 the brothers and Chester Tuschman founded Katy Steel Company (the "K" and "T" representing the two families; later became Katy Steel & Aluminum, dealing in mainly structural steel); in 1948 Toledo Paper Box Company was acquired. Joe's sons, Alvin and Richard, joined the management in the post-WW II period.

Kasle Iron was a "significant factor" in the regional market in the 1960s and 1970s. The firm specialized in serving industrial accounts, placing containers on the sites of its scrap-providing clients. It also had "a retail operation," buying scrap from a variety of customers who brought materials to its location.

The companies remained family-owned and operated until 1977 when Kasle Iron & Metal merged with two non-Toledo firms to form Magnimet Corporation, which subsequently became part of Cargill and then North Star Steel. Katy Steel was sold in 1986 and Toledo Paper Box in 1991.[42]

Kasle Iron also proved to be a training ground for Calvin Lieberman. As his second job following graduation from college in the 1930s, he became comptroller at Kasle, staying for about 10 years. That experience taught him about the scrap and steel business and in 1947 he formed Ace Steel Baling.

In an interview, he recalled attending a lecture at the Taft Institute in Cincinnati in the 1950s. The speaker talked about "recycling," including automobiles, an emerging new approach and terminology in the traditional scrap industry. That presentation gave him the intellectual and economic motivation for his subsequent efforts to improve the new "recycling sector" and make the metal salvaging business more efficient. Adopting recycling methods and patenting several processes of his own, he operated Ace Steel Baling until selling it to Kasle Iron in 1976. Thereafter he served as a consultant to Kasle and other firms and organizations in that trade. With more than sixty years of experience in the scrap and solid waste business, he is a nationally known authority on recycling and environmental issues.[43]

Sherwin Kripke was another who gained initial experience at Kasle Iron before World War II. Upon his return from military service, he joined with partners Harry and Joe Linver (father and son) to form Kripke-Linver. The firm's first yard was at Wabash and 14th streets, moving to Hill Avenue in the 1950s. About 1957 Sherwin Kripke left the firm and formed Sherwin Metal Reclaiming Company. SMR primarily handled copper and aluminum scrap, including state-of-the-art smelting. His sons, Harley, Larry and Bobby, subsequently joined the operation in the 1960s and 1970s. In 1969 SMR Company bought Kripke-Linver, bringing it back into the family. In 1976 the company merged with Tuschman Steel to form Kripke-Tuschman Industries. As another example of industry consolidation, in the early 1980s the Fort Wayne, Indiana firm of Superior Iron & Metal (later to become OmniSource) purchased Kripke-Tuschman.[44]

The scrap business was not in Harry Nistel's background. As a new accounting major just graduated from the University of Toledo, he was simply looking for a job and found one with a new scrap company, Tuschman Steel. After serving as accountant, office manager and then general manager for twelve years, he moved to Kasle Iron and in the 1960s bought part ownership, along with Harold Woodruff. Nistel subsequently bought out Woodruff. He expanded his scrap business by acquiring Ace Steel Baling, Cousins Iron and Metal, Monroe Scrap and Jackson Iron and other sites elsewhere in Michigan. He also added a brokerage firm, buying and selling scrap from other dealers and selling to foundries. He was very involved with the effective conversion of scrap car bodies into materials ready for recycling, installing one of the first auto shredders in Ohio and the country in the early 1970s. Resulting processed scrap was even shipped out of Toledo to overseas consumers.[45]

Sam Levine was another emigrant from Russia in the very early 20th Century. Age 22, he left Europe in 1903, promising to bring over his wife Ida and son Abe as soon as possible, following a very common immigration pattern. He first worked in the New York City garment district for six years, which allowed him to have his family rejoin him. That work also, however, led a doctor to prescribe that he move into an outdoor job for his health. Relocating to Toledo, he purchased a horse and wagon and traveled as far as Wauseon, Tiffin and Findlay, trading new brooms and other household items for scrap metals and rags. According to his 1977 obituary, after some years he became a partner in Shiff and Levine, headquartered on State Street. In the late 1930s he sold his interest and joined A. Edelstein & Son, originally founded in 1919, and then owned by his son Abe. He retired from the business in the mid 1960s.

With the Edelstein firm as a base, brothers Abe and Harry Levine became major players in the local scrap metal and steel business. Born in Russia in 1903, Abe came to Toledo as a young boy and attended the old Woodward Technical School (located on the site of the current Main Library). In his late teens, he began working at Kasle Iron and then Edelstein's as a bookkeeper. He and partner Abe Milstein subsequently acquired Edelstein's and Levine became sole owner following Milstein's death.

Abe Levine retired as president from Edelstein's in the mid-1970s and retired as chairman of Wabash-Lagrange Steel (see below) in 1988. His obituary said of him, "Everyone in the Jewish community knew Abe Levine. In the history of any community there are people who are the pillars – and he was one of them."[46]

Gary Beren succeeded his uncle Abe Levine in ownership of Edelstein & Son. Prior to that ownership, he recalled picking up scrap from the more than a dozen small scrap yards in the region and seeing them close up as the operators retired and the business consolidated. During his time at Edelstein's the firm also operated a "rag shop," which involved buying used clothing from Goodwill, the Salvation Army, even from New York City vendors, having a crew hand sort the pieces into categories, e.g. military surplus, for re-sale to niche markets looking for such items.[47]

A. Edelstein and Son operated as a family-owned Toledo business for 79 years, being purchased in 1998 by OmniSource Corporation of Fort Wayne, Indiana, as part of the on-going consolidation of the industry. Gary Beren retired as Edelstein's chairman and his son, Joel, remained as president and became vice president of OmniSource's Ohio Ferrous Group.[48]

There was much cross-over between the metal scrap and steel products businesses. One example of this is the Wabash-Lagrange Steel Company, founded in 1934 with the participation of Abe Levine and with a management team of Sam Isenstein and, after WW II, his brothers Ralph and Victor. In its early years, the firm was on North Summit Street, near the old Northwood Inn. In 1956 it moved into the former Frank Steel Company warehouse at 5050 N. Detroit Avenue, which was the start of its major evolution into a national integrated service center. Abe Levine's sons, Gordon and Joel, joined the company in 1956 and 1963, respectively. When Jon Levine and Larry Robbins, Gordon's son and son-in-law, joined the company in the 1970's the firm became another three-generation family concern in the community.

After World War II, Wabash-Lagrange was the first steel company in the country to use the St. Lawrence Seaway bringing salvageable material from Pearl Harbor to the Port of Toledo. Immediately following the war it was very difficult to purchase steel from U.S. mills whose production was tied up with government priorities in rebuilding the war devastated regions of the world. In the late 1940's when government restrictions were lifted, Wabash-Lagrange began its relationship with all the major domestic mills in the United States. In 1966 the company acquired 15 acres of land in the Lucas County-sponsored Fort Industry Industrial Park near I-75 in the North East corridor of Toledo. By 1969, the company had completed its first expansion to this new service center and added additional capacity to its material handling and processing capabilities. That move positioned the company to service its customer base in all contiguous 48 states, Canada and Mexico.

The decades of the 1970s and 1980s saw continued business growth and expansion via acquisition of other similar firms, in the Toledo area, elsewhere in Ohio and across the nation. In 1986 the O'Neal Steel Company of Birmingham, Alabama contacted the Levines to explore the possibility of acquiring Wabash-Lagrange. Being a family owned business for 54 years, the decision did not come easy. The determining factor to sell to the O'Neal firm was that company's philosophy of family first, followed closely by its loyalty to employees, customers and suppliers, country, community and friends and the importance of philanthropy. In January of 1999, Wabash-Lagrange became O'Neal Steel, which is now the largest family-owned metals servicing company in the nation.[49]

His sons Gordon and Joel joined their father in the 1940s. They saw that during the war, new steel production went to war goods, while scrap metals fueled secondary, domestic manufacturing. That experience promoted the steel service center concept within the industry and their firm expanded sales to end-users throughout the country and to other steel service centers. That pattern shifted in the 1970s as the industry evolved and end-users became the primary buyers with less and less going to other service centers.

The Tuschman family is another example of the intermingled nature of the scrap and steel businesses, as well as family connections within Toledo's Jewish community. In the early 1900's, Morris Tuschman emigrated from Russia to Toledo and became a peddler, which included acquiring scrap metal, paper, hides and bones. Using a horse and wagon, he regularly traveled from Toledo to Monroe and Dundee, Michigan. In turn, he sold the scrap metals to Sam Kasle, another Jewish immigrant from Russia who operated a Toledo scrap yard called Kasle Iron & Metal. Subsequently, Sam Kasle married Morris Tuschman's oldest daughter, Hannah.

Morris Tuschman married Rachael Kripke. Morris and Rachael had three sons; Sidney, Frank and Chester. Sidney and Chester were lawyers and shared a law practice located in the Spitzer Building on Madison Avenue. Frank and Chester also carried on their father's scrap business by founding Marine Steel Company in the early 1940's. In 1944 Marine Steel became the Tuschman Steel Company, located on Detroit Avenue. The brothers also opened similar operations in East St. Louis, Illinois and Fort Wayne and Muncie, Indiana.

The Tuschman Steel Company, headed by Chester Tuschman, assumed a major role in the scrap processing industry. It was known as one of the industry's more progressive companies, having installed modern baling, shearing, and containerized transportation equipment. During the Korean War, Chester Tuschman represented many of the major steel mills to the Office of Price Stabilization, then headed by former Toledo mayor Michael DiSalle.

Beginning in 1945, Chester Tuschman was also a partner with Joe Kasle in Katy Steel. Katy Steel stood for the name, Kasle-Tuschman or KT. Chester sold his interest in Katy Steel and entered into another partnership called Toledo Steel Supply. Toledo Steel Supply was started by the Abe Levine family, Milford Meyers and the Chester Tuschman family. Toledo Steel Supply was a steel warehouse specializing in plates and other long bars products. Chester died in 1969 and his son, Thomas, became President and CEO of the Tuschman Steel Company.

The evolution and consolidation continued. In 1976, the Tuschman Steel Company merged with Linver-Kripke and Sherwin Metal Reclaiming, founded by Sherwin Kripke and his family, to form Kripke-Tuschman Industries Inc. In 1980, Superior Iron & Metal, owned by the Leonard Rifkin family of Fort Wayne, Indiana, acquired Kripke-Tuschman. The merged entity later became OmniSource Corporation. In 1998, OmniSource further expanded its presence in Toledo by acquiring another long-time Toledo owned scrap metal company, A. Edelstein and Sons Inc.

OmniSource, through its various acquisitions and its organic growth including the development of its Scrap Management Group, eventually became the largest scrap processor, broker and scrap management company in North America with over 45 locations and annual sales of $2.5 billion. Thomas Tuschman, Senior Vice President and Robert Kripke, Vice President remain with OmniSource Corporation. In October, 2007, OmniSource was acquired by Steel Dynamics of Fort Wayne, Indiana for $1.1 billion.[50]

Universal Metals is another firm focused more tightly on steel products. Yale Feniger was part of the local industry with his own company, Northwest Ohio Steel, from the 1950s to 1972. At that time, the company was sold to National Steel. Yale's son, Bill, joined Northwest Steel of Pittsburgh following his graduation from college in 1969. In 1972 he moved to Colorado and opened his own steel company, returning to Toledo in 1986 and began Meridian National, a steel service center and recycler of paint waste. In 2001 he left Meridian National and established Universal Metals in North Toledo. That firm offers its customers slitting, leveling, shearing and pickling services.[51]

Local and Regional Businesses: Automotive parts and services

The relationship between the scrap/recycling industry and the automobile industry was a symbiotic one and the same might be said about the families involved in each of the fields in the Toledo Jewish community.

For example, Ben Solomon moved from Jackson, Michigan to Toledo in the early 1930s to take a job in the local scrap business. When that did not work out, he started Ben's Auto Parts on Westwood with his brother Art. By 1935 Ben moved to Monroe Street between 11th and 12th street; Art remained on Westwood. Beginning in 1940, the firm also had an auto salvage yard on north Detroit Avenue. At the end of WW II, he moved into marketing surplus military vehicles and parts. His son Don joined the operation in the mid-1950s, by which time the firm was dealing in vehicles and parts worldwide, and in 1960 the company became Ben's Truck Parts and Equipment, Inc.. In the late 1960s and on into early the1980s the business grew to include more work with dealers who were building other machines using the surplus military vehicles, e.g. dune buggies and front-end loaders. Another facet was helping to liquidate inventories of vehicle manufacturers going out of business. Ben Solomon died in 1984 and the business was closed. Subsequently, Don Solomon has been engaged in the factory liquidation of overruns and heavy duty truck parts worldwide via Stour Limited.[52]

The Liber family is another example in the auto-related network. Harry Liber founded Woodville Auto & Truck Parts in Northwood, Ohio. His son, Joseph said that his father saw the auto parts business as offering greater opportunity during the Great Depression. Harry died in 1998, but his son and grandson, Erich, continues to operate the business, making it another three-generation firm in the community.[53]

Goodman "Goody" Liber, brother of Harry, was also in the auto parts sector. He started Goody's Truck Parts & Equipment on Lewis Avenue in 1939, following work in the scrap business with Samuel, his father, and an uncle, Morris Rozenman, in Tiffin, according to his son Mickey. The business continues today under the ownership of his sons and grandsons. His reputation and prominence in the industry led Goody to being elected president of two trade groups, the National Auto and Truck Wreckers Association and the Ohio State Auto Parts Association.[54]

Meyer (Mike) and Charles Liber were two other brothers of Harry and Goodman. After working at Goody's firm, following WW II, Chuck and Mike bought Cherry Auto Parts at 716 Cherry, between Erie and Ontario streets. The store sold a variety of auto parts, but later concentrated on auto glass. The company later included a lot on Detroit Avenue, selling used car parts. Toledo Auto Trim was also acquired as part of the firm. Sales were to retail and wholesale customers locally, regionally and nationally.

Yet another player in the field is Westwood Auto Parts, on Westwood Avenue, established by brothers Gary and Zale Reinstein. They gained initial experience working for their uncle Harry Liber's company, Woodville Auto Parts. In the late 1970s the brothers wanted to establish their own firm and also preferred to remain in Toledo and thus bought a former factory on Westwood. Their customer base is retail to walk-ins, as well as to local body shops.[55]

Max Katz, an immigrant from Romania to Toledo, entered the business when he opened his Checker Auto Parts. Besides becoming successful, he provided a learning experience for his two sons, Art and Calvin, who joined him and later operated their firm, Max Auto Supply Company. They subsequently became major players by being among the first fifteen purchasers of Midas Muffler franchises in 1956. Over the years they expanded their ownership to between 150 and 160 shops in the eastern half of the country. At the time of Calvin's death in 2006, the family still operated about 100 Midas shops in Ohio, Michigan, New York and Pennsylvania. Calvin's son, Randy, continues the family's involvement in the business.[56]

Local and Regional Businesses: Wholesale Garments

Many local Jews worked in the Toledo factories. Anecdotally, the mother of Erwin Katz, who came to the U. S. in 1913 and roomed with her sister, sewed button holes for $3 per week in the local garment business. Other persons interviewed for this history mentioned having family in the garment trade as well. Several major firms appear and disappear through a search of city directories.

Redfern Manufacturing was said to be on Washington and made both women's and men's apparel. But curiously, city directories for the period 1910 – 1936 did not list such a firm. However, when the Cohen, Friedlander and Martin garment firm was sold to out-of-town interests in 1946, the "Redfern" trademark was specifically mentioned in the news story.

Rothmoor Corporation, another firm mentioned in a video interview, could not be found in city directories covering the period 1910 – 1936 under that name. However, it was the Rothmoor firm that bought Toledo's last garment factory in 1946.

Conde Cloak Company was incorporated in 1913 with M. R. Cohn as president and with a capitalization of $100,000. In 1926 the directory still listed M. R. Cohn as president, with Joseph Applebaum as vice president and J. F. Delaplane as secretary at 501 – 513 Superior Street. By 1930 the firm had consolidated on Superior to number 505. There was no listing in the 1936 city directory, but a Manuel R. Cohn was listed as an insurance agent in the Spitzer Building. Perhaps the Depression had forced a closure to the garment company.

Cohen-Friedlander-Martin was perhaps the major manufacturer. It began in 1892 at Erie and Orange and by 1910 had moved to 561 – 567 Erie Street with Alice S. Cohen as president and treasurer and L. S. Ottenheimer as vice president and secretary. Twenty years later, the firm had incorporated and moved to 1001 Washington Street. It was Toledo's sole garment manufacturer in 1946 when the Rothmoor Corporation of Chicago bought the firm. At that time it had 200 employees producing 2,000 coats per week and Rothmoor was uncertain if the "Redfern" trademark for coats would be retained.[57]

The H. Blitz Cloak Company was another player in the garment business. Incorporated in 1926 with Hyman Blitz as president and treasurer and Pearl Pund as secretary, but with only $3,000 in capital, the firm at 1003 Washington was short-lived. By 1936 Hyman Blitz was listed as vice president at Cohen, Friedlander and Martin.

A Toledo Cloak & Suit Company was one of five such firms listed in the 1926 directory. Solomon Appelbaum was president-treasurer and Jack Rosenblum was vice president-secretary, doing business at 139 Erie. The company had passed on by 1936 when the directory listed a Solomon Appelbaum as a "clothing contractor" and Jack Rosenblum did not appear at all.

The Novelty Cloak & Suit Company was another 1926 listing and was out of the "garment district" by being at 1213 – 1215 Cherry Street, with J. E. Lieberman, Max Zucker, Sander Straus and Harris Kass listed as owners. It had disappeared by 1936 when Max Zucker was listed a "clothing cleaner" and there was a Jennie Lieberman described as "widow of Jacob" living in an apartment on Warren Street.

The Western Cloak Company was right in the Jewish neighborhood in 1926, being on the third floor of the Toledo Factories Building, which still stands at E. Woodruff and North 12th. The owners and operators were listed as Samuel Steinberg and Hyman Blitz. This firm, too, had gone by 1936. Blitz was doubly involved in the garment trade for he was president of H. Blitz Cloak Company also in 1926 and ten years later both of his firms were gone from the directory but he was vice president at Cohen, Friedlander and Martin.

Neighborhood Migration

We turn from a survey of local Jewish neighborhood businesses back to the larger picture of neighborhood evolution and population migration in the second half of the 20th century. The trend to move westward continued into the 1950s and 1960s, and at a growing rate. One writer saw the local activity following the national pattern and wrote in the *Toledo Jewish News* in 1970: "Throughout the country, families were seeking to raise their children away from the inner city. Open, grassy areas and less crowded schools were attractive, as well as a new social sphere away from the old neighborhoods."[58]

Once again, the relocation of a synagogue gave unmistakable credence to this on-going migration. B'nai Israel, the oldest congregation in Toledo, broke ground in 1955 for a new synagogue at Douglas Road and Kenwood Boulevard, about four miles west of its 1913 synagogue on North 12th Street. Thus the congregation literally and figuratively jumped over the interim expansion of Jews into the Old West End and caught up with the more recent settlements in the newer western suburbs.

One interesting aspect of this westward movement is that it did not include a general dispersion of Jews within these gentile residential areas. Rather, there were pockets of Jewish settlement within these newer neighborhoods and suburbs. (*Photo 11, page 93*)

"But, for all there [sic] determination to live in 'good' middle-class neighborhoods, away from their former neighborhoods, members of this generation still preferred to live with other Jews."[59]

One noteworthy trend is that each succeeding area of Jewish settlement tended to be more expansive and less dense, and that evolution increased in speed with the passage of time. In part, this reflects the impact of automobile ownership, which enabled families to commute faster and more widely to destinations, which, in turn, could be a greater distance from the homes of those coming to them.

In 1970 Harry Rosen, executive director of the Jewish Community Center, conducted a population survey. Among the findings was that the ". . . geographic center of the Jewish population in Toledo at that time was a point near Talmadge Road and I-475." Rosen used the survey to argue that ". . . this would give credence to the selection of the 45 acre site on Sylvania Avenue next to the expressway for a new Jewish Community Center . . . and as a site for other Jewish community institutions that wish to locate in the heart of the future community."[60]

The survey's findings and Rosen's argument fitted nicely with other concurrent activities in the Jewish community. The Congregation Shomer Emunim had purchased forty-five acres on Sylvania in 1968 as a site for a new Temple and was open to other Jewish groups making it their new home as well. In 1973 worship services began in the new Temple, now nine miles west of its previous Collingwood site.

The Jewish Community Center was the prime candidate to share the parcel and a 1969 poll showed much support for such a move. Respondents overwhelmingly (74%) favored a new Center and 70% labeled the Collingwood facility as inconvenient for them to reach. Planning for a new Center moved ahead and groundbreaking occurred in 1975, with final completion in 1986 after a series of construction phases.

Another sign of this most recent westward migration was the October 30, 2005 groundbreaking for a new B'nai Israel Synagogue to join the campus already containing the Temple and the J. C. C. Services began in the new house of worship in 2007.

But the westward refocus of the Jewish community was not just on the Sylvania site. In 1975 a new Etz Chayim shul was dedicated at 3853 Woodley Road. This synagogue is two miles west of Meadowbrook Court, where the three previously-merged Orthodox congregations (B'nai Jacob, Shari Zedeck and Anshai Sfard) had been worshipping (and which, in turn, was several miles west of the three congregations' earlier shuls). It is about three miles east of the Temple-J. C. C.-B'nai Israel complex.

Demographics

This chapter began with a review of statistics to provide a setting or context for what was to follow. It is fitting to conclude the chapter in the same manner as Toledo's Jewish community pushes into the 21st century..

Contemporary Jewish historian Jonathan Sarna summarized the national Jewish population situation thusly: "Two surveys completed at the beginning of the twenty-first century confirmed that America's core Jewish population . . . is shrinking." Regardless of which survey is used, a decline of three to five percent is documented . . . .[T]he decline is . . . historic, marking the first time since colonial days that the total number of Jews in America has ever gone down. As a percentage of America's total population, moreover, Jews have been declining for decades. Having peaked in the 1940s, when they formed 3.7 percent of the population, they constitute less than 2 percent of America's overall population at the turn of the twenty-first century, the first time the numbers have fallen that low since 1910.[61]

Sarna continues with four reasons for this decline: "First, the American Jewish community suffers from low fertility and is not reproducing itself. . . .In addition, Jewish immigration, which for years compensated for the low birthrate, has declined drastically.

. . . Third, conversions to Judaism have also plummeted. . . . Today, the number of annual conversions to Judaism has slowed to a trickle. . . . Finally, and most important, intermarriage has cut into America's Jewish population totals. The National Jewish Population Survey of 1990 uncovered 1,325,000 individuals whose grandparents had been Jews but who now practice other religions, mostly as a result of marrying non-Jews. The more recent American Jewish Identity Survey ups that number to 2,345,000. These and other surveys demonstrate that the children of mixed Jewish-Christian marriages identify overwhelmingly either with Christianity or with no religion; only 25 percent of them, in a 1999 national survey of incoming college freshmen, identified themselves as Jews.[62]

The Toledo Jewish community resembles this national situation and local surveys can provide more detail. Three fairly extensive population surveys have been detected since WW II.

The first survey was done in September 1973 under the auspices of the Jewish Welfare Federation. The data came from interviews of 268 local Jewish households, about one in seven of the total. The total community's size was estimated to be 7,250 individuals.

The two more recent surveys give a more current picture of the local community.

A *Greater Toledo Jewish Community Population Survey* was undertaken in 1994.[63] The survey estimated the local Jewish population at 6,000, about 1% of Greater Toledo's overall population, with 42% of the people having lived in Toledo all their lives.

Jewish households number 2,588. Within those households, 21% included a spouse who was not raised Jewish; in turn, 64% of those spouses have converted to Judaism. (Nationally, the conversion rate of marriage partners not raised as Jews is 5% to 10%.) Related to this finding, more than 75% of respondents felt it was "important" that their child marry a Jew. Eight per cent of local Jewish households include a non-Jewish spouse.

Synagogue membership extends to 84% of Toledo's Jewish households. That membership is divided among Congregation Etz Chayim (31%), Temple B'nai Israel (36%) and Temple Shomer Emunim (40%). Nineteen per cent of households belong to more than one congregation.

The local Jewish population continues to age. The survey found 25% is 65 years of age or older. (Nationally, seniors make up 17% of the Jewish population, while the total of U. S. citizens 65 or older is 13%.) Other age categories locally: about 25% are between 47 and 64; 28% are between 19 and 46; 21% are under 18 years old.

In terms of local work habits and income, 43% of Jewish adults work fulltime; 15% work part time; more than 25% are retired. The median income (half of the people make less, half make more) is $58,545 and one-fourth of Toledo Jews report incomes exceeding $100,000, while one-third make less than $40,000.

In 2000 another census of the local Jewish population was conducted. At that time the total population was estimated to be 5,461 individuals. For comparison, the census gave the following total population figures for earlier years: 1994 – 6,370; 1982 – 6,300; 1974 – 7,300.[64]

The 5,461 persons were distributed among 2,211 households, for an average size of 2.47 persons per household. Of those households, 64.8% consisted of one or two members. In 1994 one-or two-person households made up 63.2% of all Jewish households and in 1984 similar households constituted 61.2. The trend is clear: a growing percentage of households are on the one- and two-person variety.

In the census, 91.4% of the individuals in Jewish households indicated they were raised Jewish or were converts. Of the 71% of individuals who were married, 68.1% were both raised Jewish.

References

1   Anderson, Elaine, *The Jews of Toledo, 1845 – 1895*, University of Toledo doctoral dissertation, 1974, pp. 279 – 289 and *passim*

2   Sarna, Jonathan D., *American Judaism: A History*, Yale University Press, 2004, pp. 1, 375.

3   Sarna, pp. 63, 65

4   Sarna, p. 64

5   Sarna, p. 64

6   Sarna, p. 64

7   Sarna, p. 65

8   Lerner, Marvin G., pp. 1-2 *History of Jewish Philanthropic Organizations in Toledo, Ohio*, 1959, pp. 1-2 (included in Leaders' Manual, Jewish Welfare Federation).

9   For a discussion of these two issues, see Sarna, p. 66

10   Feuer, Leon, *An Autobiographical Sketch*, 1969, p. 28

11   Sarna, p. 65

12   Sarna, p. 65

13   Ford, Harvey, *The Toledo Blade*, April 24, 1955, clipping, n.p.

14   Quoted in Seymour Rothman, *After 100 Years: A Sparse History of Temple B'nai Israel*, 1970, Preface.

15   Ford, Harvey, *The Toledo Blade*, April 24, 1955, clipping, n.p.

16   Anderson, p. 223

17 Anderson, p. 232

18 Anderson, pp. 279 – 289 and *passim*.   This population calculation complements the figure of Marvin G. Lerner, who estimated about 3,000 Toledo Jews in 1900, reflecting another five years of growing immigration, in his *History of Jewish Philanthropic Organizations in Toledo, Ohio*, 1959, p. 1 (included in Leaders' Manual, Jewish Welfare Federation).

19 Hughes, Susan M., *The Growth and Development of the Jewish Community Center in Toledo, Ohio 1906 – 1976*, 1987, p. 13 citing Mrs. Irving E. Goldman, *History of Collingwood Avenue Temple: 1875-1952*, 1962. Papers of Temple Shomer Emunim.

20 Anderson, pp. 284 - 285

21 Sarna, pp. 220-221

22 Hughes, p. 13 citing Glazer, Nathan, *American Judaism*, Chicago: University of Chicago Press, 1972.

23 See the history of B'nai Jacob in the chapter on congregations for another version of its early days.

24 Hughes, Susan M., p. 13 citing Glazer, Nathan, *American Judaism*, Chicago: University of Chicago Press, 1972.

25 *80th Anniversary* booklet of Toledo Federation, p. 37

26 Hughes, p. 14 citing *Population Census*, [no other reference]

27 "Often, the choice of location for a new Jewish community center can accelerate the exodus of Jews away from an old area of settlement or even reverse the trend.– Hughes, p. 14 citing Silberman, p. 213
In Toledo's case, however, the [population] movement was well underway and the building of the Jewish Community Center on Collingwood Avenue did nothing to halt it. Within five years of the decision to build, the Community Center was already becoming obsolete. [perhaps obsolescent a better term]– Hughes, p. 14-15 citing *Minutes, Long Range Planning Committee*, 1976 in Jewish Federation of Greater Toledo papers.

28 Hughes, p. 14 citing *Population Census*, [no other reference].

29 Marvin Jacobs and Erwin Katz, videotape interview at the J. C. C., June 25, 2003.

30 The following description of businesses in neighborhoods predominantly Jewish or frequented by Jews is a composite view, drawing on city directories, video taped interviews and statements made to the author. It covers the period approximately 1940 to the present. It is intended to be evocative of a place and time, not a complete recreation of a neighborhood.

31 Interview of Betty Applebaum, daughter of Joseph and Dorothy, by Alice Applebaum, March 1, 2006.

32 Thomas "Yonnie" Licavoli came to Toledo in 1931 from Detroit

and soon controlled most bootlegging and gambling in the city. He was eventually sent to prison, later paroled, and died in the early 1970s. For one account of his colorful life, see Harry Illman's *Unholy Toledo,* San Francisco: Polemic Press Publications, Inc., 1985. Sam Schuster reportedly had a run-in with Licavoli and lived to receive an apology and compensation from the gangster, a very rare occurrence; see Illman, p. 117.

33 *Blade,* April 5, 1959, clipping, n.p. and *Blade,* January 30, 1981, clipping, n.p.

34 *Blade,* May 19, 2003, online archive, n.p. and Daryl Yourist, telephone interview with the author, July 10, 2008.

35 Larry Friedman, e-mail to the author, May 24, 2007 and Toledo City Directories for 1935, 1936-37.

36 *Blade,* July 9, 1987 clipping, n.p., *Blade,* December 19, 2001 clipping, n.p. and e-mail from Cyndi Romanoff Rosenthal dated July 9, 2008.

37 Telephone interview with Richard Metzger, August 2, 2007.

38 E-mail from Fred Okun to Shelly Okun, June 27, 2007, shared with the author.

39 Interview with Fred Okun, August 9, 2007.

40 http://www.jewishsf.com/content/2-0-/module/displayhistory/story_id/23275/format/html/edition_id/464/displaystory.html. Downloaded May 5, 2007.

41 Carl Zimring, a visiting professor of history at Oberlin College, was cited in http://www.clevelandjewishnews.com/articles/2005/04/14/news/local/acover0415.txt. Downloaded May 31, 2007.

42 Joseph Kasle was interviewed about his life for a story in *The Blade* on December 31, 1999 and his obituary was in *The Blade* October 31, 2000. Telephone interview with Richard Kasle, June 26, 2007.

43 Telephone interview with Calvin Lieberman, May 31, 2007. For an informative tracing of the evolution of automobile recycling, see his article, "Creative Destruction," in the Fall 2000 issue of *American Heritage* and online at AmericanHertage.com.

44 Telephone interview with Harley Kripke, June 1, 2007.

45 Telephone interview with Harry Nistel, June 27, 2007.

46 *Blade,* February 17, 1991, n.p. Telephone interview with Joel Levine, June 25, 2007.

47 Telephone interview with Gary Beren, August 16, 2007.

48 *Blade,* April 4, 1998, n.p.

49 E-mail from Arleen Levine with information from Gordon Levine, July 7, 2008.

50 Interview with Thomas Tuschman, July 2, 2007 and subsequent e-mails.

51 Telephone interview with William Feniger, June 26, 2007 and www.universalmetalsllc.com

52 Telephone interview with Don Solomon, August 15, 2007.

53 *Blade*, March 9, 1998, n.p.

54 *Blade*, March 19, 2003, n.p.

55 Telephone interview with Gary Reinstein, August 6, 2007.

56 *Blade*, July 14, 2002, n.p. and *Blade*, January 17, 2006, n.p.

57 *Toledo Times*, November 23, 1946, clipping, n. p.

58 Hughes, p. 14, citing Harry R. Rosen, "Jewish Population Survey" in *Toledo Jewish News*, April, 1970, n. p.

59 Hughes, p. 14 citing Charles E. Silberman, *A Certain People*, New York: Summit Books, 1985, p.175

60 Hughes, p. 15 citing *Toledo Jewish News*, April 1970, n. p.

61 The two surveys are the 2001 National Jewish Population Survey, which put the decline at about 5%, and the American Jewish Identity Survey of 2001, which estimated the decline at 3%. Sarna, p. 357.

62 Sarna, p. 360.

63 Based on a random sample of completed interviews with 250 adults selected from Jewish Federation of Greater Toledo files, the survey had a 95% confidence level with a +/- 6.2% of error. The firm of Stanford H. Odesky and Associates conducted the survey and analyzed the data. Laurie H. Cohen wrote a synopsis of the survey, which was the basis for the data and conclusions cited in this chapter.

64 *2000 Census of the Great Toledo Jewish Community*, Executive Summary, n.p.

Chapter 2
Congregations

Introduction

As the author of a history booklet on the B'nai Israel congregation put it so well, "The early history of Jews in Toledo is extremely sparse, . . . Earliest mention of Jews in Toledo uncovered by a moderate amount of research is in a single sentence in *The Occident and American Jewish Advocate* for September 1857. . . . The magazine, published in Philadelphia, had sent a reporter through the Midwest to learn of the size and nature of Jewish communities in this rapidly growing part of the country. The only reference to Toledo read: 'Though there are Israelites, no attempt had been made, at least as far as we heard, to organize a congregation'."[1]

That single sentence from 1857 makes the point: no Jewish population can fully be considered a "community" without one or more organized congregations. The synagogue, temple, or shul is a fundamental building block for a settlement of Jews. It provides an institutional base for collective religious practice, as well as for a host of complementary activities, such as benevolent assistance and religious instruction for children.

Toledo's Jewish history is fortunate to include a rich heritage including Conservative, Orthodox and Reform congregations. In the midst of coping with family life and making a living in a gentile-dominated country which was not a homeland for most of them, practicing Toledo Jews gave their time, talent and treasures to organizing and maintaining congregations. Records and accounts of these congregations clearly demonstrate a high level of commitment by many individuals. A number of rabbis have played vital roles with the various congregations; some were driving forces for decades.

This chapter reviews the founding and development of the Toledo synagogues, temples and shuls which have left a trail of institutional records. The various congregations are grouped by Orthodox, Conservative and Reform doctrine with their respective histories arranged chronologically. Some material from before 1895 is included, drawing heavily upon Dr. Elaine Anderson's doctoral dissertation, *The Jews of Toledo, 1845 – 1895*, to present a more complete history of the organizations for the reader.

Although confronted with the coming of the Civil War in the 1850s and with the tumult of the war years themselves (1861 – 1865), Toledo Jews achieved true community status as the country emerged from the Civil War with the formation of the first Jewish congregation.

Orthodox - Congregation B'nai Israel ("Sons of Israel")

There is supposition that families who eventually formed the B'nai Israel Congregation began gathering for worship around 1866. A history of the B'nai Israel Congregation, published as part of the dedication booklet of the 1955 synagogue on Kenwood Boulevard, said the ". . . first Jewish public service of a religious nature held in Toledo was on the High Holy Days in the fall of 1863 in Gitskey Hall on the corner of Summit and Monroe streets."

In 1866 the congregation was formally incorporated under the name B'nai Israel, following Orthodox doctrine. They first met at Clark's Hall on Cherry Street and later moved to the Old Bethel Church between Summit and Water streets.[2] That date gained official status when the B'nai Israel membership later selected 1966 as its centennial year.

Historian Elaine Anderson wrote "B'nai Israel (Sons of Israel) was established and had a rabbi for part of 1869 and 1870, and there is no question that the congregation continued after he left." She also cited a short article in the *Commercial*, a Toledo newspaper, from March 7, 1871, that noted local Jews had celebrated Purim the day before.[3]

This theory gains credence because the first mention of the B'nai Israel congregation in a Toledo City Directory was the 1871-72 edition. A "Beny Israel" was listed under the heading "Jewish Synagogue" in the city's houses of worship category. The citation included its location in the Yeager Block (which was on the south side of Madison Avenue between St. Clair and Superior streets) and listed services as every Saturday from eight to ten in the morning. Small groups of worshippers, both Jewish and gentile, typically used such rented space before they could support their own quarters.

The 1872-73 edition of the directory corrected the spelling to B'nai Israel and cited a different location, Lynn Street between Summit and Water streets.[4] This change of site reflects the strengthening of the community during the preceding six years to the level that it could acquire its own facility, so reasoned Seymour Rothman, who wrote a centennial history of B'nai Israel. Yet, the site was leased, not purchased. The new synagogue site formerly had been a church and shelter for lake sailors, sponsored by the Western Seamen's Friends Society.[5] This move towards greater congregational substance continued the next year when B'nai Israel gained a rabbi. The spiritual leader was one Abraham Goldberg.[6] The directory also listed him as a peddler residing at 30 State Street.[7]

The Blade told about the same story. It put a "Rev. Mr. Roth officiating as rabbi, assisted by Mr. Goldberger." Congregation officers mentioned in the coverage were Mr. Van Orden, president, and Mr. Oesterman, vice president. The paper reported that "a large addition to [the B'nai Israel] membership followed the dedication.[8]

The congregation progressed for the immediate future. A local paper noted that the synagogue's membership more than doubled in the next two years. The same paper also informed its readers that Passover had been celebrated in 1873 and N. D. Oesterman [later generations spelled it Osterman], had succeeded Solomon Van Noorden [probably the same Van Orden above] as president.[9]

Historian Anderson used an 1874 article from the Cincinnati-published *Israelite* to profile that early B'nai Israel congregation. "The [*Israelite*] writer said that the Jewish population of Toledo had increased during the previous few years, and that the majority of newcomers were natives of Poland and Holland. 'The Israelites here as a class are not wealthy but are industrious and well-to-do. There is a congregation [B'nai Israel] which holds divine services according to the most orthodox Polish Minhag.' . . . If the membership was seventeen as *The Toledo Blade* suggested, the total congregation, using the multiplier of three and a half which the city directories of that time employed, probably exceeded sixty."[10]

A troubling event in 1876 marred the progress thus far. One or more persons forced their way into the B'nai Israel synagogue on Lynn Street and did a great deal of damage. They tore down gas lighting fixtures, smashed the furnace, ripped books and ruined seats. Total damage was estimated at $500. The congregation put up a $50 reward payable upon the arrest of the perpetrators and member Abraham Shugarman increased the reward by another $50. *The Blade* called the incident "simply intolerable" and called for prosecution "to the fullest extent of the law." No arrests were ever made.[11]

The congregation's first public listing of all officers was in the 1877-78 city directory: N. D. Oesterman, president; A. Shugarman, vice president; A. Tyroler, secretary; S. Van Noorden, Jr., treasurer. This roster indicates that a second group of Jews had reached Toledo, from the Netherlands, to join the earlier settlers from regions of modern-day Germany. The Geleerd, Oesterman and Van Noorden (sometimes spelled Van Orden) families appeared in many subsequent periods of Toledo Jewish congregations.[12]

The 1878-79 directory placed the synagogue on State Street between Cherry and Allen (now Canton) streets, on the northwest edge of Toledo's business district, Rabbi Abraham Cohen presiding. This area would develop into Toledo's first Jewish neighborhood by the end of the century. Subsequently, all listings for the congregation are absent from the city directories for nearly a decade.

The 1887-88 edition then picked up the group again, placing a B'nai Israel synagogue in Clark's Hall at 64 Cherry Street, with Rabbi Abraham Goldberg, residence at 43 Beacon Street, in the pulpit. The 1888-89 directory had one Joseph Levin as rabbi. The following year Abraham Cohen was rabbi, with Rabbi Levin as assistant. The year after that listed one Alfred Arndt as rabbi and he later appeared as an assistant to Rabbi Levin. This frequent change of rabbis is probably due to their being laymen, performing this religious duty along with having full-time jobs.[13]

While rabbis were rotating on an annual basis, the 1889-90 directory located the B'nai Israel Synagogue at 1902 Union Street, which is now North 12th Street, corner of Woodruff Street. Seymour Rothman designated this as the "first home" that truly belonged to the congregation. Dedicated January 6, 1889, the new, $5,000 wooden frame structure had seating for 600. Following Orthodox doctrine, it had a gallery where women sat for services. The members used the building until the congregation moved into its much larger new temple at North 12th and E. Bancroft streets in 1913.[14]

The 1913 brick synagogue with stone trim was a great advance over the earlier one and carried a projected cost of $50,000. Local architects Edward Thal and Sidney Aftel designed a Greek cross plan, seventy-five by one hundred feet. The general style reflected the Arts and Crafts Movement and the Chicago School influence of Louis Sullivan. The main worship space had a capacity of 700 on the main floor and another 300 in a balcony. An impressive dome, with an apex reaching fifty feet above the floor, covered the space. Art glass windows illuminated the interior of the worship space. The congregation dedicated the cornerstone on December 11, 1913. The ceremony included depositing a handwritten list of about 150 B'nai Israel members inside the cornerstone. The cornerstone was subsequently moved to the congregation's new temple on Kenwood Boulevard and the list removed.

A *Toledo Blade* story on the 1913 cornerstone laying noted "In the culmination of the hopes and dreams of the congregation, a large part of the credit is due Rabbi Silverman and the members of the building board who have spent a great time in planning for the new temple that promises to be one [of the] handsomest in the state. The building board includes Joseph Nast, chairman; I. Gerson, treasurer; A. M. Goldberg, secretary; and A. David, D. B. Eppstein, Jos. Jacobs, Sidney E. Aftel, I. H. Parisky, F. Gindy, Louis Shurer, R. Fine, Sam Friedland, Sol. Edelstein, H. Rosen, B. M. Green, William Horwitz, A. J. Smith, H. Zanville, Max Zanville, Jos. Friendman." There was also a ladies' auxiliary to the building board, with Mrs. R. Fine, chairman; Mrs. I. H. Parisky, secretary; Mrs. A. J. Smith, treasurer.[15]

This 1913 B'nai Israel Synagogue would serve well during a period of great growth for the congregation. One of the rabbis most distinctly connected with that congregation was Michael Lichtenstein, who accepted the call of B'nai Israel in 1922. He was born in 1893 in modern-day Poland, grew up in England, and received his rabbinical training at Schecter Theological Seminary and the Jewish Theological Seminary of City College, both in New

York City. His first two pulpits were in Mobile, Alabama and Dayton, Ohio.

The B'nai Israel centennial history noted that Rabbi Lichtenstein gave much attention to improving the level of Hebrew school education. His well-based reputation as a student and interpreter of the Talmud, speaker of five languages and master of Hebrew culture and oratory led to him being much in demand in the whole Toledo community.

While the 1913 shul was an outstanding structure, several years of increasing congregation activities pointed up the need for other facilities besides formal worship. Many of the congregation's other events, including its Hebrew School, had to take place at the Jewish Educational League Building, which was some blocks away on Southard Avenue at Linwood. The laying of a cornerstone for a B'nai Israel Annex in May 1924 climaxed a fundraising drive that enabled a three-story social building to rise adjacent to the shul on the south. *(Photo 12, page 93, B'nai Israel - 12th and Bancroft)*

After fourteen years of Rabbi Lichtenstein's leadership, the congregation was understandably saddened by his death in July 1936, age 43, due to heart disease while returning from two religious meetings in New York and Rhode Island.[16]

Dr. Morton Goldberg succeeded the late Rabbi Lichtenstein. Born in 1901 at Bialystok, Poland, he grew up in Pittsburgh and initially studied medicine at the University of Pittsburgh. He quickly decided that seeing children in pain precluded a medical career. He explained to his father and with his father's blessing he transferred to New York University and completed his B. S. degree in 1922. He then graduated from the Jewish Theological Seminary of America in 1925. While serving at his first synagogue, in Fall River, Massachusetts, he finished his master's degree from Brown University. In 1937, the same year he came to Toledo, he received his Ph. D. from Webster University. He gained a second doctorate, in divinity, from the Jewish Theological Seminary in 1966. He remained at Congregation B'nai Israel until he retired in 1972 and was rabbi there when the congregation moved from Orthodox to Conservative doctrine.[17] The subsequent history of Congregation B'nai Israel is covered below in the Conservative section of the chapter.

Orthodox - Congregation B'nai Jacob ("Sons of Jacob")

According to historian Elaine Anderson, the second Jewish congregation in Toledo was B'nai Jacob. *The Toledo Blade* of December 13, 1876 carried a story that articles of association for B'nai Jacob had been filed at the county recorder's office. Initial officers were Len (Levi) Pearlstein, president; Jacob Epstein, vice president; Isadore Reis, secretary; M. Epstein, treasurer; and

Israel Epstein, Michael Davis and Jacob Epstein, Jr., trustees. All lived in an area bounded by the Maumee River, Oak and Cherry streets (actually Woodruff, Union, State, John and Allen (now Canton) streets). The city directory classified all as "peddlers" except Pearlstein, termed a "junk dealer," and Israel Epstein, called a "merchant." In the 1870s and 1880s, this neighborhood on the north side of Toledo's business district was home to most of the Polish Jews.[18] *(Photo 13, page 94, Rabbi Goldberg)*

The 1879-80 edition of the city directory was the first citation of a synagogue's location: S. W. corner of John and Union (now State) streets. This was a logical and convenient site, given the proximity of members' homes. The listing included Louis Radion, rabbi; Levi Pearlstein, president; Joseph Minsky, vice president; Adolph Coplan, secretary; Philip Cohen, treasurer; Jacob Epstein, I. Levi, and David Marx, trustees. *(Photo 14, page 94, B'nai Jacob)*

The above account is at some variance with the history presented in *Congregation B'nai Jacob Observes 75 Years of Service to G-D, Community and Torah True Judaism, 5652 – 5727, 1891 – 1966,* which was published on the occasion of the congregation's 75th anniversary. That version is that in 1891 a "small group of Jews" rented a vacant store on the northeast corner of Canton (formerly Allen) Street and Woodruff Avenue as a place of worship "in a manner they felt more in the tradition of their fathers." By 1898 the assembly had grown to 100 families and it gained its first spiritual leader, Rabbi Isaac Shapiro.[19] *(Photo 15, page 94, Rabbi Shapiro)*

B'nai Jacob Rabbi Nehemiah Katz wrote a short history of the congregation for the dedication booklet of the 1950 B'nai Jacob Synagogue. It provided some further details of the early years:

"The B'nai Jacob Congregation today is the oldest and largest true Orthodox Ashkenazic synagogue in Toledo.

"But at its inception 60 years ago, there existed a relatively strong group of Chasidic [sic] origin who succeeded in initiating the Spardic [sic] version into the services.

"As a matter of fact, it seems that the Chasidic group was the originators of the founding of B'nai Jacob as there was no other Spardic synagogue at the time in Toledo. However, several years later when the new Jewish immigrants to Toledo who joined the congregation were of Ashkenazic origin, the services were changed to the Ashkenazic version, which has remained to this day."[20]

In 1900 B'nai Jacob purchased a lot at 936 N. 12th Street (corner of State Street, then known as Union) and after two years of further planning and construction, a synagogue was completed, described in the history as ". . . a beautiful piece of architecture inside and out by standards of the day." During this formative period, Rabbi Shapiro resigned his position but remained in the congregation. (Some years later, his grandson, Dr. Donald Steinberg, served as president of the congregation.) His successor was Rabbi Abraham J. Hirschowitz, whom the history identified as bringing "prominence to the synagogue as author of many scholarly books on Judaism." Two lay members were also singled out as playing important roles in this time, David Rayman and Edward Brodsky, both of whom served as presidents of B'nai Jacob.[21]

In 1906 Rabbi Isaac Moses Silberman began his tenure at B'nai Jacob and remained until his death in 1934. While serving the needs of the synagogue's members, he also "became head rabbi of the city and was charged with the arduous task of supervising the keeping of the Kosher standards in slaughter houses and food places."[22] In 1932 all the Toledo synagogues honored Rabbi Silberman for his twenty-five years of Toledo service with a banquet and a four-month trip to Israel.[23]

The B'nai Jacob Sisterhood sprang from the desire of some twenty-five women wishing to "participate more actively in the synagogue" during the 1920s. Mrs. Morris Cannon chaired the initial meeting, at which Mrs. Kozman was elected as the first president. The 75th anniversary history listed the following women among the charter members of the Sisterhood: Mrs. David Abelowitz, Mrs. Harry Berkowitz, Mrs. Morris Cannon, Mrs. Sam Feldstein, Mrs. Sam Fisher, Mrs. David Friedman, Mrs. Kozman, Mrs. Hersch Lubitsky, Mrs. Samuel Lubitsky, Mrs. Sam Rice, Mrs. Anna Rogolsky, Mrs. Michael Samborn, Mrs. Sam Stark, Mrs. Ida Seitz, Mrs. M. R. Topper, Mrs. David Zanville, Mrs. Louis Zanville, and Miss Clara Zimmerman.[24]

Following the death of Rabbi Silberman, Rabbi Nehemiah Katz was called to assume the position in January 1935. His religious training included study at the Yeshiva of Slutzk, Russia, and attendance at the Rabbi Isaac Elchonon Seminary of America, where he was ordained in 1932. Prior to coming to Toledo, he had done post-graduate work and received various awards for academic achievements. In the same year he was elected to lead B'nai Jacob, Rabbi Katz married Eunice Silberman, the late rabbi's daughter. Rabbi Katz continued at B'nai Jacob until the congregation merged with Sherai Zedeck (and shortly thereafter also with Anshai Sfard) to form Etz Chayim; he then served as rabbi of that new Orthodox congregation.[25]
(*Photo 16, page 95, Rabbi Katz*)

Rabbi Katz was a noted Orthodox Jewish scholar and played a role in the building of five synagogues, a Kosher slaughterhouse and a Jewish day school while in Toledo. His obituary also noted that he founded the only two ritual mikvah baths in Toledo, one of which was still in use at Etz Chayim at the time of his death. He served as a chaplain of the Toledo Mental Health Center and at the Lucas County jail, as well as being a member of the Toledo Board of Jewish Education, Jewish Family Service, Jewish Community Center, the Jewish Welfare Federation and Darlington House.[26]

While Toledo suffered through the Great Depression, the B'nai Jacob membership reached 350 families in 1937. Congregation president David Friedman led the search for a site upon which to build a new, larger synagogue. Two years later two parcels at the corner of Putnam and Batavia streets in the Old West End were purchased. However, the pending turmoil of the Second World War forced postponing of building plans. The existing structure on the site was just remodeled into a meeting hall and classrooms and named the B'nai Jacob Center.[27] With the increased facilities available, the Men's Club formed that year with 121 members.

The congregation was busy during WW II. In 1942 a religious school was established with 70 children enrolled. The newly-formed Men's Club offered one year's free membership in the club and the synagogue for all Jewish servicemen in the community. All veterans were invited to take part in all activities at the synagogue and the center.[28] In 1943 an Academy of Jewish Learning was begun with 45 adults enrolled, some non-Jewish. Three courses were offered: Mendel Rayman taught "Elementary and Advanced Hebrew," Dr. Nathan Becker taught "Economic and Social History" and Rabbi Katz led a class in "Bible and Jewish History."[29]

The end of World War II brought the first issue of a bulletin, entitled *Hashomer*. The regular publication contained news of congregation activities, including the Men's Club and the Sisterhood.

War's end also saw synagogue membership reach 400 and it was necessary to once again address the need for a larger synagogue. Rabbi Katz and member Nathan Hendelman learned of the availability of a lot at 2200 Parkwood Avenue (on the corner of West Bancroft Street), also in the Old West End. This fitted nicely into the westward movement of B'nai Jacob's members and very quickly the board, under the leadership of David Friedman, president, and Ben Singer, vice president, moved to purchase the parcel.[30]

Architect and B'nai Jacob member Herman Feldstein drew up plans (completed in August 1949), which called for a synagogue and a school building on the site. The concept was "contemporary in design, with early Babylonian Temple influence, the detail with its geometric designs is derived from ancient synagogues of Moorish and Coptic influence," wrote architect Feldstein.[31] The main auditorium seated 825 persons and the chapel accommodated 45 people.[32]

In the summer of 1948, before the new synagogue was built, a large house already on the site was remodeled into seven classrooms, a library, meetings rooms and a kitchen for catering. All congregational activities occurred at this new B'nai Jacob Center, except for religious services, which were still held at the old synagogue until October 1949.[33] That move included relocating all the Torahs. Rabbi Katz led the ceremonial transfer, assisted by Cantor Eugene Schwartz, Shamus Nochim Silverman and Gaboim Nathan Hendelman and David Abelowitz. (*Photo 17, page 95, Confirmation class*)

The Putnam Street facilities were later sold and the synagogue at Twelfth and State streets was also sold shortly after it was vacated.[34] The New Light Baptist Church purchased the former B'nai Jacob shul for $30,000.[35]

Groundbreaking for the new synagogue was Sunday, October 2, 1949; the cornerstone was laid June 20, 1950. The new B'nai Jacob synagogue was dedicated September 3, 1950. At that time President Ben Singer paid special credit to

". . . the untiring efforts of Rabbi Nehemiah Katz, Joe Feldstein, Morris Lubitsky, the Building Board, the friends and members of B'nai Jacob Synagogue, the unselfish devotion of [the] Sisterhood and the unboundless [sic] enthusiasm of our Men's Club."[36]

Two events stand out in 1951. First, the congregation welcomed Cantor Jacob Spanglet to B'nai Jacob. His previous services had included Congregation Beth Aharein in Brooklyn and Moshulul Park Center in the Bronx. When he and his family first moved to Toledo, they lived with his sister, Jeanette Ulman, whose husband Julius was then cantor at Temple B'nai Israel. Cantor Spanglet served at B'nai Jacob and then, as a result of mergers, at Etz Chayim, until September 1987, when he retired at the age of 69. He also taught at the local Hebrew School.[37] (*Photo 18, page 95, B'nai Jacob Officers*)

Second, the B'nai Jacob bulletin, *Hashomer*, gained recognition when a national Jewish magazine, *P'Rakin*, reprinted an article that had originally appeared in the local periodical's New Year's edition.[38]

In 1952 the Sisterhood expanded its activities by sponsoring a Brownie troop. Mrs. Arthur Berkowitz was the leader. The 75th anniversary history said it "flourished for several years and then became part of one of the larger Girl Scout troops in the city."[39] (*Photo 19, page 96, Sisterhood officers*)

The history of B'nai Jacob includes the synagogue sponsoring religious services for Jewish residents at the Toledo State Hospital. Apparently, a synagogue committee organized this outreach, in which Rabbi Katz participated and which included treats being given to the hospital patients at Hanukkah.[40]

At the *Kol Nidrei* service in 1953, President Herman C. Moss announced that the mortgage of the shul was paid off and thus the synagogue was debt free. A "gala celebration and mortgage burning ceremony" was held before a capacity crowd.[41] (*Photo 20, page 96, Sisterhood*)

The B'nai Jacob community experienced a major growth in its facilities with the construction of a new Classrooms and Social Hall, which was dedicated May 17, 1959. The announcement had been made the previous year, with Alfred H. Samborn to be general chairman of the building program and Rabbi Katz, Morris Lubitsky and Herman Moss serving as the steering committee. As with the 1950 synagogue, Herman Feldstein drew the plans, which featured a split level design that resolved space problems. It included ten classrooms for 230 students and Grossman Auditorium, with a stage and seating for 375 theater style or 250 for meals. The addition also provided a rabbi's study and office area.[42] The Sisterhood showed its usual high level of support by forming a kitchen equipment fund, led by Mrs. Nehemiah Katz, Mrs. Herman Moss and Mrs. Morris Lubitsky.[43] The reported cost was $125,000.[44] (*Photo 21, page 96, Herman Moss*)

In 1967 the congregation voted to merge with Sharei Zedeck. For a few years, the Parkwood synagogue was the home to both B'nai Jacob and Sharei Zedeck. The building was eventually sold to the Bethel Seventh-day Adventist Church after the Jewish congregation moved to Meadowbrook Court.[45] The subsequent history is covered in the Etz Chayim section below.

Orthodox - Congregation Sharei Zedeck ("Tower of Justice")

Indicative of the growing Jewish population in Toledo during the late decades of the 19th century, Congregation Sharei Zedeck was formed around 1900 as an Orthodox synagogue of "Russian-Polish Hebrews."[46] A brief history of local congregations printed by the Jewish Federation of Greater Toledo in 1987 cites 1906 as the year "...a small group of ten, a minyan, gathered in a second floor room of a rented house to worship."[47]

The following year this new congregation met in a house at 624 Spring Street, between Mulberry and Stickney, in one of Toledo's Polish neighborhoods and northwest of the center of Toledo's Jewish settlement at the time.[48] The congregation grew to fifty by 1920 and to seventy by 1924. A new synagogue was consequently built in 1925 at 2102 Mulberry Street (corner of Moore street). By then, Sharei Zedeck numbered 100 members.[49] The congregation's shul continued to function on Spring Street for many years.[50] At both of its locations, rabbis from B'nai Jacob journeyed to the synagogue and led services.[51]

Early officers were Harry Bletterman, president; William Worshtil, vice president; John J. Zaft, secretary; S. Schechet, treasurer; Harry Hoffman, first trustee; Harry Goodleman, Morris Goodleman, Charles Kale, Abe Leibovitz, Charles Shapiro, Louis Shapiro, Isaac Wexler, and Sam Zimmerman, trustees. *Chevra Kadisha* officers were Harry Wexler, S. Levin, Morris Milstein and J. Leibovitz.[52]

In 1941 Jacob (Jake) Stein was president. He was the son of Mendel Stein, one of the charter founders of Sharei Zedeck. Lillian Kale recalled that Stein was "Blessed with a cantorial voice and a great knowledge of the Torah, he became the unofficial rabbi, cantor, gabbai, shamus, *Chevra Kadisha* chairman and anything else the shul needed. With his wife Mollie by his side, they both ran the day to day operation of the synagogue as if it was their own home.[53]

Lillian Kale also remembered that the "Sharei Zedeck Sisterhood was a very active group. Some of the early members were Lillian (Laika) Eisenstein who catered many lucheons and dinners in the basement dining hall. Others involved were Rachel Wexler, Bessie Bletterman, Bessie Fingerhut, Mary Perlman, Sarah Schwartz, Clara Essak, Sophia Worshtil, Rachil Milstein, Rose Bellman, Mrs. Olson, Blanche Kale, Kate Posner, Elsie Perlmutter, Gertrude Leibovich, Eva Shiff, Faygie Goodleman, Goldie Brandman, Fannie Foraster, Tillie Kale, and Sara Leibovitz.

"In the late 1950s the 'younger generation' began to take over, led by Lilly Foraster Yourist, Pearl Foraster Yourist, Annette Foraster Gould, Frieda Levine, Thelma Wexler, Edith Eckber, Dolores Perlman, Ruth Zimmerman, Ruth Essick, Helen Hascal, Sally Wexler, Cissy Rappaport, Jeanette Schwartz, Ruth Fingerhut, Sharon Rainwasser, Lil Kale and so many others who all worked to support the enrichment and upkeep of Sharei Zedeck Synagogue."[54]

President Stein remained in that office until 1967 when Sharei Zedeck merged with B'nai Jacob.[55] The final act of merger was the transfer of the Torah (Holy Scrolls) from Sharei Zedeck to B'nai Jacob. That July the Torah was transferred from Sharei Zedeck to B'nai Jacob. Bearers were Abe Levine of Sharei Zedeck and Irwin Fruchtman of B'nai Jacob. Although the two congregations merged in September 1967, they continued to hold separate services. The first united service was July 27. At the time, B'nai Jacob was credited with 450 families and Sharei Zedeck was listed at about 250 families.[56]

During its existence, Rabbis Isaac Silberman and Nehemiah Katz of B'nai Jacob provided spiritual leadership, and student rabbis, guest cantors, and Rabbi Lazer Schacter, a member of the congregation, also led services.[57] Rabbi Katz also provided spiritual leadership during his thirty-three years in Toledo.

Subsequently, B'nai Jacob-Sharei Zedeck merged with Anshai Sfard in 1970 to form Etz Chayim.[58] (This may be the same group as "B'nai Abraham," cited by Rabbi David Alexander in *Reform Advocate* of 1908, see below.)

Orthodox – Congregation B'nai Abraham

In June 1908 Rabbi David Alexander of Temple Shomer Emunim, included this congregation in his listing of Orthodox shuls then in Toledo. He located Congregation B'nai Abraham at the corner of Spring and Mulberry streets, and organized in September 1906. It was organized as an Orthodox congregation and "established for the purpose of affording a place of worship for those who are living at a great distance from the other orthodox Synagogs [sic]." He ascribed to it a membership of 80, with its own rabbi and cantor, and with a Hebrew school which held daily sessions. The president of B'nai Abraham was Simon Berkowitz and secretary, David Gertner.[59] This may well be another description of Sharei Zedeck; more research is needed.

Orthodox - Congregation Anshai Sfard ("Men of Spain")

Orthodox Jews established another congregation in the early 20th century at the corner of Canton and Woodruff streets. In August 1915 congregation president Sam Kasle led the community to its new synagogue on Canton and Scott streets, a short distance away. The new site, purchased for $1,700, included a residence which Cantor Louis Klein used. The new house of worship was dedicated with festivities that included a speech by Cornell Schreiber, who became Toledo's third Jewish mayor in 1918.[60] At another point in its history, the building served as the First German Reformed Church and at least one other gentile congregation. As of this writing the building is abandoned, but still standing. *(Photo 22, page 97, Anshe Sfard)*

The congregation remained in these quarters for four decades. It then moved to a temporary site at 2252 Parkwood Avenue in 1954. The Parkwood structure was remodeled for $8,000 and was to served until a new synagogue was built there, according to Marcus Friedman, president of the congregation. The newspaper story about the move said Anshai Sfard had about 250 members.[61]

Plans changed apparently. On October 15, 1961 ground was broken for a new synagogue at 3220 Meadowbrook Court, a relocation considerably westward and another example of the movement trend of Jewish synagogues in Toledo. In January of 1962 the congregants dedicated the cornerstone.[62]

In August of 1962 the congregation announced it had elected Rabbi Shaiall Zachariash to be spiritual leader. He was native of Los Angeles and a graduate of Ner Israel Rabbinical Seminary in Baltimore, Maryland.[63] Subsequently Rabbi Zimand was listed as leading the membership.[64] In 1970 the congregation merged with B'nai Jacob-Sharei Zedeck.[65]

Orthodox - Congregation Etz Chayim ("Tree of Life")

In 1967 came the first of the mergers that would ultimately result in the formation of Congregation Etz Chayim. That year the congregations of

B'nai Jacob (450 families) and Sharei Zedeck (150 families) voted to join together and be known as Congregation B'nai Jacob-Sharei Zedeck. The convergence officially occurred on Rosh Hashanah in October 1967 (5728 on the Hebrew calendar). At the time of the vote, Dr. Donald Steinberg was president of B'nai Jacob and Jacob Stein was president of Sharei Zedeck.[66]

Then in 1970 the remaining Orthodox congregation, the 150 families of Anshai Sfard (also known as Meadowbrook Court following its relocation to that site in 1962), joined. In 1973 the newly-formed congregation selected the name Etz Chayim ("Tree of Life"), wishing to evoke the sense that a single tree then grew from its multiple roots, in this case, three previously separate congregations. According to Rabbi Edward Garsek, the decline of the local Jewish population's numbers was clear and the merger was logical since the groups ". . . shared the same purpose and goals." At the same time, the rabbi acknowledged that "It was not the easiest merger because everybody had the synagogue where they grew up." The eventual three-way merger did succeed, however, because, as Elsa Leveton, administrator of Etz Chayim, said, "Once the three congregations came together, everybody worked together, they all made an effort to make it work." The new congregation worshiped in the Meadowbrook Court synagogue until the Woodley Road shul was ready. Meadowbrook was later sold to the First Free Methodist Church for $85,000.[67] *(Photo 23, page 98, Cantor Spangler and Rabbi Garsek)*

On Sunday, August 1973 a groundbreaking was conducted for a new Etz Chayim house of worship.[68] The new synagogue was built at 3853 Woodley Road, in the Sylvania Avenue-Talmadge Road area, providing additional evidence for the westward migration of Toledo's Jewish population.[69] Joe Feldstein and Morris Lubitsky were the lay leaders of the planning process; Herman Feldstein was the architect.[70] The final design of the structure included a 400-seat main sanctuary (which could be expanded), a social hall and kitchen to serve about 300 people, a chapel seating 75 for daily morning and evening services, a library and a few classrooms and offices. Reflecting the creation of the new shul from three predecessors, architect Feldstein included a memorial room featuring the memorial plates from all three earlier congregations. The shul also contains a *mikvah* or ritual bath, used in purification and conversion rituals. It also maintains the only institutional kitchen in the city following Orthodox standards. The synagogue was dedicated in January 24 – 26, 1975. Rabbi Nehemiah Katz, who was the senior Orthodox rabbi in Toledo and who had helped guide the mergers, became the first rabbi of the new synagogue and served until his retirement in 1981.[71] *(Photo 24, page 98, Cantor Rubin)*

Rabbi Edward Garsek succeeded Rabbi Katz as spiritual leader of the congregation, having originally come to Toledo in 1975 to assist Rabbi Katz.

The son and son-in-law of rabbis, he graduated from Hebrew Theological Seminary in Chicago, having known from childhood that he wanted to enter the rabbinate. Following his ordination in 1972, he assisted his father at their synagogue in Fort Worth, where he had been born, and subsequently came to Etz Chayim.[72]

Conservative – Congregation B'nai Israel

A major doctrinal shift, accomplished under Rabbi Goldberg's leadership, was the change of B'nai Israel from an Orthodox congregation to a Conservative one. The centennial history noted "The changes were made slowly, and generally speaking, the members accepted the changes."[73] Among the changes resulting from this shift of dogma was that men and women members of the congregation sat together at services. In Orthodox shuls women sat in a balcony while the males were in pews on the main floor. Rabbi Goldberg was quoted as saying "Why shouldn't a man and wife sit together at holy services? Besides [he continued], if they sat together there would be less smooshing [sic] during services."[74]

While speaking at a 1954 dinner given in his honor, Rabbi Goldberg explained his commitment to community service: "I could not possibly serve my own congregation completely if I did not also serve the community of Toledo as a whole." Consequently, Dr. Goldberg held many prominent positions within the greater Toledo community. For example, he was a charter member of both the Toledo Labor-Management Relations Citizens Committee and the Toledo Board of Community Relations and served on the boards for the Toledo Public Library, the Toledo Public Schools and Toledo Mental Hygiene. In later years, he gave his time and talents to the Legal Aid Board, the Toledo Hospital and to Jewish students at the University of Toledo.[75]

During Rabbi Goldberg's tenure, B'nai Israel grew to 1,000 members and an increase in congregational activities strongly argued for larger quarters. The case for moving gained a major boost in 1941: Sol Edelstein, a former president of the congregation and one who had discussed the need for a new temple at some length, died and bequeathed $10,000 to B'nai Israel as the start of a fund for a new synagogue.[76] (*Photo 25, page 98, Confirmation*)

By this time, Toledo's Jewish population was concentrated further west than earlier. The Old West End included many Jewish households and at one time or another Orthodox, Conservative and Reform congregations built there. B'nai Israel's role in this demographic trend began when it acquired three adjoining parcels on Collingwood Avenue at Virginia Street during 1947 and 1948. The Religious and Hebrew schools moved to the new site and the synagogue offices moved into one of the existing buildings there later in 1948, while other congregational functions continued on Bancroft Street. Even in the new improvised classrooms, enrollment increased so greatly that double sessions had to be scheduled.[77] Sydney Friedenthal, congregation president, told *The Blade* in 1949 that there was no definite timetable for a new building. The latest cost estimate was nearly $500,000 – a deterrent – and there was the pressing need to help persons displaced in Europe by the recent war to relocate to Palestine.[78]

However, just a few years' experience at the Collingwood location convinced the B'nai Israel leaders that it did not have the potential to host all the congregation's activities and needs, even with a new building. They began looking for yet another replacement site. (The B'nai Israel trustees subsequently sold the Collingwood real estate in July 1956 for a new Jewish Center facility. The congregation continued to use the one building on the site until the new Kenwood shul was ready.)[79]

Sidney Friedenthal served as president of the B'nai Israel congregation for fifteen years during this time period, concluding his presidency two years after B'nai Israel moved into its Kenwood Boulevard home. (The south entrance of the new temple was designated as the Friedenthal Terrace in honor of his many years of service.) He recalled facets of the decision-making and planning process of the relocation for the centennial history booklet: "Like every other issue in our community, there was a variety of opinions. People who lived near the [1913] synagogue objected [to the proposed move]. Some members, who had developed a great deal of attachment for the synagogue building and annex, objected." (*Photo 26, page 99, Rabbi Fishel Pearlmutter and Rabbi Morton Goldberg*)

The first step was to sample the ability to raise the necessary funds for such new construction, for if the capital was lacking, the decision would be moot. Friedenthal said that early conversations raised optimism that adequate monies could be raised. These preliminary steps also fostered greater general enthusiasm in the congregation regarding relocation.

One sign of that interest was the great number of suggestions for what the new facility should include. Friedenthal remembered that ". . . at least one prominent member was determined that we should have a swimming pool and gymnasium in the building, something that possibly should have been included in the old annex. I opposed this firmly, however, arguing that we were building for religion, education and culture."

Despite the Edelstein bequest of $10,000, much more fund raising was needed. Contributions from the general membership to the building fund were "encouraging," according to Friedenthal. Most members also agreed to an increase in congregation dues.

One touching example of financial commitment was Alix Blumberg's [now Alix Blumberg Greenblatt] unannounced presentation of her piggy bank for the construction while Friedenthal was speaking at the dedication of the cornerstone. "The idea of a child doing this at this moment meant so much to me that I almost broke down," Friedenthal said later.

Fund raising was not a cakewalk, however. At one point there was a cash flow problem and Friedenthal called some members to a meeting at the former Hillcrest Hotel on Madison Avenue and explained that $50,000 was needed in short order. Charles Fruchtman then personally asked each of the men there for help and received pledges totaling $55,000. Fulfillment of the pledges came so quickly that Fruchtman was able to deliver a check for the full amount to Friedenthal the very next day.[80]

Raising sufficient funds was essential, but finding the right site was very important too. Local Jewish residents continued to move westward within the greater Toledo area, a trend that had taken them from the near north side to the Old West End and would continue into West Toledo and beyond into Ottawa Hills and the Sylvania-Sylvania Township areas. Members of all the synagogues followed this migration pattern. In the 1930s and 1940s, the demographic center of Toledo's Jewish population was in the Old West End. B'nai Israel had reacted to this by its purchase of the three parcels at Collingwood Avenue and Virginia Street in the late 1940s.

Apparently, the congregation leadership believed that this westward movement would continue so B'nai Israel member Archie Stone, in charge of finding possible sites, included several parcels further west within the scope of their site search, e.g. opposite Ottawa Hills High School and the location where St. Ursula Academy was later built on Indian Road. Another West Toledo site was a nineteen acre parcel on the corner of Douglas Road and Kenwood Boulevard, owned by the Owens-Illinois Glass Company.

When B'nai Israel representatives approached the glass company, they learned that the local Ursuline Convent was also interested in purchasing the parcel. Owens-Illinois asked the two religious groups to resolve between themselves who should buy the land, for the firm did not wish to have the two institutions bidding against each other. Once the buyer was decided, O-I would negotiate a price. Sidney Friedenthal explained that Rabbi Goldberg conferred with the Ursulines' Mother Superior and they decided that B'nai Israel should move ahead with the purchase. The deal was struck for a price of about $23,000 or $24,000, the company charging only for its original cost and closing fees. The B'nai Israel board officially ratified the purchase on December 25, 1952.[81]

As an epilogue to the story, the congregation ended up buying the entire parcel since the price was so attractive and deeding a portion to the Ursulines for St. Ursula Academy, the reason the nuns had been looking at it. Subsequently, the holy order built at the academy's present Indian Road site instead; the property returned to Jewish ownership when it was acquired for Darlington House, whose story is told in another chapter. A portion of the original plot was also given for the current Old Orchard School and surrounding green space.

This generous action received coverage in *The New York Times* newspaper, *Newsweek*, and *Time*. A headline about the concept even appeared on a lighted sign at Broadway and 42nd Street in New York City. There was a concept considered for the area to become an interfaith campus, with all the buildings complementary to each other in design and function. That never happened, but it received some media attention as well.[82]

Sidney Friedenthal recalled that he anticipated only one problem with the new temple site: he worried about train whistles from the adjacent tracks interrupting services, especially during High Holy Days. This concern was shared with the operators of the Toledo Terminal Railroad, who promised "no whistles." They had the trains' flagmen dismount at the Kenwood crossing, halt vehicular traffic while the train passed, and then remount the train. After a few years of that, Friedenthal said, "we stopped asking for flagmen. The whistles never were a problem."[83]

The new B'nai Israel Synagogue had its groundbreaking on June 4, 1954 and the cornerstone was laid on June 5, 1955. Religious School pupils gathered in the new building for the first time on October 16, 1955. The first Friday evening service in the 750-seat worship space was on February 24, 1955. (Earlier that morning, after the last morning service in the Bancroft Street synagogue, a group of elders carried the Torahs from there to their new home.[84]

The Kenwood temple experienced the same cycle as earlier synagogues - it served well, but congregational growth after it opened and subsequent use of the building argued for change and expansion. Sidney Friedenthal explained to Seymour Rothman for the 1966 centennial history that the synagogue had one basic need: "room, room, room, room." Furthermore, an architect would need to devise "some clever way" of expanding the building without destroying the outward appearance and fitting the new space to the site. Such changes as a better place for the gift shop, a library area separate from the board room, a designated clerical work space, more convenient spaces for the rabbi and added classrooms should all be incorporated as well, he maintained.[85] Resolution of those needs would only come several decades later.

In 1969 Rabbi Fishel Pearlmutter joined the staff at B'nai Israel as Associate Rabbi. His immediate position prior to Toledo was Associate Rabbi at the Park Synagogue in Cleveland, one of the largest congregations in the United States at the time. The Baltimore native was a graduate of Yeshiva

University and the M. H. L. Jewish Theological Seminary. He was also a U. S. Navy chaplain for three years. He succeeded Rabbi Goldberg as Rabbi when Rabbi Goldberg retired in 1972, receiving the title of Rabbi Emeritus. Besides being active within the local Jewish community, including serving on various boards, he was also Jewish chaplain for the University of Toledo and was a member of the Labor-Management-Citizens Committee. While at B'nai Israel, he produced a videotape of the High Holiday Service for hospitals.[86] In 1982 the congregation sponsored a week-long tribute to Rabbi Pearlmutter, celebrating his twenty-five year rabbinical career and his services to B'nai Israel.[87]

In 1978 Rabbi Arthur Gould became Associate to Rabbi Pearlmutter after serving pulpits in Alabama, Oklahoma, North Carolina, Virginia and Pennsylvania. He was ordained by the Hebrew Union College in June of 1978.

In August 1982 Rabbi Herbert Yoskowitz accepted the position of Senior Rabbi at B'nai Israel. A native of Brooklyn, New York, and a graduate of Brooklyn College, Rabbi Yoskowitz moved to Toledo from Congregation "Brith Shalom in Bellaire, Texas, prior to that he served in Baltimore at Beth El and as a lecturer in Jewish History at Baltimore Hebrew College. Before coming to Toledo, he had received several awards for outstanding community service and adult programming.[88] (*Photo 27, page 99, Arnold Carmel and Madge Levinson*)

Rabbi Arnold Bienstock became the spiritual leader of Congregation B'nai Israel in 1984. The new Senior Rabbi was a graduate of Columbia University and the Jewish Theological Seminary. He also attended Hebrew University in Jerusalem. His previous posts included Senior Rabbi at Temple Israel in Portsmouth, New Hampshire and involvement with the New England Region of United Synagogue Youth.[89]

In August 1997 Congregation B'nai Israel gained new spiritual leadership, in fact, a double dose. That month Rabbi Michael Ungar succeeded Rabbi Arnold Bienstock, who had moved to Congregation Shaarey Tefilla in Indianapolis. A native of Detroit and familiar with Toledo due to visits via the United Synagogue Group in Detroit, Rabbi Ungar is a graduate of the Jewish Theological Seminary of America in New York City. He served as assistant rabbi at Congregational B'nai Amoona in St. Louis and as rabbi at Temple Shomei Emunah in Montclair, New Jersey before coming to Toledo.[90]

At the same time, his wife, Rabbi Wendy Ungar, became educational director at B'nai Israel. Also a graduate of the American Theological Seminary of America, she has a master's degree and a graduate degree in Hebrew Letters as well. She also worked at the Hebrew Academy. She was the first Conservative female rabbi in the city. President of Temple B'nai Israel Fagie Morse was quoted in a newspaper article saying "You just can't ignore this incredible bonus. We were unbelievably inspired by them."[91]

One of the objectives of the Ungars in Toledo was "To really try and create a venue so we can engage as many members of the congregation and community in Jewish activities and raise levels of Jewish observances," according to a statement in *The Blade*.[92]

Implementing that objective, Rabbi Ungar soon offered a series of free classes on Jewish identity. The sessions included such topics as "Conservative Jews – Who Are We? What Do We Believe?", "The Amidah Shuffle (Synagogue Choreography)," "Synagogue Do's and Don't's," and "Everything You Always Wanted to Know But Were Afraid to Ask."[93]

"Passover University" was also instituted at B'nai Israel to help Jews more thoroughly appreciate and participate in that holiday. At the shul, instruction and hands-on training was given on the making of matzah (unleavened bread) and chicken blintzes. There were also discussions on conducting the proper Passover Seder with all its rituals and how to keep young children interested in the observance and about their role. Rabbi Michael Ungar discussed the components of Passover and how to modify a family's traditional observance.[94] *(Photo 28, page 99, Cantor Jamie Gloth)*

After a five-year tenure at B'nai Israel, rabbis Michael and Wendy Ungar left for Bexley, Ohio. Michael became associate rabbi and Wendy educational director at Congregation Tifereth Israel in that Columbus suburb. While in Toledo, Rabbi Michael Ungar said he was pleased to have reintroduced Purim spiels (humorous musical plays part of the Purim observance) and "Passover University" (which ultimately included all area synagogues). Wider community involvement included initial sponsorship of the "Erase the Hate" campaign that fights bigotry and hatred in the community and participation in Habitat for Humanity's "Holy Toledo build," in which Toledo's Jewish congregations worked to build homes for families needing them.[95]

Rabbi Sylvan D. Kamens then served as an interim rabbi at B'nai Israel for two years following Rabbi Michael Ungar's relocation to Columbus, Ohio. During his tenure, Hazzan James Gloth became the new cantor at B'nai Israel. He is a graduate of the University of Cincinnati and attended the H. L. Milller Cantorial School and the College of Jewish Music at the Jewish Theological Seminary in New York City.[96] *(Photo 29, page 99, B'nai Israel)*

Space issues at Temple B'nai Israel, first described in 1966, were resolved thirty-eight years later when *The Blade* reported that the B'nai Israel Synagogue had been sold, preparatory for the congregation to move from the building and into a new temple once again. Initially, a local Christian congregation arranged to purchase the Kenwood site, with the Conservative Jewish community remaining on the site until October 31, 2004 and then moving into a new building by late 2006, holding services in a temporary location in the interim.[97] That deal fell through and a later story in *The Blade* said that the University of Toledo Foundation purchased the six-acre Kenwood property in April of 2004 for $1.75 million. Under provisions of that purchase, B'nai Israel did not have to leave until its new temple was completed.[98]

On August 1, 2004 Rabbi Barry J. Leff succeeded interim Rabbi Kamens. Rabbi Leff's background differs significantly from previous rabbis that have served the congregation. Born in New York City to a family that was generally Orthodox in background but predominantly "not very observant," Leff was in the high-tech corporate world for twenty years and had lived in Israel, Iran and Thailand, besides the United States. Only when his wife Lauri began to study for conversion to Judaism did he experience a rebirth of interest in Judaism as he read the books she was studying. "The interconnectedness of the *Kabbalah*, the mysticism, made sense of me," Rabbi Leff said. "Over the course of the next year, I became observant [of Judaism]". No longer feeling excited by his business activities, Leff sold his telecommunications firm in California's Silicon Valley and "developed a missionary zeal for Judaism," ultimately deciding to study for the rabbinate. He subsequently graduated from the Ziegler School of Rabbinic Studies in Los Angeles, which is the only Conservative Jewish rabbinical school on the West Coast. Prior to coming to B'nai Israel, Rabbi Leff served at Congregation Beth Shalom in Tucson, Arizona and Beth Tikvah Congregation in Richmond, British Columbia, Canada.[99]

Once in Toledo, Rabbi Leff's major issues involved change and preparing for the future: The capital campaign to finance the new synagogue and planning that new building were major priorities. Organizationally, B'nai Israel worked with Etz Chayim with the goal of merging their respective Sunday school programs. In the midst of these capital matters, Rabbi Barry Leff also announced the organization of an on-going class for Jews who desire to know more about their faith. The class was open also to gentiles considering conversion, interfaith couples and all others interested in Judaism. The class met once a week for a term of about six months, with meetings scheduled for the convenience of attendees.[100]

Groundbreaking for the new synagogue in Sylvania occurred on Sunday, October 30, 2005. As part of the ceremony, soil from the congregation's past, present and future sites was mixed with earth from Jerusalem.

The year 2007 (year 5768 on the Jewish calendar) witnessed two major changes for the Congregation B'nai Israel. In January members moved from their Kenwood synagogue after 50 years to a new synagogue in Sylvania, adjacent to the Jewish Community Center and The Temple-Congregation Shomer Emunim. The new building includes a circular sanctuary trimmed in oak with natural light coming in through clerestory windows. The $4 million, nearly 20,000 square feet synagogue is smaller than its predecessor and better sized to the needs of the 450 families who comprise the congregation. Abraham Musher-Eizenman, a local architect and a member of the congregation, designed the building.

Then in August of 2007 a new spiritual leader came to the Conservative congregation. Rabbi Moshe Saks is a Philadelphia native and a graduate of the Jewish Theological Seminary of American. Immediately before coming to Toledo, he served ten years at Beth Tzedec Congregation in Calgary, Alberta, Canada. One of the attractions of B'nai Israel, the rabbi noted in a newspaper interview, was the "spirit of cooperation" he found among its members. After serving ten years in western Canada, he is also pleased to be closer to his family and his wife's family, both concentrated on the U.S. East Coast. Rabbi Saks is also a certified alcohol rehabilitation counselor; he holds degrees in history and Hebrew literature from Yeshiva University as well as a degree in social work from Columbia University. Among his other studies have been pastoral psychiatry and clinical pastoral education.[101] (*Photo 30, page 100, Torah procession to new B'nai Israel Synagogue*)

Conservative - Vermont Avenue Temple

The Jewish Federation's brief history of local congregations notes B'nai Shalom, a Conservative temple, was organized on August 12, 1900. Founders of what the Federation cites as Toledo's first conservative congregation were Nathan Oesterman, L. Littleman, Jacob Sherman, M. A. Offstadt and Louis Epstein. Four years later the congregation bought a former Christian church on Vermont Avenue, between Adams and Southard and Rabbi Freund of Shomer Emunim dedicated it in September 1904. According to the city directory of 1905, Edward Benjamin Browne was the first rabbi and remained for less than two years. David H. Wittenberg succeeded Browne, leaving in April 1907. The last listing for the Vermont Avenue Temple was in the 1921 Toledo City Directory.[102]

Reform - Congregation Shomer Emunim ("Guardian of the Faith")

One source claimed there were thirty, or fewer, Jewish families in Toledo in 1870.[103] Another document put the number at "approximately forty-seven."[104] While the majority followed Orthodox practices, a minority took an interest in the Reform Judaism alternative. Reform Judaism began in Germany in the 1800s as some Jews decided that Orthodox dogma was too rigid, even backward for the time period, and an obstacle to Jews' greater acceptance into gentile (especially German) society. The variety of Reform Judaism that took root in America was more radical than the European version. Generally in American Reform Judaism, men did not wear any head covering during services, dietary and other ritual laws were not considered binding and English, not Hebrew, was the primary language at prayer services. The Reform movement deemed social activism as the main obligation of Jews, not observing rituals.[105] (*Photo 31, page 100, Shomer Emunim*)

Initially, these local practitioners assembled in their homes and other rooms, with out-of-town rabbis leading services.[106] By July 1874 the Toledo adherents were mentioned in an issue of *The Israelite* as working to form a local Reform congregation.[107] According to a history of Shomer Emunim, the following individuals were prominent in this early period: Gotthelf Bloch, A. S. Cohen, Max Eppstein, Leopold Frank [sometimes spelled Franc], S. H. Frank, Benjamin Frankenberg, Edward Goldmann, Isaac Landman, Jacob Lasalle, Julius Mack, Nathan L. Ries and Joseph Roth.[108]

The Reform movement was gaining momentum in Jewish settlements across the United States and thus the local supporters gained from their affiliation with a national trend. In the view of Rabbi Joseph Telushkin, "In its heyday in the late nineteenth century, Reform Judaism totally dominated American-Jewish religious life. There were about two hundred major Jewish congregations in the United States in 1881 and the vast majority was Reform, with only about twelve Orthodox.[109] *The Israelite* reporter wrote that the push for a local Reform congregation came from "younger [men] who have come to Toledo from places where they have enjoyed a synagogue and sabbath school."[110]

Local Reform Jews also faced obstacles. Their small numbers meant the local Reform congregation lacked tangible support. *The Israelite* reporter who saw the beginnings in 1874 noted that "lethargy" among Jews was a limiting factor, as was the disinterest of older Jews, who had been raised in the Orthodox manner.[111] The need to tend to daily affairs as part of a greater effort to become settled and successful in the new country also competed for the time and resources of the Reform-minded Jews.

In February 1875 the drive for a local Reform congregation achieved a major success. Toledo Reform Jews held several meetings that month, formed a congregation and collectively raised $1,000 or more for a synagogue.[112] Assembling in one of the rooms of the United States Express building on St. Clair Street, between thirty and forty persons adopted a constitution that included using Rabbi Isaac Mayer Wise's *Minhag America* (Religious Custom of America) as the form of worship and by-laws.[113] Accepting the suggestion of Rabbi Wise, the leading Reform clergyman in America, who lived in Cincinnati and who had established the first rabbinical seminary in America (Hebrew Union College) in 1875, the founders took the name Shomer Emunim (usually translated as "Guardian of the Faith" or "Guardian of the Faithful") for their new congregation.[114] The newly-elected officers were Emanuel Stern, president; Gustave Goldsmith, vice president; Max Eppstein, secretary; Moses Gitskey, treasurer; and Jacob Lasalle, Henry Stern and Simon Kohn as trustees. This new board of directors was charged with legally incorporating the congregation under Ohio law, locating a proper site for worship and securing a rabbi.

The proper site issue was resolved when the congregation purchased a small church at the corner of Adams and Superior streets. A Baptist group had originally built it, but local Unitarians had used it more recently. In September the Jews did some repair and remodeling to suit their needs with the intention of having it ready to observe the High Holy Days later in 1875.[115]

A two-phase plan secured a rabbi for Shomer Emunim. Initially the congregation arranged for a Mr. Gerstle of Cincinnati to come and lead services while a more permanent rabbi was sought. In October 1875 representatives of Shomer Emunim invited Rabbi Benjamin Eger of Titusville, Pennsylvania to Toledo. He offered to serve on a trial basis, subject to final congregation approval.

As part of his audition, Rabbi Eger gave an evening lecture on Sunday, October 16. The general public was invited and assured that he would speak in English. Two days later *The Blade* printed a review of the lecture that had been presented to a synagogue filled with "a very intelligent audience, composed of representatives of all creeds."[116]

Presumably that lecture was not the rabbi's only success in pleasing the congregation. On October 26 the membership unanimously voted to make Eger their leader. One member who was not named described the new rabbi: "He gave entire satisfaction as a learned man and rabbi on reform principles and all think he is the right man at the right place to instill the doctrine of Judaism in our children and to enlighten the older ones. He has awakened some of the sleepers by his sound and logical reasoning."[117]

President Abraham Lincoln had first proclaimed Thanksgiving as a national holiday during his presidency and Shomer Emunim observed it along with the rest of the country in 1875 with special services. The congregation's efforts were included in a local newspaper's listing of community observances. Historian Elaine Anderson commented that "This was a degree of recognition which had not previously been given to a Jewish congregation. Shomer Emunim had been launched with a flurry of activity and someone made sure that the press was well informed of each development."[118] Reading Anderson's account of the start-up of Shomer Emunim, Max Eppstein stands out as the most energetic and involved person among the charter members, at least based on newspaper coverage. It seems likely that he made sure the local media knew of the synagogue's Thanksgiving services, among its other activities.

The flurry of founding activity in 1875 continued into early 1876. On January 6 Jennie Stern of Toledo married Gates Thalheimer of Syracuse, New York in Shomer Emunim Temple. Rabbi Eger performed the ceremony, with Max Eppstein and Jacob Landman as ushers. A newspaper account credited the wedding with special significance: since services began in the new synagogue on the eve of Rosh Hashanah without a consecration service, the bridal ceremony was used for that purpose as well.[119]

Reform Judaism appeared in good health and growing at a robust pace, both in Toledo and around the nation as the 1870s progressed. As an example, Shomer Emunim sponsored the first Purim Ball in Toledo on March 9, 1876. Five days before the event, one newspaper announced that 500 tickets had been sold already! Two large rooms at the Oliver House accommodated the gala.[120] Another positive sign for the future was the first Shomer Emunim confirmation in May 1878. (The young people confirmed were Minnie Eger, Albert Friendlander, Ida Friedlander, Albert Goldsmith, Lizzie Goldsmith, Ida Koch, Sara Koch, Solomon Lasalle, and Abraham Stern.)[121]

Elaine Anderson noted that the "community climate in which the Reform congregation was launched was an extremely receptive one. There was curiosity, but it was combined with what appears to be a genuine interest in Jewish activities, Jewish traditions, and in the Jewish position in the contemporary religious scene." Furthermore, she credits Rabbi Eger with working well within this environment. He was a skilled and bilingual speaker (English and German, the languages of Toledo's primary gentile population groups) and took an active part in Toledo's life. He even arranged a pulpit exchange with his counterpart in a local Unitarian church.[122]

But after just a few years, the Shomer Emunim congregation had apparently fallen into decline. Contemporary records do not fully explain the circumstances, but at least three factors were divisions within the congregation, a falling away of some members and Rabbi Eger's too-fervent calls for greater religious commitment. Compounding this characteristic, Eger became involved in a probate court case revolving about what was best for two young Jewish children who had been abandoned in Toledo. The "Englander children" case was not settled to the rabbi's liking and he gained the reputation as a "trouble-maker" and "religious fanatic," as well as fostering the involvement of a civil court into Jewish family matters. Sometime in early 1880 Eger left the Shomer Emunim pulpit and moved to Jackson, Michigan and later Madison, Indiana.[123]

Symbolic of the congregation's disintegration was the sale of the synagogue at Adams and Superior in the late spring of 1880. The building was jacked up and moved the short distance to Huron Street between Adams and Madison streets to make space for the new Masonic Temple on its former site. The former synagogue was converted into the headquarters of the Third Ward Republicans.[124]

Fortunately for the long-term survival of Toledo's Reform congregation, at least two former members were not prepared to allow the group to disappear. Max Eppstein had been one of the earliest and strongest Reform advocates in the city. He had also been secretary of the earlier Shomer Emunim congregation. Gotthilf Bloch was a second local Reform Jew who wanted to re-establish the congregation. Both Eppstein and Bloch were sons of rabbis and they brought their determination to several meetings in late spring 1885 with the purpose of re-organizing the defunct community.

With a positive consensus achieved in the spring meetings, the local Reform cadre invited Rabbi Isaac M. Wise, the leading Reform cleric who resided in Cincinnati, to visit Toledo in June to assist in the rejuvenation. He breakfasted with Eppstein and Bloch, as well as E. J. Cohn and Jacob Lasalle. The next day he addressed potential congregation members in the GAR Hall. Apparently he was very persuasive and the listeners equally receptive, for at the conclusion of his address those present resolved Shomer Emunim should be reborn. New officers were elected by the thirty-six members; the group also included seven young men who did not have full membership status, but who had donated funds. As a further sign of this enthusiasm for congregational rebirth, the members voted to join the Union of American Hebrew Congregations (the nationwide organization of Reform congregations) and selected Max Eppstein to attend the Union's meeting in St. Louis in July.

The re-formed congregation moved ahead to celebrate the High Holy Days of 1885. Quarters were rented in the Central Congregational Church at Tenth and Adams streets and M. S. Manheimer, a preceptor of Hebrew Union College in Cincinnati, came north to lead the services. While Manheimer had compliments for the choir and the renewed sabbath school, he also urged the ladies of the primarily female Shomer Emunim community to inspire their "lukewarm and indifferent husbands and brothers" to aspire to greater religious commitment.[125]

Rabbi Wise continued to aid the renewed congregation by providing a new rabbi. He arranged for Tobias Shanfarber, a student in his last year at Hebrew Union College, to have no classes on Friday or Monday and thus be able to commute to Toledo and lead Sabbath services. Furthermore, if the people of Shomer Emunim liked Shanfarber, he could become their rabbi. Local Reform leader Max Eppstein liked the young man and no doubt helped see that he was elected rabbi by a unanimous voice vote.[126] Shanfarber's popularity continued into 1886 as he was hired as a full-time rabbi at a salary of $1,500 per year upon being graduated and ordained at Hebrew Union College. In fact, the congregation sent the new rabbi a three-foot-tall floral arrangement and Gotthilf Bloch, E. J. Cohn and Max Eppstein personally attended the ceremony in Cincinnati. The Shanfarber period ended quickly, however. Rabbi Shanfarber left Toledo in the early summer of 1887 to take a pulpit in Fort Wayne, Indiana. His departure was apparently amiable and he was welcomed back for visits over the years.[127]

Meanwhile, the congregation moved ahead on other fronts. It held a very successful Hanukkah festival in 1885. Some three hundred Toledoans, some of them gentiles, participated in the December 7 program. Success continued in 1886: a Purim Ball raised $432 for the temple's women auxiliary's building fund. That year more than 100 children attended Sabbath school on a regular basis, including some whose parents were not congregational members.

Shanfarber's departure meant that the congregation experienced a brief period without a rabbi. The community observed the High Holy Days of 1887 in rented quarters in the Soldiers Memorial Hall, located on the southwest corner of Adams and Ontario streets. The services included another Hebrew Union College senior student, Clifton H. Levy, presiding. Levy pleased the congregation and the leaders tried to retain him with the same arrangements they had secured for Shanfarber. This time, the powers-that-be at the college declined, saying that Levy's studies couldn't stand the time demands of the deal. Shomer Emunim had to advertise for a new rabbi.

With a revitalized congregation, but no permanent synagogue for eight years, Shomer Emunim took action in June 1888. The membership decided to build a new temple. In the fall of 1888 Max Eppstein, Leopold Frank and Henry Stern traveled to Youngstown, Ohio with an architect to examine the synagogue of Congregation Rodef Sholem. The trip was well worthwhile and Eppstein reported that he was positive that his Toledo synagogue would do what was needed.[128]

By the spring of 1889 plans had progressed sufficiently so that a drawing of the new Shomer Emunim Temple was featured in an *American Israelite* article. The congregation paid $2,500 for a lot on the east side of Tenth Street, between Washington and Monroe streets. The proposed building was expected to cost $10,000 and include a 150-seat sanctuary and room in the basement for a Sabbath school.[129] The goal was dedication before the fall High Holy Days.[130]

The dedication was September 20. Rabbi Clifton Levy remained the congregation's temporary spiritual leader. Rabbi Isaac Wise and Rabbi Louis Grossman of Detroit journeyed to Toledo to participate. Toledo Mayor Hamilton and several Protestant clergymen were also present. *The Blade* gave the event space on page one of the next day's newspaper, describing the congregation as the families of "twenty-four of the best and wealthiest Hebrews in the city, among whom are those of Messrs. G. Bloch, Jacob Lasalle, M. M. Eppstein, Isaac Landman, Leopold Franc, Julius Mack, Joseph Roth, N. N. Ries, Henry Stern, S. H. Frank, E. Goldman, Henry Thorner, Louis Strasburger, D. Hubert and others.[131]

Shomer Emunim had a new temple, but still no permanent rabbi. Shortly after the new synagogue was dedicated, Edward Benjamin Morris Browne was named as its rabbi. He had lived a more eventful life than his two youthful predecessors. A one-time professor of medical jurisprudence and newspaper editor, he had managed to become "ostracized by the Rabbinical fraternity in New York, especially by the representatives of the Reform congregations." the *American Israelite* reported in 1887. Thus, the congregation could have known it was getting a rabbi of some controversy. Discord followed him to Toledo and among his local antagonists were the president and vice president of the congregation. Plus, he was described as "restless" and "personally ambitious" by one local historian. He pursued other projects outside of Toledo and aggressively sought to become the first Jewish chaplain of the U. S. Congress – all of which kept him away from Shomer Emunim for some time. In the end, he stayed through the High Holy Days of 1891, then departed for a Chicago congregation. By the end of that year Max Eppstein wrote that the temple was nearly closed, including no Chanukah festival.[132] For most of the following year, Shomer Emunim had to make do with temporary rabbis when one could be obtained.

For some twelve years Shomer Emunim either had lacked a rabbi completely or not for more than two years at a time. With the selection of Emanuel Schreiber in November 1892 that situation improved as he remained until June 1897. Rabbi Schreiber brought a wide perspective and undeniable scholarship to the temple. Born in Austria, he studied in Vienna and received a Ph.D. from the University of Berlin (1872). He had been a rabbi in Germany, but immigrated to America seeking greater freedom for his Reform ideas. He had served congregations in Mobile, Alabama, Denver and Los Angeles prior to Toledo. The author of some twenty books and pamphlets before his arrival in Toledo, he would also present a paper at the 1893 Chicago's World Fair.[133] His selection must have pleased Max Eppstein, for Schreiber fit Eppstein's vision of what a Reform Jew should be, especially a Reform rabbi. With the construction of the new Tenth Street Temple and the appointment of Rabbi Schreiber, Eppstein would seemingly have been pleased with Reform Judaism in Toledo when he passed away in February 1894.

Congregation Shomer Emunim continued to grow in membership and by 1907 the synagogue's leadership was looking for more adequate quarters and a location more convenient as the Jewish population moved westward. The need for larger facilities also forced Epworth Methodist Episcopal Church to seek a new building and Shomer Emunim purchased Epworth's former church on Scottwood Avenue, between Monroe and Bancroft streets, in what would much later be called the "Old West End."[134]

An account of the Scottwood Temple stressed its pleasant, socially enjoyable ambiance as a gathering place for the membership.[135] Attractive as it was, and an improvement over the Tenth Street Temple, the Scottwood location sufficed only until 1917, when the congregation moved to its new Collingwood Avenue Temple.

The relocation from Tenth Street to Scottwood nearly coincided with the arrival of Rabbi David Alexander. He served for fourteen years, the longest tenure thus far among Temple Shomer Emunim rabbis. After the more cosmopolitan background of Emanuel Schreiber, David Alexander presented the congregation with a more typical American Reform background, i.e. a graduate of Hebrew Union College.

One of the few surviving newspaper accounts of Shomer Emunim during its Scottwood Temple period noted that the congregation claimed a membership of 110 families, which was increasing. Prophetically, the article closed with "The congregation expects to build a new temple within the next few years." The leadership during the Scottwood period was A. S. Cohen, president; Charles K. Friedman, vice president; Joseph I. Kobacker, treasurer; Herman Hirsch, secretary; trustees D. B. Eppstein, Benjamin Frankenberg, E. A. Herzog, Harry J. Kaufman and J. M. Weil.[136] The concurrent ladies' society officers were: Mrs. M. Wise, president; Mrs. Julius Geleerd, vice president; Mrs. M. Dreyfus, treasurer; Mrs. David Alexander, secretary.[137]

In reviewing the campaign that would result in the Collingwood Avenue Temple, the unrecorded author of that Temple's history strongly hinted that Rabbi Alexander had only one primary objective prior to 1917: persuading the congregation that the Scottwood Temple would need to be replaced with a greater facility that would serve the congregation itself and enable Shomer Emunim to better serve the greater Toledo community. (*Photo 32, page 101, The Collingwood Temple*)

Not surprisingly then, after only ten years in the Scottwood Temple, the Shomer Emunim congregation built a totally new, larger, synagogue on Collingwood Avenue, corner of Acklin. No doubt with a great sense of congregational accomplishment, Rabbi Alexander led the dedication ceremonies on February 16, 1917. The lay leaders of the congregation at this time were – Charles K. Friedman, president; Isidor Silverman, vice-president; Leon Netzorg, secretary; Maurice Moyer, treasurer, and trustees A. S. Cohen, Abe Koch, Morris Rosenberg, Edwin M. Rosenthal and Morris H. Lempert.[138]

The new temple proved to be a fine facility for organizations affiliated with the congregation. There had been a Men's Club for some years. "The history of the Collingwood Avenue Temple Brotherhood is a story without written record. It exists in the memories of those men who enjoyed this brotherly association. At that time the organization was know as the Men's Club. The Brotherhood succeeded the Men's Club in 1935, the year Rabbi Feuer came to the Temple. For some years the Brotherhood "sponsored and financially supported" Troop 37 of the Boy Scouts of America, which under the leadership of Jules Houseman and Louis Michael "became one of the leading troops in the area." . . . In 1950 a Bowling League was formed."[139]

"Since the very founding of the Congregation in 1875, there always has been an active women's organization of the Temple, interested in promoting its welfare. Soon after [the men began the congregation] their wives met to organize the Temple Ladies Auxiliary for the purpose of stimulating interest in the Congregational life, improving the place of worship, and establishing a Religious School wherein their children might learn the principles of Reform Judaism. . . . The local group was among the first to join the National Federation of Temple Sisterhoods when the national organization began shortly after 1900. It soon changed its name to the Sisterhood of the Temple, following the national federation's recommendation. It was also a charter member of the Ohio State Federation of Temple Sisterhoods that was formed in 1919. One of its most noteworthy fundraising events was a "Bazaar" held c. 1926 in the Coliseum on Ashland Avenue, which raised $14,000 "to alleviate the mortgage on the Temple."[140]

The congregation's religious classes began ". . .in 1884 in the little building on Tenth Street. . .From the handful of children who in 1884 shared their school room with the building's furnace, until 1935 when 150 children were enrolled, the school grew rapidly with each forward step of the Temple. . . . In 1935, the year Rabbi Feuer became rabbi and led the complete reorganization of the school, the school has grown further, with some 400 children enrolled, 52 of them forming the largest Kindergarten class in the Temple's history [this being in 1956]".[141]

Rabbi David Alexander left Shomer Emunim in 1921, having seen the congregation grow considerably during tenure. After a three-year interval, Rabbi Joseph Kornfeld became spiritual leader of the Temple in 1924. He brought a unique distinction to the profiles of the temple's rabbis: he had served as ambassador to Persia for three years during Warren Harding's presidential administration. He remained for ten years, leaving to become Rabbi of Holy Blossom Temple in Toronto, Canada.[142]

The next rabbi at Shomer Emunim was Leon Israel Feuer, who came to the Temple in 1935 and retired as Senior Rabbi in 1972. A native of Pennsylvania, while still a child, Feuer moved with his family to Cleveland and while in high school there he met Abba Hillel Silver, who had just become the rabbi at The Temple there and who was deeply impressing congregants. In his later autobiography, Rabbi Feuer credited Rabbi Silver's encouragement with being a major factor in his decision to enter the rabbinate. Consequently, he entered Hebrew Union College after the High Holy Days in 1920. After ordination in 1927, Rabbi Feuer returned to Cleveland as an assistant to Rabbi Silver. He worked under Silver until called to succeed Rabbi Kornfeld at Toledo, where Rabbi Silver installed him at the Collingwood Avenue Temple in January 1935.[143]

In addition to his Toledo activities, Rabbi Feuer was known nationally as an ardent Zionist and worked with Rabbi Silver to further that cause.[144] In the summer of 1943 Rabbi Silver became leader of the American Zionist Emergency Council and shortly thereafter asked the Shomer Emunim board of trustees to grant Feuer a year's leave of absence to work on this greater issue. The board agreed and Rabbi Feuer did not return to Toledo until June 1944. However, he continued his strong and active involvement in Zionism, which included many trips from the city. His Zionist activity also had a local facet as he worked hard to discourage the formation of a local chapter of the American Council for Judaism, a movement within Reform Judaism opposed to Zionism.[145] (*Photo 33, page 101, Rabbi Leon Israel Feuer*)

The original 1917 Collingwood Avenue Temple served for thirty-four years, but as Shomer Emunim observed its 75th anniversary in 1950, planning was advocated for a physical expansion. Its membership had grown from the 300 families when Rabbi Feuer came to Toledo to nearly triple that size. There was some controversy about this plan, however, according to Rabbi Feuer. The fund raising necessary for the proposed expansion would be concurrent with fund raising for a new Jewish Community Center and some argued that the J.C.C. should have priority. Feuer's position, ". . . that the needs of the Temple were more urgent, and their fulfillment from every point of view more important." carried the day.[146]

An addition at the existing site was judged to be the best solution and a campaign, headed by Lewis N. Osterman as General Chairman of the Expansion Committee, successfully raised $250,000 for the work. The addition's cornerstone was laid on April 29, 1951 and the completed structure was dedicated on January 25, 1952. It included a 550-seat auditorium.[147] The Collingwood Avenue Temple complex then stretched along Collingwood for an entire block, from Acklin to Winthrop streets.

Local architects Nelson Thal and Herman Feldstein designed the temple addition, with Stanford E. Thal as general contractor. The architects explained that their major objectives were to provide additional seating for the High Holy Days and to generally accommodate an increasing membership, without making major structure changes and expenditures. Good lighting and a suitable Ark for the main sanctuary were also requirements. Breaking through part of the north wall of the main Temple for the Chapel and Auditorium solved the seating problem. These rooms featured folding doors, which, when opened, provided a clear vista to the pulpit in the main Temple. The two rooms sat between 300 and 400 for dinner and more can be seated in auditorium style.[148]

Ironically, within about a decade the congregation began to again confront the issue of whether to move. Demographically, Toledo's Jewish population continued its residential shift westward within the city and beyond into suburban communities, especially Sylvania. This was a local example of a national trend, according to Professor Jonathan Sarna, and followed similar patterns for Catholics and Protestant denominations. Such building campaigns "conveyed a message of life and hope. . . It aroused a spirit of religious activity, enthusiasm, and mission even among people who rarely attended worship services themselves." [149]

The membership, however, was divided over a proposed move. Shomer Emunim had resided in the Old West End for more than half a century (Scottwood Temple from 1907 to 1917 and then the Collingwood Temple) and was an anchor of the neighborhood. Moreover, the entire Old West End was experiencing a housing transition as black Americans formed a growing percentage of the population and more of the houses were sub-divided to accommodate renters, rather than owners.[150] New facilities would require fund raising as well. Lastly, the proposed new site was a much greater move in terms of geographical distance than the Temple had ever made before.

According to Rabbi Sokobin, a majority of the congregation approved the move at "a turbulent congregational meeting." By the time Sokobin arrived in 1972, the Collingwood Temple building had been sold to Toledo Public Schools and plans for the new structure were nearly complete.[151] The sale contract provided that the congregation could continue to have offices in the Collingwood building and conduct worship services and other functions there on weekends; the Board of Education could use the classrooms during the week. (*Photo 34, page 101, Rabbi Feuer and Lewis Osterman*)

In 1971 the congregation purchased forty-eight acres in the Toledo suburb of Sylvania, on the south side of Sylvania Avenue, just west of I-475/ US 23. The vision was for this tract to accommodate a new Temple, a new Jewish Community Center, a new Orthodox shul and apartments for senior citizens.[152]

Rabbinical leadership at the Temple changed in 1972. Long-serving Senior Rabbi Leon Feuer anticipated his pending retirement and urged the congregation's lay leaders to seek his successor so that the two rabbis could handle a smooth transfer of authority. One of the persons responding to the

Temple's recruitment call was Alan Sokobin.

Rabbi Sokobin's association with this Toledo congregation actually began while he was a third-year student at Hebrew Union College in Cincinnati. In an autobiographical essay, Rabbi Sokobin recalled being interviewed in Cincinnati by Rabbi Leon Feuer and Temple President Norman Thal. Having been selected, he served as youth advisor, educational assistant and student rabbi on weekends in 1952-54.[153] (*Photo 2 7, page 102, Rabbi Sokobin*)

His next official contact came eighteen years later when he learned that Rabbi Feuer was retiring and the Temple was seeking his successor. Sokobin applied for the position and he was subsequently invited to Toledo for an interview. The Temple's Selection Committee had four requirements for a new rabbi: 1) He should be a Hebraist. 2) He should be a "passionate Zionist". 3) He should have an earned doctorate or taught at a university. 4) He would not preside at mixed marriages. Rabbi Sokobin recalled his five-hour meeting with the Selection Committee, which included representatives of all the Temple's activities and the congregation's viewpoints. In response to one question, he replied that "the single most important quality of a good rabbi" is "leadership." At one point in the interview, Rabbi Sokobin expressed his doubt that he would be a good fit for the Collingwood Temple. He described his "own life-style" as more "traditional" and anticipated advocating changes that the congregation might not be ready for. Lynn Jacobs replied to his concern: "[the congregation] had forty years of one style of rabbinic direction and perhaps they were ready for innovation and change."[154] On June 14, 1972 the board of trustees of the Collingwood Avenue Temple announced the formal appointment of Alan Sokobin as Co-Rabbi.[155]

Congregation Shomer Emunim moved westward once again when it relocated to its current site on Sylvania Avenue between Holland-Sylvania and McCord roads in Sylvania Township, adjacent to the Jewish Community Center.[156] More than 250 people gathered at the future location on Sunday, May 21, 1972 to symbolically break ground. The congregation's 97th annual meeting was held immediately preceding the ceremony.[157] Rabbi Sokobin summarized the transition: "At the end of May we broke ground for the new building in Sylvania. On June 6 [1973] we celebrated the final Service of Confirmation in the Collingwood Avenue Temple. At the conclusion of the Shavuot service the Torah scrolls were carried out of the building, signifying the end of an era."[158]

In 1975 the members of Shomer Emunim celebrated their Temple's Centenary Anniversary. Senior Rabbi Alan Sokobin presided at the first evening service of the High Holy Days during the Centenary observance; Rabbi Emeritus Leon Feuer led the service on Rosh Hashanah morning.[159]

Mr. Alfred Samborn, a principal and founder of the local firm Samborn,

Steketee, Otis & Evans [now known as SSOE] and a member of B'nai Jacob (later Etz Chayim), designed the new Temple to a "superplan," a configuration and set of features that enabled it to function for worship, education and social affairs. Thus it reflects that "Judaism is more than a religion. It is educational and social in its outreach."[160] The 500-seat sanctuary constitutes the largest area of the Temple and features a beamed, wooden ceiling. Adjacent to this worship area is a social hall that can be joined to the sanctuary with the moving of a partition, thus providing an additional 1,000 seats when needed for services. The hall can also hold 250 persons for dinners and other social events. It may also be sub-divided into three portions for simultaneous activities. The complex includes a 200-seat chapel for weddings, small funerals and other appropriate functions. Another major component is the classroom-library, with bookshelves defining the area and a carpeted floor and moveable furniture enable the space to also host various meetings, and even weekend sleepovers for teenagers participating in *sabbatons* ("Sabbath experiences").[161]

Also in 1975 the congregation faced the decision to change prayer books. Following past practice, the Central Conference of American Rabbis had reviewed the continued suitability of the *Union Prayer Book*, first published in 1895 and subsequently revised several times. It was clearly a graphic and philosophical statement of Reform Judaism: "it opened from left to right (rather than from right to left, as traditional Hebrew prayer books do) and contained only minimal amounts of Hebrew; the bulk of the service was in English."[162] After deliberation, the Conference issued a replacement, the *Gates of Prayer*. The Temple's Board charged the Ritual Committee with comparing the old and new prayer books and making a recommendation to the membership. The then-current Temple rabbi characterized the two books thusly: The *Union Prayer Book* was physically thin, required little knowledge of Hebrew, and was familiar to several generations of Reform Jews. In contrast, *Gates of Prayer* was a larger publication, "an abundant liturgy and a serious Hebraic element." Furthermore, *Gates of Power* was a definite turn towards more traditional Judaism and away from conventional Reform Judaism.[163]

Another sign of Reform Judaism practice shifting concerned the coming of age ceremony, *Bar Mitzvah* (for males) or *Bat Mitzvah* (for females). Only for about the last twenty years had Reform congregations even observed the coming of age, and then usually only for males. Prior to the spread of the *Bar/Bat Mitzvah* ceremony, Reform Judaism had introduced confirmation in the 19th century as a group service for both boys and girls (though usually at a later stage of their teenage years), resembling the Christian practice. (In about the same timeframe, there was a grassroots trend in Conservative synagogues to add the *Bat Mitzvah* ceremony for girls to the existing one for boys.)[164]

A local manifestation of this changing outlook was what was reported to be the first adult *Bar/Bat Mitzvah* in the history of The Temple, held in December 1989. Six adults ranging in age from 29 to 62 spent several months preparing for the service.[165] (*Photo 37, page 102, Rabbi Samuel R. Weinstein*)

On July 1, 1992 The Temple congregation elected Rabbi Samuel R. Weinstein to be the congregation's spiritual leader, succeeding the recently retired Rabbi Sokobin.[166] A native of Pittsburgh, Rabbi Weinstein left Temple Anshe Hesed in Erie, Pennsylvania, to come to Toledo. Under his leadership, the Congregation Shomer Emunim continued to offer multi-faceted programming to the Temple's 680 member families, reflecting the findings of a congregational survey and the concerns of the 18-member search committee that reviewed candidates for the rabbinical position.[167]

Besides his Temple-related work, Rabbi Weinstein also is active within the larger Toledo community and beyond. For example, he has been involved with the Interracial Religious Coalition, including serving on the Executive Committee. Other efforts in the cause of greater understanding include teaching communal classes for local multi-faith organizations and hosting local school and church groups coming to The Temple. He has also been a member of the St. Vincent's Health Center's Pastoral Advisory Board for many years. Among his activity there has been assisting in the certification of Pastoral Care professionals.[168]

For twenty-four years, he has served as a military chaplain in the United States Air Force. Currently he is the senior rabbi in the Air Force's Chaplain Service and holds the rank of colonel.[169] As part of his varied duties, he has represented the Air Force on National Prayer Day at the White House and currently visits Jewish and Christian seminaries to interest students in serving as chaplains in the armed forces.[170]

In September of 2005 the ties between the Temple and the Hebrew Union College-Jewish Institute of Religion in Cincinnati, Ohio were strengthened with the appointment of Rabbi Weinstein to the clinical faculty. A graduate of H. U. C. himself, the rabbi will be mentoring rabbinical student Marshal Klaven as part of the Mayerson Mentoring Program.[171]

In 1993 Ida Rae Cahana succeeded Robert Borman as cantor at The Temple. Thus becoming the first female cantor in Toledo, she represented a wave of change in cantorial practice. Entering the Hebrew Union College's school of sacred music in 1989, Cantor Cahana was one of fourteen women in the group totaling seventeen. In a newspaper interview, Cahana said that while a cantor of either gender was a trend, another evolution of the last fifty years was the broadening of the cantorial mission. No longer was the cantor only a worship leader, a messenger of the people. Newer tasks include co-officiating at weddings, funerals, baby-namings, making hospital visits, and assisting in preparing youths for their bar and bat mitzvahs. The growth of duties is matched with greater education, now a four-year master's degree with a strong concentration in Jewish topics.[172] Following Cantor Cahana was Judy Seplowin and then Cantor Daniel Pincus.

Temple Shomer Emunim celebrated its 125th anniversary with several activities beginning with a Sabbath service on Friday, June 2, 1995. Rabbi Stephen Schafer, associate rabbi at The Temple from 1954 to 1961, spoke. A social hour and reception followed the service for the congregation's 700 families.[173]

Diane Yomtov became cantor at The Temple in July 2002, following Ida Rae Cahana. A native of Long Island, New York, she first pursued a career in opera and musical theater, attaining bachelor's and master's degrees in music. Subsequently she decided to become a cantor and entered Hebrew Union College in 1996. She came to Toledo after serving as cantor at Temple Emanu-El in Atlanta.[174] (*Photo 36, page 101, Cantor Jennifer Roher*)

In September of 2005 Jennifer Roher became the third female cantor at Shomer Emunim, succeeding Diane Yomtov. A native of New York City, she has a music degree from the University of Hartford (Connecticut) and she graduated from the Hebrew Union College-Jewish Institute of Religion in 2005 as a member of the first class which followed the five-year curriculum. The additional year of education reflects Reform Judaism's commitment to an equal partnership between the roles of rabbi and cantor, according to Cantor Roher. This complementary parity of those roles was a major attraction to Roher for becoming a cantor. She credited Shomer Emunim Rabbi Samuel Weinstein with being very committed towards such equality. [175]

For more photos of Toledo temples, see photos 38, B'nai Israel; photo 39, Collingwood Temple; photo 40, Sharei Zedeck; photo 41, Anshe Sfard on pages 103 and 104.

References

[1] Rothman, Seymour, *After 100 Years; A Sparse History of Temple B'nai Israel*, 1970, Preface.

[2] Dedication booklet, B'nai Israel Congregation, p. 5.

[3] Anderson, p. 148.

[4] Rothman, p. 6.

[5] This may have been the same site and building as the Old Bethel Church cited earlier. Further research is needed.

[6] Anderson places Abraham Goldberg as rabbi but not until 1873, serving

until at least 1878, p. 151, and a congregation history at the time of the 1955 synagogue dedication lists Solomon Van Noorden as the first rabbi.

[7] Rothman, Preface and p. 7.

[8] *Toledo Blade*, March 18, 1872, cited in Anderson, p. 149.

[9] The paper was and is cited in Anderson, p. 150.

[10] Anderson, p. 152.

[11] The incident is recounted in Anderson, pp. 170-171.

[12] Rothman, p. 8.

[13] Rothman, pp. 8-9.

[14] Rothman, p. 9 and Anderson, p. 258.

[15] Rothman, pp. 9-11 and *The Blade*, August 7, 2005, no page (online archive). In 2005 the Ohio Historic Site Preservation Advisory Board recommended that the 1914 temple be added to the National Register of Historic Places due to the building's architectural significance.

[16] Rothman, pp. 11-12.

[17] *The Blade*, January 8, 1999, n. p.

[18] Anderson, pp. 180, 283.

[19] *Congregation B'nai Jacob Observes* 75 Years, p. 3.

[20] *Dedication of B'nai Jacob Synagogue*, p. 3.

[21] *Congregation B'nai Jacob Observes 75 Years*, p. 4.

[22] *Congregation B'nai Jacob Observes 75 Years*, p. 4.

[23] *Dedication of B'nai Jacob Synagogue*, p. 4.

[24] *Congregation B'nai Jacob Observes 75 Years*, p. 4.

[25] *Congregation B'nai Jacob Observes 75 Years*, pp. 4, 10.

[26] *Blade*, May 27, 1996, n. p.

[27] *Congregation B'nai Jacob Observes 75 Years*, p. 4 – 5.

[28] There is a slight discrepancy regarding the founding of the men's Club. The *Congregation B'nai Jacob Observes 75 Years* says it was just before WW II and *Dedication of B'nai Jacob Synagogue* places that action in 1942.

[29] *Dedication of B'nai Jacob Synagogue*, p. 5.

[30] *Toledo Blade*, October 21, 1948, clipping, n.p.

[31] *Dedication of B'nai Jacob Synagogue*, p. 11.

[32] *Toledo Blade*, September 2, 1950, clipping, n. p.

[33] *Dedication of B'nai Jacob Synagogue*, p. 6.

[34] *Congregation B'nai Jacob Observes 75 Years*, pp. 5 - 6

[35] *Toledo Times*, September 8, 1949, clipping, n. p.

[36] *Congregation B'nai Jacob Observes 75 Years*, p 6.

[37] *Blade*, September 19, 1987, no page (clipping).

[38] *Congregation B'nai Jacob Observes 75 Years*, p 6.

[39] *Congregation B'nai Jacob Observes 75 Years*, p 6.

40 *Congregation B'nai Jacob Observes 75 Years,* p 6.

41 *Congregation B'nai Jacob Observes 75 Years,* p 7.

42 Dedication of B'nai Jacob School booklet, p. 6.

43 *Congregation B'nai Jacob Observes 75 Years,* pp. 7 – 8.

44 *Blade,* May 16, 1959, clipping, n. p.

45 *Blade,* clipping, no date, but probably 1973.

46 These were the words of Reform Jew Max Eppstein, quoted in Anderson, p. 266.

47 80th Anniversary; from Generation to Generation, 1907 – 1987, p. 32.

48 Recollections of Sharei Zedeck by Kale and Rainwasser, p. 1.

49 80th Anniversary; from Generation to Generation, 1907 – 1987, p. 32; two former members of Sharei Zedeck put the date at 1933 (Kale and Rainwasser).

50 Recollections of Sharei Zedeck by Kale and Rainwasser, p. 1.

51 *Blade,* September 30, 1967, clipping, n. p.

52 Recollections of Sharei Zedeck by Kale and Rainwasser, p. 1.

53 Recollections of Sharei Zedeck by Kale and Rainwasser, p. 1.

54 Recollections of Sharei Zedeck by Kale and Rainwasser, p. 2.

55 Recollections of Sharei Zedeck by Kale and Rainwasser, p. 2.

56 *Blade,* July 20, 1968, clipping, n.p.

57 *Blade,* September 30, 1967, clipping, n.p..

58 80th Anniversary; from Generation to Generation, 1907 – 1987, p. 33. Sharei Zedeck shares some confusion with a Congregation B'nai Abraham, which a 1908 issue of *The Reform Advocate* credited with having been formed in September 1906. The Advocate story said the Jews needed their own synagogue because they were living too far from the other orthodox synagogues. The 1906 Toledo City Directory puts a B'nai Abraham on Spring Street between Mulberry and Stickney (the same location of Sharei Zedeck at the time).

59 Alexander, *The Reform Advocate,* n. p. The rabbi also listed B'nai Sholom, a Conservative congregation. No further information has yet been discovered.

60 80th Anniversary; from Generation to Generation, 1907 – 1987, p. 33.

61 *Blade,* June 5, 1954, clipping, n. p.

62 *The Blade,* January 29, 1962, clipping, n.p.

63 *The Blade,* August 25, 1962, clipping, n.p.

64 80th Anniversary; from Generation to Generation, 1907 – 1987, p. 30.

65 80th Anniversary; from Generation to Generation, 1907 – 1987, p. 33.

66 *The Blade,* September 30, 1967, no page (clipping).

67 *The Blade,* August 20, 1974, clipping, n.p..

68 *Toledo Jewish News,* August 1973, p. 1.

69 *The Blade,* May 27, 1996, no page (online archive), and Recollections of

Sharei Zedeck by Kale and Rainwasser, p. 2 The 1970 merger date is four years later than the date given in 80th Anniversary; from Generation to Generation, 1907 – 1987. *The Blade* of November 6, 2004, no page (online archive) gives a date of 1974 for the final merger and contains the comments of Rabbi Garsek and Elsa Leveton.

[70] Sharon Rainwasser, Recollections of Etz Chayim, p. 1

[71] 80th Anniversary; from Generation to Generation, 1907 – 1987, p. 30 and *Dedication Book*, Congregation Etz Chayim, 1975, p.5 and Sharon Rainwasser, Recollections of Etz Chayim, p. 1.

[72] *The Blade*, November 6, 2004, no page (online archive) and Sharon Rainwasser, Recollections of Etz Chayim, p. 1.

[73] Rothman, p.. 31.

[74] Rothman, p. 32.

[75] Rothman, p. 16 and *The Blade*, January 8, 1999, no page.

[76] Rothman, pp. 23-24 regarding his conversation with Sidney Friedenthal.

[77] Dedication booklet, B'nai Israel Congregation, p. 5.

[78] *The Blade*, April 15, 1949, clipping, n.p.

[79] *Dedication booklet*, B'nai Israel Congregation, p. 5.

[80] Rothman, pp. 30-31.

[81] Accounts of this episode are in *The Blade*, January 8, 1999, no page (online archive), and the *Dedication booklet*, B'nai Israel Congregation, p. 6, (which cites Libbey-Owens-Ford as the corporate owner of the parcel).

[82] For Friedenthal's account of the land deal, see Rothman, pp. 27-28 and samples of the coverage regarding the interfaith campus are in the *Dedication booklet*, B'nai Israel Congregation, p. 9.

[83] Rothman, p. 31.

[84] *Dedication booklet*, B'nai Israel Congregation, p. 7; a photo on page 8 shows elders Michael Binzer, Sam Brassloff, Herman Fishbein, Gustave Ganch, William Horwitz, Jacob Kaplan, Sam Mostov, Max Newmark, Max Sack, William Shapiro, and Jacob Yuro moving the Torahs on February 19.

[85] Rothman, p. 31.

[86] *Toledo Jewish News*, December 1983, p. 1

[87] *Temple B'nai Israel Bulletin*, Summer Issue, August 8, 1969 and *Toledo Jewish News*, 6-1972, p. 1. Rabbi Pearlmutter died late in 1983.

[88] *The B. I. Connection*, July 15, 1982, p. 1.

[89] *Bulletin Temple B'nai Israel*, August, 1984.

[90] *The Blade*, May 31, 1997, no page (online archive) and *The Blade*, July 13, 2002, no page (online archive).

[91] *The Blade*, May 31, 1997, no page (online archive).

[92] *The Blade*, May 31, 1997, no page (online archive).

[93] *The Blade*, August 30, 1997, no page (online archive).

[94] *The Blade*, April 7, 2001, no page (online archive).

[95] *The Blade*, July 13, 2002, no page (online archive).

[96] *The Blade*, March 25, 2000, clipping, n. p.

[97] *The Blade*, September 27, 2003, Section B, p. 3.

[98] *The Blade*, May 1, 2004, no page (online archive).

[99] *The Blade*, August 28, 2004, no page (online archive). At about the same time, it was also announced that the congregation had studied and ruled the possibility of "co-locating" with Congregation Etz Chayim in a shared building project, see *The Blade*, May 1, clipping, n.p.

[100] *The Blade*, September 24, 2005, Section B, p. 3.

[101] *Blade*, September 8, 2007, Section B, p. 7

[102] *80th Anniversary; from Generation to Generation*, 1907 – 1987, p. 33.

[103] History of Collingwood Avenue Temple," Congregation Shomer Emunim library, n.d. p. 1.

[104] *80th Anniversary; from Generation to Generation*, 1907 – 1987, p. 28.

[105] For a fuller description of Reform Judaism's beginning, see Rabbi Joseph Telushkin, *Jewish Literacy*, pp.230-232, 392-395.

[106] History of Collingwood Avenue Temple," Congregation Shomer Emunim library, n.d. p. 1

[107] Anderson, p. 155.

[108] History of Collingwood Avenue Temple," Congregation Shomer Emunim library, n.d. p.2.

[109] Telushkin, *Jewish Literacy*, p. 392.

[110] *The Israelite* quoted in Anderson, p. 155.

[111] Cited in Anderson, p. 156.

[112] Anderson, p. 157, cites a *Toledo Commercial* story that said $1,500, while the *120th Jubilee of Shomer Emunim* booklet claimed $1,000.

[113] Accounts differ slightly as to the number involved. The 120th Jubilee booklet of the Shomer Emunim congregation cites "30 potential members" while the *Toledo Commercial* newspaper account of February 19 says 40. *The History of the Congregation 1875-1950* by Mrs. Irving E. Goldmann locates the initial meeting in a room of the American Express Company office on Summit Street, from a photocopy of the Goldmann history provided to the author by Rosemary Bramson.

[114] *The Blade*, May 27, 2000, no page (online archive) reports that the phrase occurs only once in the Bible, the 26th chapter of Isaiah, and "the Sylvania synagogue is believed to be the only one in the world to have taken it as its name." There was some earlier confusion about the name, but Rabbi Alan Sokobin, Rabbi Emeritus of The Temple, termed it a "mis-transliteration."

[115] There is mention in *History of Collingwood Avenue Temple* of "the first

place of worship was a small church rented from a Christian Congregation located in [sic] 11th Street, between Madison and Jefferson, approximately at the site of the present YMCA building [in 2005 the Court Rehabilitation and Corrections Services building]." The same source also says it was the site of the wedding between Rosetta Landman and Solomon Wiler in 1875. The Goldmann history says Rabbi Eger presided at the service. Presumably this site was used before the congregation purchased the Adams-Superior site.

116 *The Blade*, cited in Anderson, p. 160.

117 This quotation came from a letter signed "One of Ours" that appeared in the *American Israelite* of November 12, 1875 and is cited in Anderson, p. 161.

118 Anderson, p. 161.

119 Anderson, p. 162.

120 The Oliver House was one of Toledo's outstanding hotels at the time. It still stands on Oliver Street in the shadow of the Anthony Wayne Bridge and has been extensively renovated for several businesses.

121 *The Blade* published their names, cited in Anderson, p. 181.

122 Anderson, pp. 165-167.

123 For more on Eger's career in Toledo and the details of the "Englander children case," see Anderson, pp. 181-190.

124 Anderson, p. 190.

125 Anderson, p. 247.

126 The *American Israelite*, November 13, 1885, p. 8, as cited in Anderson, p. 247.

127 Anderson, p. 250.

128 *American Israelite*, October 5, 1888, p. 5. As cited in Anderson, p. 257.

129 *The Blade*, May 27, 2000, no page (online archive)

130 *American Israelite*, April 18, 1889, p. 1 As cited in Anderson, p. 258-259. The Goldmann history states that ". . . the first permanent Temple was erected in 1884. This small edifice was built on Tenth Street between Washington and Monroe." While the location agrees with Anderson, no confirmation of the earlier date has been found.

131 *The Blade*, September 21, 1889, p. 1 as cited in Anderson, p. 259.

132 For details of Browne's career and brief stay in Toledo, see Anderson, pp. 261-266.

133 Anderson, p. 267.

134 *The Blade*, May 27, 2000, no page (online archive) notes that the Tenth Street Temple was sold in 1909 to the Friendship Baptist Church. In 2005 the Toledo Repertory Theatre has occupied the building for some years.

135 *History of Collingwood Avenue Temple*, p. 3.

136 *Toledo Times*, clipping, n. p., ca. 1910.

137 *Toledo Times*, clipping, n. p. ca. 1910.

[138] *Dedication Program, Newly Enlarged Collingwood Avenue Temple*, 1952, p. 1.

[139] *History of Collingwood Avenue Temple*, p. 13.

[140] *History of Collingwood Avenue Temple*, p. 14

[141] *History of Collingwood Avenue Temple*, p. 16

[142] *120th Jubilee of Shomer Emunim* booklet. p. 6

[143] Feuer, pp. 1-7

[144] *120th Jubilee of Shomer Emunim* booklet. p. 6

[145] Rabbi Feuer's autobiographical essay is an interesting account of his personal Zionist involvement and how it complemented his Toledo experience. For another source regarding anti-Zionism, see Sarna, *American Judaism: A History*.

[146] Feuer, *Autobiographical Sketch*, pp. 8, 20

[147] *The Blade*, May 27, 2000, no page (online archive). The expansion caused the former residence of pioneer glass maker Michael J. Owens to be razed.

[148] *Dedication Program, Newly Enlarged Collingwood Avenue Temple*, 1952, p. 11.

[149] Sarna, *American Judaism: A History*, p. 279

[150] Rabbi Sokobin speculated that some Temple members were reluctant to move away from this shifting population, believing they would thereby "abandon the principles of prophetic Judaism." from Sokobin, *Autobiographical Essay* excerpt, p. 2

[151] Sokobin, *Autobiographical Essay* excerpt, p. 2

[152] This description of the vision comes from Sokobin, *Autobiographical Essay* excerpt, p. 2

[153] Sokobin, *Autobiographical Essay* excerpt, p. 1

[154] Sokobin, *Autobiographical Essay* excerpt, p. 3

[155] *Toledo Jewish News*, August 1972, p. 1.

[156] Sokobin, *Autobiographical Essay* excerpt, p. 2

[157] *Toledo Jewish News*, June 1972, p. 1.

[158] Sokobin, *Autobiographical Essay* excerpt, p. 11-12

[159] Sokobin, *Autobiographical Essay* excerpt, p. 20

[160] *Brotherhood*, "Guardian of the Faith," National Federation of Temple Brotherhoods, September-October, 1975, pp. 8-9

[161] *Brotherhood*, "Guardian of the Faith," National Federation of Temple Brotherhoods, September-October, 1975, pp. 8-9

[162] Sarna, *American Judaism: A History*, p. 194

[163] Sokobin, *Autobiographical Essay* excerpt, p. 18

[164] For a more complete description of this change, see Sarna, *American Judaism: A History*, pp. 287-88

[165] The people were Ann Albert, Rosemary Bramson, Rachel Chabon, Don Lorenzen, Bernie Solomon and Bella Wagner.

[166] Weinstein, Samuel, in e-mail to author, dated July 15, 2005.

[167] *The Blade*, January 11, 1992, clipping, n. p.

[168] Biographical information for Rabbi Samuel Weinstein, provided by Marvin Jacobs, August 25, 2004.

[169] Weinstein, Samuel, in e-mail to author, dated July 15, 2005.

[170] Biographical information for Rabbi Samuel Weinstein, provided by Marvin Jacobs, August 25, 2004.

[171] *The Blade*, September 24, 2005, Section B, p. 3

[172] *The Blade*, August 14, 1993, n. p.

[173] *The Blade*, May 27, 2000, no page (online archive)

[174] *The Blade*, September 14, 2002, no page (online archive)

[175] *The Blade*, September 24, 2005, Section B, pp. 3, 5

Window from the J.E.L. building now
in the Sekach building on the UJC
campus in Sylvania.

Photo 1, **J.E.L. Building 1912-1953**

Photo 2, **Sam Davis Co.**

From top, photos 3, 4, & 5

Photo 6, **1937 Canton Ave**

Photo 7, **Kosher market on Canton Avenue**

Photo 8 **Siegle's**

Photo 9, **Gross Electric founder, George (Joe) Gross (right) with Jack Gross, circa 1910. Originally The Toledo Gas Appliance Company was located at 612 Jefferson Street.**

Photo 10, **Window cleaners of Toledo Window Cleaning Company cleaning the inside of the dome of B'nai Israel.**

Photo 11

Photo 12, **B'nai Israel - 12th and Bancroft**

Photo 13, **Rabbi Goldberg**

Photo 15, **Rabbi Shapiro**

Photo 14, **B'nai Jacob, 12th Street**

Photo 17, **Confirmation class, B'nai Jacob - 1950**

Photo 16, **Rabbi Katz**

Photo 18, **B'nai Jacob officers**

OFFICERS OF THE SYNAGOGUE: (left to right) standing: Joseph Grassman, recording secretary; George Goldman, treasurer; Morris Lubitsky, secretary; Nathan Hendelman, gabai; Nathan Silverman, shamus; Max Abrams, assistant secretary; Jacob Spanglet, cantor. Seated: Jack Frank, vice president; Herman C. Moss, president; Rabbi Katz; Rabbi Bencion Tawlicki; David Abelowitz, vice gabai.

Photo 19, **Sisterhood officers**

Photo 20, **Sisterhood**

Photo 21, **Herman Moss, Mae Lubitsky**

Photo 22, **Anshe Sfard**

Photo 23 **Left to right, Cantor Jacob Spanglet and Rabbi Edward Garsek**

Photo 24 **Cantor Evan Rubin**

Photo 25 **Confirmation**

Photo 26 **Rabbi Fishel Pearlmutter & Rabbi Morton Goldberg**

Photo 27 **Arnold Carmel and Madge Levinson**

Photo 28, **Cantor Jamie Gloth**

Photo 29 **B'nai Israel Kenwood Blvd.**

Photo 30, **Rabbi Barry Leff, left, carries the torah in procession to the new synagogue on the Jewish Community Campus in Sylvania.**

Photo 31, **Shomer Emunim**

Photo 32, **The Collingwood Temple**

Photo 33, **Rabbi Leon Israel Feuer**

Photo 34, **Rabbi Feuer and Lewis Osterman**

Photo 35, **Rabbi Sokobin**

Photo 36, **Cantor Jennifer Roher**

Photo 37, **Rabbi Samuel R. Weinstein**

Photo 38, **B'nai Israel - 12th Street and Bancroft**

Photo 39, **Collingwood Temple**

Photo 40, **Sharei Zedeck Orthodox Congregation, Mulberry Street**

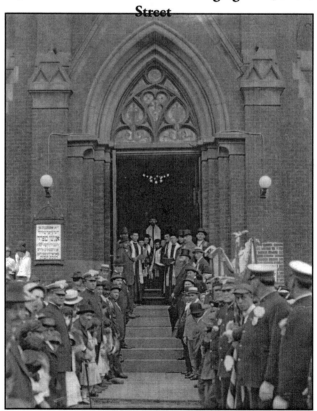

Photo 41, **Congregation Anshe Sfard**

Toledo
Federation of Jewish Charities

BOARD OF DIRECTORS
FOR 1913-14

Terms Expire April 1, 1914.

MORRIS ROSENBERG
SAMUEL TREUHAFT
JOSEPH ROTH *
HENRY STREETMAN
MORRIS H. LEMPERT

Terms Expire April 1, 1915.

SYLVAIN BASCH
RABBI DAVID ALEXANDER
HENRY ROSEN
SAM COHN
MYER GELEERD

Terms Expire April 1, 1916.

I. SILVERMAN
JACOB LASALLE
A S. COHEN
ISAAC GERSON
CHAS. K. FRIEDMAN

Photo 42

Photo 43, **Bernard Lempert**

Photo 44, **Progress Club - Monroe Street**

Photo 45, **Harry Boykoff and JCC Traveling Team**

Photo 46

Photo 47, **Albert M. Brown**

Photo 48,
**Lester Alexander and
the Army and Navy
Welfare Committee**

Photo 49, **Albert M. Brown**

Photo 50, **Center Players**

Eleanor Roosevelt

Golda Meier

Moishe Dayan

Photo 54,
**George H.W.
Bush and Roy
Treuhaft**

Photo 55,
**Solomon Smullin
and students**

Photo 56,
**Center
Orchestra**

Photo 57, **JCC committee at work**

Photo 58, Jewish Center Fund Drive

Photo 59, **Jewish Community Center
Collingwood Boulevard**

Photo 60, **Rose Lippman and JCC pre-school students**

Photo 61, **Center Orchestra**

Photo 62, **JCC senior citizens**

Photo 63, **Harry Boykoff and Irving Brenner**

Moe Berger and Marion Odesky

At Camp Ma Hi Ya

THE CENTER PLAYERS

of the

JEWISH COMMUNITY CENTER

(by special arrangement with Tams Witmark Music Library, Inc.)

present

Morris   Helen   Bernie   Marcia

Fruchtman Devenow Landis Okun

in

"ANYTHING GOES"

by

Guy Bolton   P. G. Wodehouse
Howard Lindsay   Russell Crouse

music and lyrics by

COLE PORTER

with

BARBARA OKUN   GENE RUSH   MURIEL STENBUCK

directed by

Harold Miller

ladies' clothes conceived, designed, and executed by

Lillian Greenberg

music director	choreography	set design
Rose Mary Locke	Lillian Hanham	Paul Slovak

entire production under the supervision of
Martha Jo Fruchtman

Photo 67, **Murray Guttman and Leo Shible**

Photo 68, **Future JCC Sports Stars with coaches Larry Wilk, Jim Sack, Rich Lerner and Barry Moses**

Photo 69, **Sid Levine**

Photo 70, **JFS Planning Session**

Photo 71, **Jewish Family Service building
Sylvania Campus**

Photo 72, **Toledo Jewish Orthodox Home for the Aged**

Photo 73, **Darlington House**

Photo 74, **Steve Weiner, Dr. Eva Shapiro, and Art Solomon**

Photo 75, **Hebrew Academy students**

Photo 76, **Hebrew School students**

Photo 77, **Lodge 183 IOBB**

Photo 78, **Leo Goldner and Ben Solomon**

Photo 79, **Day Camp at the JCC around mid 1940s**

Photo 80, **Jack Gallon**

Photo 81, **Toledo Bath House**

Photo 82, **Boy Scout Planning Committee**

Photo 83, **Iota Phi Kappa founding members**

Photo 84, **Sorority fun**

Photo 85, **Toledo Jewish Times**

Photo 86, **Holocaust Memorial**

Photo 87, **Joseph Nathanson**

Chapter 3
Community Support
Organizations

Introduction

This chapter is best introduced with a quotation from Jonathan Sarna, a current Jewish scholar: "The concept of mutual assistance formed part of the tool kit of cultural resources that Jews brought with them from Europe. A central Jewish religious precept, summed up in the rabbinic phrase 'all Israel is responsible for one another,' was widely practiced and remains so today. During the era of mass immigration, mutual assistance translated into philanthropy, free loans, and employment help. Those longer in the country aided those who arrived more recently; wealthier Jews helped out poorer cousins. These patterns carried over to the interwar years. Jews who made it into the white-collar world helped those with aspirations and talent to follow in their footsteps. Jewish organizations, fraternities, and synagogues disseminated news of appropriate openings through their membership and kinship networks."[1]

The story of the various Toledo Jewish organizations helping the needy, youths, recent immigrants, families and senior citizens clearly illustrates Sarna's observation. The local record of such mutual assistance abounds with examples of commendable commitment on the part of both individuals and persons acting collectively in various organizations. Their efforts dealt with on-going local needs, such as recreation and self-improvement. They also coped with evolving international situations, such as the Holocaust and the creation of the state of Israel. In a 1994 survey of Toledo Jews, 92% said that the Jewish community should maintain those agencies dealing with such important issues.[2]

This account also records many changes of organizations' names and shifting responsibilities as the Jewish community sought the most effective structure to cope with all the needs and requests. These changes of name and place within the local organizational framework can be confusing, but should not detract from appreciating all the good work done.

This history of benevolent, recreational and social programs is organized in chronological order, with the one hundred-plus years divided into three periods: Beginnings (1890s to 1920), Growth to Consolidation (1920 to 1946) and Diversification back to Consolidation (1946 to the present). These three time periods suggested themselves as each included major organizational changes. Within each time period, the narrative begins with

125

a brief introduction that highlights the forthcoming developments. The first mention of each organization in each period is printed in bold type so that readers wishing to trace just one organization through the years can more easily find it in the text.[3]

The Beginnings (1890s to 1920)

As the 19th century gave way to the 20th, the local Jewish community included a number of benevolent organizations, each assisting more recently-arrived Jews and helping all local Jews experiencing sickness or other problems. These organizations were in addition to direct aid that each congregation gave its struggling members. Some private individuals gave aid personally as well.[4]

A feature common in all such instances was the initial concentration on English-as-a-second-language classes and other efforts to help sustain the recent immigrants while they learned the manners and practices of their new homes.[5] While virtually all of the actual assistance came from the individual groups, by 1907 most people involved agreed on the need for some overall coordination.

The specific organizations then operating included the Council of Jewish Women, the Hebrew Educational Alliance, the Hebrew Ladies' Benevolent Society, the Hungarian Aid Society, the Jewish Ladies' Charity Association, the Toledo Auxiliary of the Industrial Removal Office (which helped settle indigent and unemployed Jews) and a Young People's Hebrew Society.[6] Also functioning as a community support organization was the forerunner of the Toledo Jewish Cemetery Association, described below.

Toledo Jewish Cemetery Association

With life comes eventual death and death was a fundamental factor for every member of Toledo's Jewish community. The first local Jewish burials were in Forest Cemetery in north Toledo, according to local tradition.

Perhaps the senior Jewish community support organization outside of congregations, a Jewish burial society became a formal entity in 1867 when a local *Chevra Kedusha* or benevolent society was established. Membership dues were levied based on one's age and physical condition. The *Chevra Kedusha* also extended weekly benefits to local Jews who were sick or needed temporary assistance.[7]

The major benefit was a grave in the organization's own cemetery, which was established in the same year. The cemetery was at Eagle Point overlooking the Maumee River and today is surrounded by the city of

Rossford. The society purchased the land from a local farmer, Ebie Lammers. One account alleges that Lammers was originally told the property would be used for a cider mill, implying that he would not have been willing to sell it for a Jewish cemetery. This seems questionable as Lammers' sons became the caretakers for the cemetery. Solomon Rosenbush was the first burial, occurring in 1868. Subsequent purchases of adjacent land enlarged the original cemetery in several phases as more room was needed.[8]

The *Chevra Kedusha* joined with another Jewish organization seeking a burial ground for its members in 1872 and established the **Toledo Hebrew Benevolent and Cemetery Association**. Initially the new group's focus went beyond just burials, but eventually the association's mission became solely operating its cemetery.[9]

In 1875, the association constructed a building at the cemetery that could shelter burial services and hold bodies until weather permitted internment.[10] (As of 1997, that building's cornerstone was preserved when the building was razed and is on display at the entrance to the cemetery, thanks to the family of Nathan D. Oesterman [sic], a charter member of the association.[11]) Eventually four parcels of land would total 8.2 acres .[12]

By about 1892 several local Orthodox synagogues had each purchased land and established adjacent cemeteries for their respective members, sited just outside Toledo in the suburb of Oregon on Otter Creek Road. Named Beth Shalom Cemetery, B'nai Jacob congregants came first, followed shortly by B'nai Israel and Sharei Zedeck. The United Hebrew Sick and Benevolent Association also used this Oregon location.[13] There is a small chapel on site. A total of nine land parcels were ultimately included for a total of 13.29 acres.[14]

A history of Woodlawn Cemetery, on Central Avenue in West Toledo, states that several sections have been set aside for members of the Reform Congregation Shomer Emunim, with the earliest burials done in the second half of the 19th century. The oldest area is Section 27 and is full. Rabbi Joseph Kornfeld dedicated Section 38 in 1921 and a few lots are still available as of 2005. In 1971 Rabbi Leon Feuer consecrated Section 38A and many lots are still available. In late 2001 the Temple Congregation Shomer Emunim donated a vessel for small stones that was located in Section 38A to facilitate following the Jewish custom of placing a pebble on a loved one's gravesite to indicate he or she is still remembered.[15]

Toledo Federation of Jewish Charities

By 1907, "several leading members of the Toledo Jewish community recognized the need for a more organized approach to charity in the city."

Thus, the **Toledo Federation of Jewish Charities** was formed in April of 1907. Early officers of the Federation included Nathan Kaufman, president; Sam Cohn, vice president; Henry Rosen, second vice president; Charles K. Friedman, secretary (later president); and Morris Rosenberg, treasurer. Other trustees of the Federation in these early days were Morris Kobacker, Jacob LaSalle and Samuel Treuhauft.[16] (*Photo 42, page 105, Toledo Charities*)

The newly-formed Federation stated its purpose as "the collection and properly distributing all the funds needed by the various local Jewish charity societies." The charitable organizations that had previously collected monies on their own now received funds from the Federation. In the first year's collection, 250 donors provide $6,000 for disbursement.[17] Sample activities at this early time include the Council of Jewish Women's Philanthropic Branch purchasing clothing and food for needy school children, the Jewish Shelter Home giving board and lodging to indigent travelers and the Hebrew Ladies' Benevolent Society practicing general charity.[18]

The Federation also undertook to manage funds collected in Toledo and intended for Jewish causes beyond Toledo. Early donations of this type include $850 to the Jewish Orphan Asylum in Cleveland (the largest non-Toledo contribution the Federation made in 1908), with amounts ranging from $50 to $450 to such groups as the National Jewish Home for Consumptives and the Rumanian Relief Fund.

The Federation also allocated $50 to the City of Toledo for civic relief, a sign of some commitment beyond the Jewish community itself.[19]

The Federation met in various local synagogues and in the private offices of its officers. For some years early in its history, the group met in the Progress Club Building, located at Monroe and 15th streets.[20]

In 1914 World War I began in Europe, involving the homelands of most of Toledo's Jewish residents. Three years later, the United States joined the war on the side of the Allied and Associated Powers, whose other primary members were the United Kingdom, France and Russia. The Jewish Federation of Toledo's booklet published on the occasion of the organization's 80th anniversary noted that during World War I the Jewish Federation became "affiliated" with the War Chest, a fundraising campaign reaching all across Toledo. The 80th anniversary publication said it was ". . . unclear as to whether or not fundraising for national and overseas Jewish causes was continued through the Federation of Jewish Charities. This affiliation continued in the post-war era when the War Chest was re-named the Community Chest. However, as the community changed with the years and new needs and concerns were identified, there came the realization that the Federation, as it had been set up, was unable to meet those needs."[21]

Jewish Family Service

According to Marvin Lerner's history of the Jewish Family Service in Toledo, the "Bene Israel [sic] *Chevra Kadusha* was organized in 1867 to aid the sick and distress" and Lerner saw that as the symbolic beginning of the Family Service tradition in Toledo and its original focus.[22] During the rest of the 19th century, other benevolent societies came into existence to help local Jews cope with living in the community. Sid Levine cites these organizations as the Ladies Aid Hebrew Society at B'nai Israel [Synagogue], Council of Jewish Women, local chapter of B'nai B'rith, Hungarian Aid Society, Jewish Ladies Charity Association, Jewish Relief Office, Industrial Removal Office [for resettling indigent Jews], Hebrew Ladies Benevolent Society, Jewish Free Loan Association and the Jewish Shelter Home.[23]

As mentioned earlier, the Toledo Federation of Jewish Charities was organized in 1907 as a coordinating agency to collect and distribute charitable funds, both through member groups and directly, to local Jews and to other Jewish causes beyond Toledo. Expanding its operation in 1909, the Federation took responsibility for a shelter house for indigent Jews arriving in Toledo.[24] During the first half of the 20th century a Resettlement Committee also existed. Eventually, according to Levine's history, the Resettlement Committee merged with the Federation of Jewish Charities since both groups' activities included finding homes and jobs for displaced persons.[25]

Toledo Board of Jewish Education

The story of Jews and education (loosely defined) in Toledo has two major threads in the context of this history. One thread traces the Jews' belief that their own community bore the primary responsibility for educating their children about their faith and heritage. This includes Sunday schools, the least intensive format, and Talmud/Torah instruction. These forms are traditionally offered by individual congregations and sometimes via cooperative agreements involving more than one congregation.

The second thread is the desire for self-improvement via broader education, especially learning or improving skills that empowered a person to cope more successfully with daily life. This includes "day school" classes under the auspices of a Jewish community-wide school system, such as the Board of Jewish Education and the Hebrew Academy, analogous to any other parochial school.[26]

Simultaneously with the above threads, most Jewish youths were attending Toledo Public School classes.

The other over-riding theme regarding local Jewish education is that it waxed and waned with considerable volatility between 1895 and the present. Interest in Sunday schools, Talmud/Torah and day schools rose and fell due to economic circumstances, parental mindset and available leadership.

The responsibility of instilling the Jewish faith and cultural heritage was fulfilled individually largely through family life and collectively in the various congregations in the city. In 1876 B'nai Israel and Shomer Emunim both operated "Sunday schools". From about 1913 B'nai Israel operated its Hebrew School at its synagogue, located on Bancroft at North Twelfth street.

One former B'nai Israel student, Meyer Straus, remembered his schooling there: Michael Lichtenstein was the rabbi and a ". . . Mr. Michlin was the head of the Talmud Torah. He was basically the teacher we had most of the time. . . . Mr. Michlin also taught us at his home." Straus graduated in 1926, one of seven in the class that also included Sol Boyk, Meyer Kripke, Warren Rayman, Sam Schuller, William Schuller and Harry Sherman. (Straus subsequently graduated from Scott High School while living on Franklin and Columbia streets. He later attended City College of New York, the University of Pennsylvania and received a Master's Degree in Education from Temple University in Philadelphia. He taught school from 1939 to 1978 then retired to California.)[27]

The Reform Temple, Shomer Emunim, held its religious training on Mulberry Street, as did Congregation Sharei Zedeck. Rabbis of the respective congregations also oversaw the tuition-free schools, which were supported with annual fund raising campaigns. Each of the synagogues also contributed financial support and the schools raised money by the annual sale of Manischewitz matzos (for which the local Hebrew schools had a monopoly).[28]

Marvin Lerner's history of Jewish Toledo says "We believe the origins of the Toledo Hebrew School system were established in 1892 and at the turn of the century in Toledo there were approximately 3,000 Jews.[29]

A lengthy newspaper article illustrates the self-improvement facet of education in the early 20th century. *The Toledo Blade* for February 23, 1907 contained a lengthy article by Lucas J. Beecher entitled "Primer Class for Men of the Ghetto" and with subheads reading "Scenes in the Night Shifts of the Toledo Schools Where the Ends of the Earth Meet and the Alien Becomes a Citizen" and "Deserters from the Russian Army Who Battle with Indigence by Day and with Ignorance by Night." For some sixty column-inches the reporter described classes held at the Jewish Council House, 522 Scott Street in the near north end, at the time the primary area of Toledo's Jewish settlement. Members of Toledo's Council of Jewish Women formed the night school "in an unostentatious manner" in October of 1906, the school's formation coming out of the Council's own resources and ". . . was an accomplishment characteristic of their organization of practical charity workers." The women paid the rent on the two-story residence, whose interior has been set-up as five classrooms and outfitted with electric lights, tables, chairs, blackboards and second hand primary level text books.

"The principal of one of the largest public school buildings, in a fashionable residence [sic] district of Toledo, consented to serve as supervisor. Other public school teachers and busy women who have large family and social responsibilities volunteered to work in the teaching corps." The teachers were required to have knowledge of German as well as English, though the pupils spoke Yiddish among themselves. Ten teachers were ready when classes began.

As of the article's writing, forty students, aged from twenty-one to forty, were enrolled, all men except for two women, a teenage boy and a teenage girl. Some were single while others had families yet in Europe, awaiting passage money. The sponsors had expected students to come just from the immediate neighborhood, but some pupils gave addresses at a distance from the Council House on Scott Street. All were generally ignorant of spoken and written English, but some had had education in their native lands. Five classes were scheduled, with sessions on Tuesdays and Thursdays at 7:30 p.m., with the teachers working alternate evenings.

The first task was to teach rudiments of spoken English. After several months, the newspaper reporter said that most of the classroom conversation was in English. The second task was written English and here the reporter termed the progress "remarkable" and ranked most of the students' writing legibility as "far superior to the writing of the average American professional or business man." The final goal was to prepare the students for completing citizenship applications and give them some training in civics.

As noted above, the Council House women were eminently practical and so complemented the English classes with sewing classes. Every Thursday afternoon at the Council House fourteen teachers and six assistants instructed seventy girls in "plain sewing."[30]

The Jewish Community Center

Recreation (as a means of individual physical and moral improvement) was another component of the local Jewish education network. One historical anecdote traced what would become the **Jewish Educational League** to a conversation in the spring of 1906. The story goes that Nathan

Kaufman and Charles Friedman were walking along Canton Avenue on their way to a meeting for organizing a Red Cross chapter in Toledo. As they progressed along Canton, the two saw many Jewish youngsters at play and heard many adults speaking Yiddish. They resolved to establish an organization to help these neighborhood residents and subsequently began contacting others in the Jewish community for support.[31]

Another account of the roots of the J. E. L. leads to Miss Sara Kaufman [a relative of Nathan Kaufman perhaps], described as "a Toledo juvenile social worker and member of the Council of Jewish Women," and founder of the **Banner Boys Club**. She felt the need for a local character-building organization and she focused specifically on less-privileged Jewish boys aged 12 or 13 years. An article in *The Toledo Blade* for 1907 mentions a "Jewish Council House" at 522 Scott Street and it is plausible that this was the Banner Club site.[32]

A corresponding **Girls Banner Club** was soon organized as well. Mrs. Leroy (Anne) Newmyer served as advisor, along with Sara Kaufman.

One earlier history of the Banner Clubs cited the recollection of Anna Berkowitz, a young member. She recalled the boys and girls would meet informally every week. At those sessions, Miss Kaufman talked to youths on various topics intended to make them better men and women as they grew up.[33]

Kaufman also wanted to improve the physical condition of the young members, especially the boys. Aware of the power of an athlete to inspire young boys, Kaufman persuaded Bernard Lempert, the first Toledoan to run 100 yards in ten seconds, to give physical training to the boys. (These early workout sessions for about thirty boys were in the living room of the Meyer Levy residence on Scott Street. For showers after the exercises, ". . . each boy would stand in a galvanized tub while another would sponge him off."[34]) This site was subsequently called the Council House.[35] Lempert gained an assistant in 1910 when Aaron B. Cohen joined the team. A very recent graduation of The Ohio State University, Cohen not only did some of the physical education, but he also instructed the boys in "religious character building and citizenship".[36]

A noteworthy personal legacy of the Boys' Banner Club was that one of the boys from this early period was William Hirsch, who was elected in 1952 as Lucas County's first Jewish sheriff and who subsequently served three more terms. (*Photo 43, page 106, Bernard Lempert*)

Another piece in the ancestry of the J. E. L. relates to the **Progress Club**. It was organized in 1889 as a social organization and held its early functions in a rented hall on Jefferson Avenue. In either 1906 or 1907 the group moved into its own building, a two-story structure at the corner of Monroe and 15th streets. The building's facilities included two bowling alleys and two showers. A large auditorium was also available for larger-scale meetings and exercises.[37] The site's facilities helped the club grow and prosper. (*Photo 44, page 106, Progress Club*)

Illustrating the inter-relatedness of the local Jewish community, a connection was formed between the Council House or Banner Clubs and the Progress Club. The connecting link was Ben Frankenberg, president of the Progress Club, who was also the uncle of Bernard Lempert, physical training instructor at the Council House. The Progress Club allowed the boys and girls to use the facilities of the Club as activities permitted, especially the locker rooms - with showers - and the auditorium.

The auditorium's availability one night a week for the Council House youths proved to be quite a catalyst in the cause of Toledo's Jewish support organizations. Twenty-eight boys of the Banner Club once demonstrated various exercises in a program for Progress Club members. After viewing the boys' fine work, Jewish community leaders agreed that a better facility was needed and deserved. The Progress Club itself, the Council of Jewish Women and all "those who were increasingly concerned with club work and with children and newcomers" collaborated to create such a center. In 1911 the momentum continued when the Philanthropic Branch of the Council of Jewish Women received permission for a fund raising campaign focused on building that desired center.[38]

Apparently many in the community responded generously to the appeal for in July of 1912 a letter went to all the donors announcing that construction was already underway on the new $20,000 **Jewish Educational League Building**, located on a 100 foot by 110 foot parcel at 1900 Linwood Avenue, on the corner of Southard Street, in the near north side, the center of Jewish Toledo at the time. Later that same year the building opened. Morris Lempert was president and an annual membership was $10.00.[39] (*Photo 45, page 107, Harry Boykoff*)

The official motto of the J. E. L. was "To develop and maintain a high standard of American citizenship among the Jewish residents of Toledo." The design and layout of the building exemplified the breadth of this goal. The raised basement summarized the J. E. L.'s commitment to both strong minds and strong bodies: that level contained classrooms for instruction on a variety of topics as well as a handball court and a locker room. The first floor consisted of the reading, sewing and domestic science rooms, and a gymnasium that could double as an auditorium. The second floor contained meeting rooms for various Jewish organizations, thus making J.E.L. a firm anchor for the community.[40]   the

For the next forty-one years "the J.E.L.," both the organizati building, for the two seemed to have symbolically merged in many minds, was a non-religious nucleus for so much going on in the Jewish community.

Physical activities formed one major category of J.E.L. activities. Several generations of young Jewish males recall the basketball games there that were such a feature of their childhood. The Banner Clubs' legacy was clearly apparent with the continued offering of physical education classes.

Social events were a second staple of J.E.L. activities. With so many of the organizations then meeting at the site having charitable purposes, it is no surprise that fund-raising card parties, teas and other ladies' socials were frequently on the schedule. One attendee remembered "For a small fee, maybe fifty cents, you could come in, sit down, play cards and have coffee and cake." Within two years of the building opening, it hosted the wedding of Bill and Rose Hamerman, the first of only two marriages performed at the J.E.L.[41]

The third category of activities could be termed self-improvement endeavors, again well within the tradition of pre-J.E.L. organizations. With, at one point, some seventeen organizations based in the building, classes were available on cooking, folk dancing, dramatics and sewing. Classes in English and preparing for U. S. citizenship testified to the on-going immigration into the local community. A circulating library permitted members to take materials home, complementing their on-site learning. A Sunday School was also offered.[42]

Growth and Consolidation
(1920 to 1946)

The post-WW I period witnessed the continuation of earlier activities, as well as reaction to events elsewhere in the world. The local Jewish organizational structure needed to change to better cope with both the on-going and new situations.

Jewish Federation of Toledo

Thus, in 1920 the Toledo Federation of Jewish Charities and the Jewish Educational League merged to form the Jewish Federation of Toledo, thereby unifying nearly all benevolent, recreational and fund raising under one entity. Maurice Sievers was hired as the first full-time director and oversaw all aspects of the Federation. Sievers served simultaneously in the same capacity for the component organizations, the Jewish Community Council, Jewish Family ce and the United Jewish Fund, Inc.. He served until 1926, when Joseph ucceeded him, working until 1935.[43]

Beginning in the 1920s, the Federation included one staff member to handle "family services" and this position operated throughout WW II, with the person working out of the J.E.L. Building on Linwood Avenue.[44] A newspaper account generally corroborated this effort by describing the Federation's "family welfare department." A reporter credited 500 families and individuals with being assisted during one six-month period in the early 1920s. The Federation even had a representative at Toledo's juvenile court every Saturday morning and a majority of the youths brought in were placed in the custody of the Federation or of its members.[45]

Yet another function was sponsoring the Reuben Sheltering Home at 520 State Street. The home provided a one or two nights' shelter for transients without other choices.[46]

Jewish Community Center

When the Collingwood Boulevard J. C. C. opened in 1953, then-Executive Director Albert M. Brown wrote a brief history of the Center. In it, Brown noted an earlier drive to build a new J. C. C.. He cited a story in the *Toledo News-Bee* newspaper, dated April 14, 1928, which reported that at the 16th annual meeting of the Jewish Federation, held in the Progress Club building, ". . . a campaign to erect a new and more adequate Jewish Social Center to supplant the present outgrown Jewish Educational League Building at Linwood and Southard was launched . . .".[47]. There was no doubt that the place was busy. A *Toledo Times* story in 1923 reported ". . . an average of 400 children use the building daily and 500 adults weekly, while 2500 grown-ups are connected with it in some capacity." The paper noted that activities included twenty-five different basketball teams and "about 63" organizations regularly used the building.[48] The onset of the Great Depression and then World War II were two major reasons the campaign did not reach its objective until twenty-five later. (*Photo 46, page 107*)

Elmer Louis succeeded Joseph Woolf as Jewish Federation executive director in 1936. By this time, the J. E. L. Building was known officially as the Community Center and operated as a department of the Jewish Federation, along with such others as Family Service and Transient Service. Louis' vision of the Center's mission for the future could just as well summarize its past efforts: the Center was to ". . . organize clubs and classes designed to bring out the potentialities in people and develop a generation of Jewish men and women who will be a credit to themselves, their families and the Jewish community and the general community." During his administration, a journalism club, airplane modeling group and a tap dance class were added to previously-organized activities.[49] (*Photo 47, page 107, Albert Brown*)

The effort to obtain better quarters for the Community Center surfaced again in September of 1941. The Federation's board of trustees considered buying the former local headquarters of the Knights of Columbus, whose building was at Jefferson and 16th streets. After some discussion at a special meeting, the trustees decided that the building posed too many problems for adapting it as the next Community Center and the issue died.[50] (*Photo 48, page 107, Army and Navy Welfare Committee*)

World War II was a period of great activity as the Community Center reacted to global events. It was the headquarters of the Jewish Welfare Board and United Service Organization (the U. S. O.) Local service men and women occasionally home on leave joined with all those serving at Camp Perry, the Erie Proving Ground, the Toledo Naval Armory and the Marblehead Coast Guard Station to keep the Center humming. The Federation established the Army and Navy Welfare Committee under Lester D. Alexander to help feed and entertain the troops who visited the J. E. L. Building, sometimes via chartered buses from the bases east of Toledo along the Lake Erie shore. Sometimes Community Center volunteers also delivered cigarettes and other treats to the nearby military camps.[51] Another form of communication with Toledo's service personnel was the newsletter sent overseas during the war. One newspaper account cited Sade Selker Gallon as the primary responsible person, with help from her husband Joseph.[52] (*Photo 49, page 108, Albert Brown*)

While busy throughout the week, the highlight of the Center's support of the armed services came on Sundays. On those days only service personnel and Center volunteers were allowed into the building after 3 p.m.. A buffet supper was provided for all the troops present, thanks to contributions from Jewish community organizations, followed by dancing. Single Jewish women served as "Junior Hostesses" who danced with the men to music from a juke box. One account mentioned that Albert Brown, executive director of the Center from 1942 to 1954, sometimes played the piano and conducted sing-alongs at these Sunday functions also.[53] (*Photo 50, page 108, Center Players*)

At the same time, the post-war future was also considered. Earl Rosengarten assumed the Federation's presidency in 1942 (and continued into 1947) and after discussing the matter with other Federation trustees and the Jewish Community Council, he established a Post War Planning Committee on October 12, 1944. Maurice Davis was chair with members Lester Alexander, Abe J. Levine, Eliot Meisel, Arthur Edelstein, Harry Entine, Charles Fruchtman and Sidney Freidenthal. The committee's primary charge was to plan for a new J. C. C.. The committee submitted a report recommending a new building on December 12, 1944. The

Federation's board adopted the report the same day. By March of 1945 Jules D. Lippmann had been selected to chair a fund-raising committee and Arthur Edelstein headed a site-finding committee for the new building.[54]

On May 13, 1945, as Allied forces gained military victory in Europe, some 300 local Jews dined at the Commodore Perry Hotel and collected pledges of $220,000 towards a new Community Center building. A history of the Federation records that further efforts for a new building were postponed due to the greater need of caring for survivors of the Holocaust.[55]

Jewish Community Council

At meetings in May and June of 1935 the need for a "central council" was discussed, as was the growing anti-Semitism movement in Europe.[56] Under the leadership of Manuel E. Treuhaft, a new organization, The Jewish Community Council was formed at an organizational meeting on January 16, 1936. It was to act as an umbrella group for a number of local Jewish groups, including the Jewish Federation.[57]

The new organization immediately focused on raising funds for those European Jews seeking refuge from Hitler's Nazi government, then in power for two years. Even before it was formally established, the council issued a call in November 1935 for a fund drive with a goal of $20,000. "So, again, after a lapse of many years, the Jewish community of Toledo undertook a united fund raising campaign to meet the needs of the day."[58] (*Photo 51 page 109, Eleanor Roosevelt*)

The Jewish Community Council soon undertook two other functions as well. At a June 1937 meeting of the new Council Rabbi Leon Feuer had submitted an organizational plan for the body and a committee of the Council submitted a very similar proposal to the Council. Subsequently enacted by the Council, the plan was to add three standing committees: a Public Relations Committee, an Internal Affairs Committee and a United Jewish Fund Committee.[59] (*Photo 52, page 109, Golda Meir*)

The **Public Relations Committee** (later named Community Relations) was charged to cooperate in all civic and community affairs, work with the Anti-Defamation League of the B'nai B'rith, monitor Jewish-related news items and generally represent the local Jewish community to the greater Toledo population. The Community Relations Committee continues to operate today; see the post-WW II section below for more details.

The **Internal Affairs Committee** dealt with matters within the Jewish community, such as ". . . proper compliance with Kasruth laws, encourage the observance of Jewish holidays and mediate between [Jewish] individuals, groups and organizations. Two of the issues dealt with fairly soon was the perception that some Jewish merchants were not observing the rules of the federal Office of Price Administration regarding the retail price of their goods and that some of the advertising for "kosher style" wieners was misleading. A reoccurring topic seemed to be inter-synagogue relations, judging by the minutes of the committee. (*Photo 53, page 109, Moishe Dayan*)

The **United Jewish Fund Committee** was to oversee all fund raising within the local Jewish community by the various organizations and congregations.[60] (The United Jewish Fund would officially incorporate in 1948, see below.) (*Photo 54, page 110, George H.W. Bush and Roy Treuhaft*)

Education – Toledo Hebrew School

As the Jewish community moved on from the WW I years, it began with its pre-war education structure. In 1923 The Hebrew Free School of Toledo was incorporated under the laws of Ohio, formalizing the pre-incorporation set-up. The "School" consisted of three "branches," one each in B'nai Israel, Shomer Emunim and Sharei Zedeck.[61]

By this time, the B'nai Israel branch used classrooms in the annex of the synagogue at Bancroft and North Twelfth streets. A newspaper clipping reported that the school had been in existence for forty years. The average daily attendance for the 1929 school year was 200, covering elementary and high school ages. The students receive instruction in the Hebrew language, literature and history. The story also noted that the Women's Auxiliary of B'nai Israel and a men's committee had raised $1,600 in ticket sales for a picture show at the Rivoli Theater to benefit the school.[62] (*Photo 55, page 110, Solomon Smullin*)

The earlier fund raising mix of selling matzos and receiving some aid directly from local congregations changed in 1938. At that time the Jewish Community Council urged that the United Jewish Fund coordinate all local financial campaigns and the various Hebrew schools cooperated. The schools began to receive a portion of these coordinated funds in 1940.

Also in 1938, a total of 213 students attended the various Hebrew school branches. This number was 44% of the total of 480 Jewish children attending public schools (grades 1 through 7) for the rest of their training. The branches were still at B'nai Israel and Shomer Emunim (Sharei Zedeck's closed that year), but students whose parents belonged to B'nai Jacob, Anshe Sfard and Sharei Zedeck also attended.[63] Thirty years later a Jewish educator looked back at "the lean 1930s" and gave the community high marks for not charging tuition and yet managing ". . . to remain solvent, contrary to the experience of most Jewish communities."[64]

The evolution of Jewish education in Toledo continued in 1941 with the establishment of a Bureau of Jewish Education. Eliot Kaplan led this organizing effort and the goal was to expand the support of the schools to throughout the community. According to Federations records, Lester D. Alexander was the first president and Solomon Smullin was the first director in 1943. Tuition was first charged in 1955.[65]

Post-War Diversification and Reconsolidation (1946 – present)

In 1946 the Jewish Federation changed its name to the **Jewish Community Service Association** to better portray the wide extent of the organization's operations. The organization would continue under this title until 1952. By this time, the old J. E. L. Building was increasingly becoming called the "Jewish Community Center," a name that would be transferred to each of its successors.[66]

Jewish Community Center

The immediate post-war period also saw an important evolution in the history of the J.C.C.. In 1949 trustees of the Jewish Community Service Association re-started the drive for a new Community Center building. Association president Joe Nathanson named Sidney Tuschman as chair of the "Survey for the New Jewish Center Building," which would be a jointly-sponsored project of the Jewish Community Council and the Association. The National Jewish Welfare Board's Department of Surveys provided assistance.[67] (*Photo 56, page 110, Center Orchestra*)

The subsequent local survey found much support. Implementation was entrusted to a Center Building Committee, with Jules D. Lippmann as chair, subject to the approval of the Association's trustees. Fund raising and site selection began soon thereafter. In May of 1951 Toledoan Herman Feldstein received the contract as project architect, with the Architectural Bureau of the National Jewish Welfare Board serving in an advisory capacity. The Henry J. Spieker Company was general contractor. Groundbreaking occurred on December 16, 1951 at the 2275 Collingwood Boulevard site. By this time Jules Lippmann had been elected president of the Center, following the July 28, 1951 death of Sidney Tushman. The cornerstone was laid on September 7, 1952. Sufficient construction progress was made so the annual meeting of Center was held in the new building's auditorium on March 29, 1953. Equipment and activities were relocated from the old J. C. C. in May 1953 and in a new enrollment program, Joel Levine received Membership Card Number One. The formal dedication was Sunday, September 13, 1953.[68] (*Photo 57, page 111, JCC Committee*)

The new building and a revised constitution supported the Center's new mission – to serve the entire Jewish community - adults, juveniles and children - with a full range of recreational, cultural and self-improvement activities. The new J. C. C. continued its predecessors' offerings of sports such as basketball and handball and broadened the list to include squash, volleyball and, thanks to an indoor pool, swimming. The Collingwood site also permitted the continuance of such traditional activities as the Council of Jewish Women's English-as-a-second-language classes. A day nursery, summer day camp, an orchestra and a drama club were examples of how the Center sought to serve a wider range of clients. Success soon followed. Within three years, nearly 108,000 persons used the J. C. C., with sixty-three clubs based at the building holding 1,550 meetings and 284 other organizations gathered there as well.[69] (*Photo 58, page 111, Jewish Center Fund Drive*)

The cause of providing outstanding recreational facilities for the Jewish community received another boost when Jewish Welfare Federation President Stanford Thal announced in September 1968 that title had been taken to an overnight camp site in Chelsea, Michigan. More than two years of negotiations, and some possibility that several other Jewish communities would participate, preceded this purchase of 140 acres about 60 miles northwest of Toledo. The J. C. C. Day Camp had already used it for a three-day camp out the previous summer and the young campers liked it. This would become Camp Ma-Hi-Ya.[70] (*Photo 59, page 112, Collingwood JCC*)

The recurring theme of migration in the local Jewish community again came to the forefront in the late 1960s. The relocation of many Jewish families from their initial neighborhood on the north edge of the downtown into the Old West End and, in the post-WW II decades, further westward into West Toledo and Sylvania was a pattern again affecting the J. C. C.. By the late 1960s more than eighty per-cent of the Center's membership lived west of Secor Road. (*Photo 60, page 112, Rose Lippman*)

In 1969 the Steering Committee of the J. C. C. undertook another survey concerned with use of the current Center and a possible new facility. Of respondents to the poll, 74% favored a new Center and 81% wanted it expanded into a complete complex, featuring indoor and outdoor attractions. In addition, 70% criticized the Collingwood site as inconvenient for them to reach, and nearly 50% said this location limited their use of the Center. A large number of those surveyed added that the Center should "bring a sense of unity to the Jewish community."[71]

A combination of foresight, planning and good fortune led to a solution that would carry the J. C. C. into the 21st century. In 1968 the local Reform congregation, Temple Shomer Emunim, purchased forty-five acres of land on the south side of Sylvania Avenue in Sylvania Township, just west of Interstate 475/U. S. 23. The congregation intended to build a new Temple there, replacing the one on Collingwood then in use. The new site could accommodate both a new Temple and a new J.C.C. and collaboration between those two groups led to an outstanding manifestation of that potential. (*Photo 61, page 112, Center Orchestra*)

The move of the J. C. C. was complex, in part because the Center wished to continue to offer its services while the construction and relocation was underway. Some of the activities requiring special facilities, such as swimming, handball and squash, remained at the Collingwood site until the new facility was done, thanks to an agreement between the Center and the Toledo Red Cross Chapter, which bought the Collingwood building in July 1972. Another arrangement with Sylvania Public Schools enabled other J. C. C. programs to use school gyms and auditoriums. Lastly, local synagogues and even private homes were used for activities drawing fewer persons and needing little or no special equipment.[72]

Just as complicated as maintaining the Center's multitude of programs was the construction of the new complex. The preliminary phase was done in 1973: the pool, temporary office buildings and the "teen house". The official groundbreaking for the main building was November 17, 1975, with U. S. Senator John Glenn as the main speaker. At that time, J. C. C. President Melvin G. Nusbaum reported that $1 million had been raised towards a goal of $2.3 million.[73] Within the next three years the physical recreation component was completed, including the health club, gymnasium, racket ball courts and rooms for weight training and lockers. The last portion to be constructed opened in January 1986, providing administrative space, group activities and meetings. In addition, the J.C.C. campus now included those outdoors assets not available at the land-locked Collingwood site.[74] An abundance of landscaped grounds surrounded a man-made lake, a lodge and picnic area.[75] Indicative of the J.C.C.'s good reputation and its decades of service is a 1994 finding that 96% of the members of the Jewish community were aware of the Center and nearly three-quarters of the local Jewish population were or had been members of the facility.[76] (*Photo 62, page 113, JCC Seniors*)

In 1974, during this relocation process, the J.C.C. was opened to non-Jews as members, who were primarily interested in using the athletic and recreational resources. By the about end of the century, 60% of the membership was non-Jewish and the J.C.C. affiliated with the Young Men's Christian Association in an initial four-year agreement that designated the J.C.C. as the Sylvania Branch of the local Y.M.C.A. Members of either organization could use the facility.[77] (*Photo 63, page 113, Harry Boykoff and Irving Brenner*)

The sale of the Collingwood building necessitated the movement of the Jewish Welfare Federation offices to Monroe Street quarters in 1974 and then in 1979 the Federation moved again to the Sylvania Avenue complex, joining The Temple and the Community Center.[78] (More Community Center *Photos 64, 65, 66, 67 and 68 on page 114, 115 and 116*)

Jewish Family Service

In preparation for operating the new Collingwood Boulevard facility, in March of 1953 the Jewish Community Service Association, originally formed in 1946 when the Jewish Federation changed its name, turned over its financial assets and holdings to the new **Jewish Community Center** organization. The Center's revised constitution also focused the organization on programming for the community, not responsible for fundraising or disbursing funds for charitable purposes.[79]

This also meant that the Jewish Community Council now had responsibility for those functions that would evolve into today's Jewish Family Service. Thus, according to one historical account, "This same Family Service, which had its origins in the Hebrew Ladies Benevolent Society and the Philanthropic Branch of the Council of Jewish Women back at the turn of the century, had, in a sense, come home to 'The Federation' again."[80]

In the early 1950s, Family Service collaborated with the Council of Jewish Women to provide English classes for adults at Scott High School, a good location given the concentration of Jews in the Old West End (although the migration to western suburbs was underway at the time).[81]

The Family Service agency had been a component of the Jewish Community Council since 1953. It remained a part until 1960 when the Jewish Welfare Federation was created and Family Service became part of that new organization. Family Service became an autonomous organization in 1965. With its new status, Family Service also undertook child placement, including adoptions, and working with Jewish senior citizens in the community generally and the residents of Darlington House, Toledo Jewish Home for Aged.[82] (*Photo 69, page 117, Sid Levine*)

Sid Levine, J. F. S. director from 1957 to 1969, recalled that during the mid-century period Family Service ". . . was a pioneer with the JFS agencies in the U. S. in developing comprehensive social service programs for the aged, mental health treatment for individuals, children and families, family life education programs, training of professional psychotherapists, etc."[83]

A particularly close relationship developed with Darlington House residents. The agency worked with Darlington House staff on initial counseling and screening for prospective residents. J. F. S workers continued to assist new residents adjust to life at Darlington as well.[84]

Jewish Family Service also expanded its activities regarding family counseling and child placement. Increasingly well-trained staff members applied family therapy skills to resolve household problems. When emotionally disturbed youths could not continue to live in their homes, J. F. S. helped place them in residential treatment schools in Cleveland and New York and provided some financial assistance.

Mentally ill members of the community also received counseling and material assistance, even including J. F. S. volunteers and staff refurbishing a family's home to better suit needs. This care extended to Jewish patients at the Toledo State Hospital as well, with Family Service representatives enabling Rabbi Katz to make regular visits there [and presumably other rabbis also].[85] (*Photo 70, page 117, JFS Planning Session*)

Family Service maintained the tradition of helping relocate recent immigrants as another function. The problem of displaced persons following WW II persisted for many years, joined later by refugees from the Hungarian Revolution. J. F. S assisted members of both groups to begin their new lives here.[86] (*Photo 71, page 117, JFS Sylvania Campus*)

The 1970s and 1980s were years of expanded activities and increased efforts in traditional areas for Jewish Family Service. The resettlement of refugees continued, with the most recent wave coming from Russia as the Soviet Union broke apart and non-Communist governments eased immigration restrictions. A Resettlement Coordinator was hired, symbolizing the growing attention to this responsibility.[87]

Among other activities during this period were Family Life Education workshops, the handling of more requests for adoptions (of both local children and from other countries), requests for consultations from the Hebrew Academy for students and staff, the preparation and distribution of Holiday food baskets to needy individuals and families, and the creation of a homemaker service for seniors. A Friendly Visitor and Kosher Mobile Meals service and a vocational service were attempted for a brief period, but a shortage of volunteers for these labor-intensive duties and a decline in the local unemployment rate led to their cancellation.[88]

The major administrative event of this period was the 1973 relocation of the J.F.S. offices from Collingwood Boulevard to Monroe Street. This was, in part, another sign of the Jewish community's migration westward within the urban area.

During the 1990s and into the 21st century, Jewish Family Service responded to two major influences. One was the continued need for most of the existing services and the realization that the aging local Jewish population required more assistance for its seniors. To provide that help, J. F. S. entered into service contracts with several home health agencies, Darlington House and the Great Lakes Credit Union. Family Service also became a provider with Medicare and other insurance companies. Frail Jewish seniors received assistance in their homes via the Specialized Homemaker Service. The sale of Darlington House in 2000 affected the delivery of services to seniors. More collaboration between J. F. S. and Jewish Senior Services began, with an expansion of the Specialized Homemaker Service, the resumption of the Friendly Visitor Program and the creation of a Concierge Service.[89]

Immigrant resettlement and child placement responsibilities evolved as well. In the early years of this period a VISTA volunteer was added to coordinate citizenship services. After 1995 the numbers of immigrants and resettlement activity declined due to international factors, actually stopping temporarily in 2001. Family Service did, however, continue to work with previously resettled refugees in such areas as language translation services and preparation for citizenship. Also by the mid-1990s the adoption program was scaled back due to more birthmothers choosing placement through private attorneys. First a staff position was eliminated, with remaining staffers taking on those duties, and then in 2000 J.F.S. ceased making placements at all. One staff person and one contracted professional continued home studies and post-placement services.[90]

On November 7, 1999 Jewish Family Service celebrated its Fiftieth Anniversary. In a service at Temple Shomer Emunim, former Toledo J.F.S. Executive Director Lou Albert was the keynote speaker.

The second major influence was financial pressure. By the nature of their mission and clientele, the programs of the J.F.S. do not produce much income. Support had always come primarily from the local Jewish community, either through central organizations or private donations. The United Jewish Council fund drive of 2001 produced a "no growth" total of pledges and in 2002 the UJC requested all local Jewish agencies to evaluate their operations in the face of stagnant funding. The mutually-agreed upon decision between the United Way of Greater Toledo, the J.F.S. and the U.J.C. for J.F.S. to stop receiving United Way funding also impacted the financial situation.[91]

The results, which began in the 2003-2004 operating year, saw retention of some services and down-sizing of others. The Friendly Visitor program was seen as "a real winner" for both the clients, whose quality of life was definitely enhanced, and the volunteers who provided the dedicated services. The Food Bank and Financial Services programs continued to aid individuals and families needing food at holidays and sometimes year-long, as well as small loans or actual stipends to qualified Jews facing crises. The Home Help Referral Service and the Specialized Homemaker Service also continued because they clearly enabled seniors to have greater independence and stay in their own homes. (Non-Jews previously admitted to the programs remained, but future new clients needed to be Jewish.) The declining level of émigrés to Toledo permitted the reduction of the program, with it being re-named Refugee Services. The CARES program ended, due in large measure to issues of transportation liability issues under Ohio law. Lastly, the adoption and counseling programs functioned ". . . only to refer individuals and families to appropriate professionals for service." J.F.S. retained a Licensed Independent Social Worker to work with indigent Jewish clients as appropriate.[92]

In December 2001 the J.F.S. and the J.S.S. offices moved to 5166 Monroe Street, Suite 301 as part of an agreement with the United Jewish Council of Greater Toledo that the previous Sylvania Avenue site was too small and lacked client privacy.

More recently Family Service operations gained much better quarters in the form of the Sekach Community Services Building. Located on the Jewish Community Campus on Sylvania Avenue, the facility is both a substantial new asset for several campus organizations and an impressive testimony to the vitality and generosity of the Toledo Jewish community.

The initial bequest that enabled this facility to happen came from Leo and Vera Sekach, who were their families' sole survivors of the Holocaust. With the assistance of the Hebrew Immigrant Aid Society, the young married couple relocated from Europe following the end of World War II and settled in Toledo, with help from the local Jewish Family Service. For many years they lived on Gramercy while Leo worked for Columbia Gas and Vera used her talent as a seamstress. Leo died in 2001 at age 91 and Vera passed away in 2005 at age 90.

Following Vera's passing, the Jewish Family Service, the United Jewish Council of Greater Toledo and the Toledo Jewish Community Foundation received bequests of $300,000 each from the Sekach estate.

Given the nature and size of the bequests, it was decided to construct a new building on the Campus which would serve the entire local Jewish community. The building consists of approximately 9,000 square feet in two sections. The Leizerman Jewish Family Service Wing fronts on Sylvania Avenue while the Helen Goldman JCC/YMCA Childcare Wing faces west. The facility also includes a storage room for the Jewish community food bank. This newest building contains thoughtful ties to earlier structures that played important roles in the community in the past. Memorial plaques from Darlington House, cornerstones from the Jewish Education League building and Darlington House and a Star of David window frame from the original J. E. L. Building are all included in the Sekach Building. Ground was officially broken in October 2006 and the building was dedicated and occupied the following year.[93]

United Jewish Fund

A sign of the growing complexity of the local Jewish support network was the 1948 incorporation of the United Jewish Fund. Prior to this action, the Fund operated with volunteers while the Jewish Community Council provided administrative support. The Council members decided that the founding of the state of Israel on May 14, 1948, with its subsequent need for assistance, and the general level of need among Jews worldwide, were both reasons for putting the United Jewish Fund on a more formal footing. The incorporation process included hiring Julian Stone as a full-time director. In its first year of operation the Fund raised the record-breaking sum of $816,000 to aid the new Israeli state and displaced persons following the war.[94] In 1994 nearly 80% of local Jews contributed $1.58 million to the Fund.[95]

Jewish Welfare Federation of Toledo

The next milestone for local Jewish benevolent efforts came on July 12, 1960. After five years of study and planning, the United Jewish Fund (established in 1948) and the Jewish Community Council (established in 1935) merged to form the **Jewish Welfare Federation of Toledo**. The previous leader of the United Jewish Fund, Arthur Edelstein, became the Welfare Federation's first president.[96] Burt Silverman, former Council president, became the new group's vice president. The merger was said to not affect the status of Jewish Family Service and the Council in terms of receiving funds from the Red Feather (precursor of United Way) campaign. That was important because in the year prior to the merger, the J.F.S. had received $20,000 and the council had received $46,000 to supplement funds from the United Jewish Fund.[97]

In 1985 the Federation changed its name to the **Jewish Federation of Greater Toledo**.[98]

On July 1, 2000 the Federation assumed the name **United Jewish Council of Greater Toledo**. *The Blade* later reported that the new organization's first Chief Operating Officer was Marvin Goldberg.[99] Joel S. Beren became C.E.O. in 2003, serving until 2008. Currently, Abby Suckow is Interim Chief Executive Officer.

Community Relations Committee

Regardless of the name of its parent organization, the Community Relations Committee (formerly the Public Relations Committee) continued to operate in this time period. A brief review of some of the issues that can be traced in its records in the United Jewish Council archives show the range and nature of its work.[100]

In 1949 a local company owner distributed a pamphlet to ". . . many people in Toledo, particularly physicians and dentists . . . that purported to be against socialized medicine. In fact, the pamphlet was a "spring-board" to make "anti-Semitic statements, and asserted that the Jews were behind socialized medicine and that a great majority of Jews were communists. The committee agreed that its chairman, King Baer, should meet with the company owner. Dr. Louis Ravin, committee member, also suggested that a statement be prepared for the Toledo Academy of Medicine's "Bulletin" contesting the attack.

Ten years later the committee considered the ramifications of a new Toledo City Council statute that required stores to be closed one day a week, Sundays generally, unless religious beliefs supported a different day. The local Roman Catholic diocese and the Council of Churches had supported the new law. The discussion stretched over several sessions with little major substantive action taken and the law was eventually repealed.

Other topics that reappear in the minutes include instances of the Christian religion being observed in public schools, some editorial positions of *The Blade* and related news coverage, e.g. when Arab representatives visited the city, housing or employment discrimination, the actions of a Bible Club at Woodward High School and the appearance of anti-Semitic speakers, e.g. George Rockwell (a neo-Nazi of the 1960s).

Toledo Jewish Cemetery Association

The earlier cemetery association merged in 1963 with the congregations using the Oregon cemeteries site to establish the Toledo Jewish Cemetery Association. The new association oversaw all the separate Oregon cemeteries, subsequently collectively named the Beth Shalom Cemetery. The association incorporated in 1965. The association is now responsible for the upkeep and operation of both Beth Shalom and Eagle Point cemeteries.[101]

The Toledo Jewish Orthodox Home for the Aged

Helping care for senior members of the Toledo Jewish community is a long-standing tradition, but one honored primarily through the efforts of individual families and congregations.

The Toledo Jewish Orthodox Home for the Aged officially joined the local care-giving network with its incorporation in 1936. Early fund raising included efforts by a group of women under the leadership of Rebecca Topper. They sponsored card parties, rummage sales, donor luncheon and other activities. One of the curious activities missing from modern fund raising was the collecting of tax stamps, sorting them and sending them to Columbus for payment, as Rose Hamerman, one of the ladies who participated, recalled. Mrs. Sol (Molly) Silverman assumed leadership upon the death of Mrs. Topper.[102] (*Photo 72 page 118, Home for the Aged*)

Given the hard times locally during the Great Depression, the home did not begin operating its first facility until 1946.[103] That was a former residence at 2220 Ashland Avenue (corner of Batavia Street), well-situated within the then-Jewish community. Five residents moved in on August 5, 1946. The home included sixteen rooms able to accommodate 20 residents, a kitchen equipped to comply with Orthodox dietary laws and quarters for a live-in staff of three, including a nurse. Joseph Ringold was president of the home's Board of Directors at the time and Mr. and Mrs. Joseph Plaut were the first superintendents, having had previous similar experience in Cincinnati. A women's auxiliary provided the daily care and longer-term support.[104] (*Photo 73, page 118, Darlington House*)

While a commendable start, the home soon became inadequate as more and more people sought entrance and the lack of an elevator proved to be a major hindrance. Thus, a larger, three-story brick house at 2233 Collingwood Avenue replaced the first home in 1951, accommodating more residents and featuring an elevator.[105]

As caring for the community's elderly became a larger job, Benjamin E. Lane was hired in 1955 as the first professionally trained director. In addition, a salaried staff, which included a dietician, housekeeper and nurses, assumed some tasks from the auxiliary.

In 1958 the Jewish Community Council sponsored a study of the care resources available for senior Jews. The outcome was a proposal for a new facility, which also would be expandable to meet future needs. Three years of fund-raising succeeded and enabled the laying of a cornerstone for a new building on Darlington Road in the Old Orchard neighborhood, another sign of the westward movement of the Jewish population of Toledo. The new home was named Darlington House the Jewish Home for the Aged. At the time of its cornerstone dedication on October 8, 1961, the anticipated cost was to be $846,000 and $700,000 had already been raised.[106] It officially opened on the eve of Passover (April 22) in 1962 and twenty-two residents moved in.

Darlington House proved a great success and by 1965 it was filled to capacity. Lester Alexander chaired a Self-Study Committee to plan for the future. Just three years later ground was broken for an additional wing to Darlington House and it was named the Lester Alexander Pavilion, to honor the man who had died November 1, 1968. He had been a president of the J. C. C. and had served as secretary of the Collingwood Temple for twenty years.[107] (*Photo 74, page 118, Steve Weiner, Dr. Eva Shapiro, and Art Solomon*)

On October 7, 1984 the new Dr. Eva Shapiro wing was dedicated at Darlington House. It was named to honor Dr. Shapiro, who was credited to be "the first female dentist in private practice in the Toledo area." The addition included a second dining room, recreational spaces and a nursing station. It increased the facility's total capacity from 116 to 125 residents.[108]

A women's auxiliary and a volunteer corps assisted the professional staff to provide an enjoyable life for the residents.[109] Shirley Yaffee, president of the auxiliary in 1978 and a Darlington House Board member, said the auxiliary played a major role at Darlington. For example, it cared for the linens, it purchased at least one electric bed each year and the group paid for the Occupational Therapy Room and its equipment. During her presidency, the auxiliary began sponsoring the Saturday afternoon teas, responding to a resident's regret that Saturdays were "dull." The auxiliary also presented a bus to Jewish Senior Services for excursions.[110] Roy Treuhaft, a former board member, recalled in a 2003 interview that ". . . the volunteers made the place special. Everyone in the community volunteered. They did many little jobs."[111]

In 1980 Pelham Manor was built on land adjacent to Darlington House. Roy Treuhaft led the dedication ceremonies on October 19, with local Congressman Thomas Ludlow Ashley and Martin Janis, Director of the State of Ohio's Commission on Aging, speaking.[112] This new facility was for seniors capable of more independent living.[113] A Housing and Urban Development Department grant helped finance the project.[114]

As the century closed the Darlington House Board became very concerned about several matters. Those areas of concern were the possibility of legislative action that would have a negative effect of the facility, the future of Medicare and Medicaid reimbursements, the need for substantial capital improvements to maintain the standard that was the hallmark of Darlington House and the diminishing Jewish population in the area.

In consideration of these factors the Darlington House Board of trustees approved the creation of a Long Range Planning Committee to evaluate the future options for the facility. After an extensive study of the alternatives, the Committee recommended that the Darlington House facility should be sold. The sale was consummated to Royal Manor Health Care on July 31, 2000. By that time only 35% of its residents were Jewish.

The placement, investment and utilization of Darlington House funds (now Jewish Senior Services) was of great concern to the Board. After extensive study the Task Force recommended that various funds of Jewish Senior Services, including proceeds from the sale of Darlington House, be placed in a supporting organization within the Toledo Jewish Community Foundation. It was agreed that the mission statement of this organization would conform to the mission statement of Jewish Senior Services and that control of the Board would remain with Jewish Senior Services.

The Jewish Senior Services Supporting Organization was officially created on December 24, 2001. Since that time grants have been approved providing substantial funds for the benefit of Jewish elderly of the greater Toledo area.[115]

Board of Jewish Education

Local educational organizations grew in 1953 with the opening of the Progressive Hebrew Day School at the B'nai Jacob Center on Parkwood and Bancroft streets. It operated on an irregular basis, according to the history of the Federation. In 1962 a "high school department" began and shortly thereafter a Toledo College of Hebrew Studies opened.

In the early 1960s Morris Horowitz of the Bureau of Jewish Education reported that the three operating branches had a total enrollment of 300 students (B'nai Israel 185; the Temple 60; B'nai Jacob 55). Tuition had been introduced in 1955, it was raised in 1960 and by the time of the report it ranged from $25 to $75 per year, based on the age and gender of the child.[116]

Dr. Judah Pilch, a specialist in Jewish education systems, was hired to study the local system in 1963. In his report he complimented the facilities and their physical condition. He concluded that nearly 1,100 children of all ages received some kind of Jewish education in these classes, about one-fourth of the total Jewish school-age population in Toledo. Almost two-thirds of these children were aged ten to twelve. This age concentration was because their parents were primarily interested in Bar Mitzah preparations and the youngsters dropped out of school immediately afterwards, Dr. Pilch said. He recommended a consolidated school be organized.[117]

As an outcome of that study, the **Toledo Board of Jewish Education** was established in 1970, with an operating constitution approved the following year. The Board included representatives from each Toledo congregation and ". . . the Jewish Welfare Federation helped mold policy for curriculum and facilities." The new organization provided centralized services and supervision for local Jewish schools affiliated with it. The T. J. B. E. directly supervised the David Stone Hebrew Academy, the Community Hebrew School, the High School for Jewish Studies and the Adult Institute of Jewish Studies.[118] (*Photos 75 & 76, page 119, Hebrew Academy students*)

According to a *Blade* story in January 1964, a "Hebrew Academy" was planned to begin at Meadowbrook Court Synagogue in September with a kindergarten and perhaps a first grade class. The Academy was incorporated in the fall of 1963 and Dr. Joseph Judis was the president. All Jewish children in Toledo, not just those with an Orthodox affiliation, are eligible to enroll, the story said.[119]

Apparently start-up needed a little more time, but in the September 1966 issue of the *Toledo Jewish News* Dr. Joseph Judis announced that "After many years and a number of attempts a Hebrew Day School will open its door in Toledo once again. The school will be known as the Hebrew Academy of Toledo, and will begin classes on Wednesday, September 7, 1966 with a Nursery and Kindergarten at 3220 Meadowbrook Court." Rabbi Ephraim Zimand was designated as Administrator. The newspaper gave credit for this success to Rabbis Nehemiah Katz and Ephraim Zimand, as well as Dr. Judis and the Academy's board of trustees.[120]

By 1969 the picture had dimmed. A report on the "Bureau Hebrew School" noted that the enrollment of 202 children (142 boys and 60 girls) is ". . . the smallest in the history of the Bureau." The reasons given were the decline in birth rate, the old problem of retaining post-Bar Mitzah boys and the loss of potential students to the new Hebrew Academy.[121]

But if it was competition, the Academy experienced its own ups and downs. It opened in 1966 with 25 children in two pre-school classes. By 1969 there were 110 children enrolled in pre-school through fifth grade. Two years later there were only 60 children from pre-school through third grade. There were plans at the time to add a fourth grade again in 1972 and eventually fifth and sixth grades. The curriculum had gained state accreditation. The 1971 tuition was $500 for nursery school and $550 for elementary levels. This constitutes most of the operating funds, with other revenue coming from the Toledo Jewish Welfare Fund, private gifts and state and local funds. The classes met at B'nai Israel Synagogue.[122]

In 1996, the Academy enrollment was 86 students, with a gender division nearly fifty-fifty. The pupils represented Toledo's three congregations about evenly. There was an active Hebrew Academy Parents Association and the

Toledo Board of Jewish Education gave special attention to recruitment. An annual report of the time stated the Academy's philosophy: ". . . to provide every child with an environment in which s/he can learn and grow – in every way – with a climate of solid Jewish mores, ethics, and values."[123]

In 1999 the Academy gained its Middle School, grades six and seven, thanks to a four-year $275,000 grant from the Partnership for Excellence in Jewish Education. An eighth grade was anticipated for the following year.[124]

The Toledo Jewish Community Foundation

The Toledo Jewish Community Foundation began operations in 1980 under the auspices of the Federation. Marvin Kobacker was the first chairman of the board and was subsequently succeeded in that office by Gordon Levine, Harley Kripke, Frederick Treuhaft and Donald L. Solomon. Sidney Mostov served as the first part-time director. It may receive cash donations, contributions of property, stocks and bonds and can be the beneficiary of bequests in fulfilling its role as the endowment program of the Jewish Federation. It is a long-range and continuing effort to build for the future needs of the local community and to institute innovative programs and services. The Foundation is a separate fund, whose uses are for special purposes and are segregated from the annual campaign funds. By the end of 1985, the Foundation had assets of $2,250,000.[125]

The Foundation soon began making grants to local Jewish community groups and soliciting funds. In 1992 the Foundation decided the time had come to hire a full-time endowment director and Arleen Levine joined the Foundation in March 1993.[126] By 1997 Foundation assets totaled $12,000,000. The 2001/2002 Annual Report noted that there were then 31 Special Purpose Founds, 12 Agency Funds and 2 Supporting Organizations. The following year's report announced that the Jewish Senior Services Supporting Organization had been established, using the proceeds from the sale of Darlington House, as well as other endowment funds of Jewish Senior Services.[127] Summarizing its first twenty-five years of operations, Donald L. Solomon, Chairman of the Foundation's Board, said that from its beginning, ". . . the Foundation has grown into the thriving enterprise that its founders envisioned . . ." The 2004/2005 Annual Report listed a grand total of all funds of $24,180,931 and by December 31, 2006 foundation assets were valued at $32.4 million.[128]

In September of 2006, the Foundation awarded a grant of $50,000 to the Israel Emergency campaign for the reconstruction of the Ophthalmology Department of the Western Galilee Hospital-Nahariya in honor of Dr. Louis and Sophie Ravin for their many years of leadership and dedication to the Toledo Jewish community.

B'nai B'rith

The Independent Order of B'nai B'rith began in New York City in 1843 and is generally recognized as the oldest continuously-operating Jewish service organization in the world.[129] A local presence began with the establishment of a lodge, Ephraim Lodge #183, on September 15, 1872. The growth of the local community, and presumably interest in B'nai B'rith activities, fostered the formation of a second lodge on November 10, 1907, the Toledo Lodge #631. The two lodges consolidated on May 10, 1910 into the Toledo Lodge #183, with Isaac Rosenthal, its first president.[130]

The activities of the local B'nai B'rith proved to be very difficult to research. However, one encounters the organization helping support Boy Scout troops and sponsoring very popular bowling leagues in Toledo. Furthermore, individual members honored the goals and philosophy of B'nai B'rith by their active and outstanding participation in many other Jewish community activities. (*Photo 77, page 119, Lodge 183 I.O.B.B.*)

Hadassah

Henrietta Szold founded the Women's Zionist Organization of American in 1912 in New York City. The current Hadassah website gives this description: ". . . the largest volunteer organization and the largest women's organization in America, Hadassah is committed to strengthening the unity of the Jewish people. . . . In the U. S. we reach our goals through Jewish and Zionist education programs, Zionist Youth programs, and health awareness programs, as well as by advocating for issues of importance to women and to the American Jewish community."[131]

Hadassah reached Toledo in 1924 with the formation of a chapter, composed of two groups, Seniors and Juniors. Eva Epstein Shaw was the first president of the Seniors. Dues were $4.00 per year, with $1.25 being retained for Toledo activities and the balance being forwarded to fulfill national quotas. The early years included luncheons at the Lasalle and Koch department store, rummage sales, card parties, showers for Hadassah supplies and sewing groups.[132]

Given the international focus of the organization, the primary effort of local chapters was fund raising. As Toledo moved into the Depression, the local chapter's "chief money maker event" was the Ten Dollar Donor luncheon. The pressure was great, for the Toledo women had annual quotas of $2,500 for medical work, $500 for the Jewish national fund for the purchase of land in Palestine, $300 for the upkeep of twenty-two infant welfare stations and $175 for school lunches. Supplementing the fund raising, the chapter's sewing group had produced more than 500 garments and shipped them to Palestine. During WW II the local chapter participated in bond drives and also provided Hanukkah dinners for area service men and women, as well as being hostesses at the J. E. L. Building for the Sunday buffet suppers and dancing.[133] A joint fund-raising and social event was the Zionist Family Night Bazaar and Youth Festival held at B'nai Israel.[134]

The local organization continued to grow in the 1950s and 1960s. Major events included fashion shows and the chapter even sponsored a Toledo performance of the Israel Symphony Orchestra, with Leonard Bernstein as conductor and soloist. During this period the chapter was comprised of three groups, Henrietta Szold (met afternoons), Lilah (met evenings) and Devorim (a continuation of the earlier Business and Professional Group, met on Sundays).

In the 1970s the Lilah group attracted young married couples with family Chanukah parties, holiday workshops, garage sales, progressive dinners, gourmet auctions, Night at the Races, Summer Bar-B-Ques, all of which required lots of member involvement. In the same period, increased national quotas needed new fund raising methods. Lilah group sponsored Oy Vegas Casino Night and Hadassah theater parties assumed a new look by utilizing the Westgate Dinner Theater. That new shopping center was also the venue for The Westgate Super Shopping Spree, where long hours of volunteer labor raised thousands of dollars.

The national trend of more women working full-time impacted Hadassah in the 1980s and by the latter years of the decade the Toledo chapter saw a need to re-organize and re-invigorate. The major organizational change was the consolidation of the three groups into one. As the new century opened, local Hadassah membership numbered more than 400 women and they remained fully dedicated to the organization's principles and goals.

Women's American ORT

This movement began with the 1880 formation of O.R.T. (or the Russian acronym for *Organization for the Distribution of Artisanal and Agricultural Skills*) in St. Petersburg, Russia. More affluent, socially-conscious members of that city's Jewish community sought to aid impoverished Jews living mainly in Russian rural areas and small villages. Their goal was not simply charitable handouts but to provide vocational training and tools so that families could improve their condition.

The American Women's O.R.T. followed in 1927, being organized in a Brooklyn, New York kitchen. As the century progressed, the organization established vocational training facilities both in the United States and in Israel. It sought to expand its membership as well and a representative of national O.R.T. visited Toledo in the spring of 1960. As a result of that visit, an organizational meeting was held in the fall at the Innisbrook home of Mrs. Max Shulak. The charter group included Mrs. Richard Kasle, Mrs. Ronald Harris, Mrs. Louis Millman, Mrs. Alan Konop, Mrs. Richard Helburn, Mrs. Allan Cohn, Mrs. Henry Silverman, Jr., Mrs. Jack Romanoff and Mrs. Leonard Fruchtman.[135]

As with the local chapters of other national and international organizations, O.R.T. units need to focus mainly on fund raising to finance the greater goals. Over the years, Toledo's O.R.T. has sold box lunches for such special events as Super Bowl football games and the "Art for O.R.T." galas. One year's gala included donated art works by internationally-known Toledo artist Israel Abramofsky and talented sculptor LeMaxis Glover.[136]

In 1978, U. S. Secretary of State Cyrus Vance appointed ORT member Marla R. Levine to the U. S. National Commission for the United Nations Educational, Scientific, and Cultural Organization. She represented O.R.T., in which she served as national vice-president and national bulletin chairman at the time. This action came in partial recognition of her being named Outstanding Leader of 1972 by the Toledo Council of Jewish Welfare Funds and the Toledo Area Chamber of Commerce; she had recently completed a term as president of the Toledo Board of Jewish Education as well.[137]

Chabad of Toledo

The Chabad movement permanently reached the Toledo community in April 1987 with the arrival of Rabbi Yossi and Raizel Shemtov and their one-year-old son, Mendel. They came as the emissaries of the Lubavitcher Rebbe of Righteous memory, Menachem Mendel Schneerson. Under the doctrine of the Chabad movement, such emissaries enter a community to "kindle the spark of Judaism in all those around them."[138]

Both Yossi and Raizel were born into Chassidic families, his in Detroit, Michigan and hers in Brooklyn, New York. In 1985 Yossi Shemtov received his Rabbinic Ordination and two years later he was ordained as a Rabbinic Judge.

Using funds from the Lubavitch Foundation of Michigan, the original Toledo Chabad House was at 2350 Secor Road. In 1997 Chabad relocated to 4020 Nantucket Drive, at the corner of Sylvania Avenue. The programs reach out to synagogues, schools, homes, offices, prisons, onto the streets, into cyberspace and one-on-one anywhere.

Local Chabad programming for children has been very active. *Camp Gan Israel* began in 1990 with seventeen children. It grew to eighty-five ". . . of the happiest campers in town." In 1992, Raizel Shemtov started a preschool program called *Gan Yeladim*. That afternoon program has grown into a certified preschool ". . . that specializes in provided an early childhood development program in a warm Jewish environment." Little wonder that "Morah" Raizel has become so well-known to more than 500 children in the community.

Programs have been organized for special groups. In 1993 the "Food and Learning Center" opened, catering to the "financial, emotional and spiritual need of new Americans in our community, although its outreach is available to all those in the Toledo Jewish community." Then in 2001, Chabad and the United Jewish Council entered into a partnership to meet the needs of college and university students. This joint effort resuscitated the Hillel/Chai Jewish Student Center at the University of Toledo.

All this activity necessitated an additional family in the local Chabad establishment and Rabbi Shumuly and Chani Rothman joined a few years ago. Rabbi Shumuly completed his rabbinic training in Houston, Texas and Chani, his wife, received her education at Montreal Seminary, Canada. One of the first activities of the new rabbi was initiating his "Living Legacy" program, which takes extra-curricular Jewish-centered activities and celebrations into classrooms.

In 2005 the New Jewish Learning Institute was established as another forum for Jewish education with the task of ". . . bring[ing] to Toledo new Jewish voices and perspectives in the most accessible way possible." Rabbi Shemtov described such activities as ". . . a key concept of Chabad's growth in the Toledo community. Chabad is relentless in finding new approaches, new programs, and new means to reach the heart of every Jew and to create the specific program and opportunity that will meet the comfort level of every single individual."

Hillel

Hillel began in 1923 at the University of Illinois when Dr. Chauncey Baldwin, professor of Biblical literature, wrote an article in *The American Israelite* that highlighted the Jews' need ". . . to provide for the ethical and spiritual training of its young people." Consequently the "first Jewish student ministry on an American campus" began. "The new agency was named "Hillel" after one of the great teachers in Jewish history, whose patience and devotion to study marked him as the ideal symbol of the

Jewish spirit in the campus setting." After a year, Rabbi Benjamin Frankel convinced B'nai B'rith to sponsor the group. At this time the Hillel network extends to 279 universities in 13 countries on 5 continents.

The Hillel chapter at the University of Toledo apparently began in 1972; Dr. Stephen Goldman was named Hillel Counselor and Leo Goldner was Coordinator. Dr. David Weinberg succeeded Goldman as Hillel Counselor at UT in October 1975. A examination of flyers and other news items in the United Jewish Council archives shows that the campus group's activities included encouraging fellowship among Jews on campus, understanding world issues and learning more about local institutions. An example of the latter is a luncheon in 1976 that featured Lou Etchoff, assistant director of the Jewish Welfare Federation, as speaker. The UT chapter also sometimes joined with the active Hillel chapter at Bowling Green State University, such as ". . . a *Shabat Oneg* – a joint service and oneg with BGSU Jewish Students Group." Fun was on the agenda sometimes too, as with a " Purim Party – The Whole Megillah!"[139]

(Photo 78, page 120, Leo Goldner and Ben Solomon)
(Photo 79, page 120, Day Camp at JCC around mid 1940s)

References

1   Sarna, pp. 220 – 221.

2   *1994 Greater Toledo Jewish Community Population Survey*, p. 3.

3   The J. C. C.'s *60 Years 'in pursuit of excellence;' a commemorative pictorial of the Jewish Community Center of Toledo* has a simple but most helpful chart tracking the evolution of local Jewish social agencies from 1906 to 1966, on p. 12. Past presidents and executive directors are also listed in the booklet.

4   *80th Anniversary; from generation to generation, 1907 – 1987*, Jewish Federation of Greater Toledo, p. 34.

5   Hughes, p. 1.

6   *80th Anniversary*, p. 34. In *A History of Jewish Philanthropic Organizations in Toledo, Ohio* by Marvin G. Lerner, done in 1959 and included in the Jewish Welfare Federation's *Leaders' Manual*, the following groups are also listed as "beneficiaries:" Jewish Relief Office, Jewish Free Loan Association and the Jewish Shelter House.

7   *80th Anniversary*, p. 43. Rabbi Joseph Telushkin, in *Jewish Literacy*, pp. 626-7, spells the term *"Chevra Kadisha"* and gives it a literal translation of "Holy Society". He also describes it as only a burial society, whose

members physically and ritually prepare a body for interment in a process called *tahara* ("purification"). In some cases, members sit with the body continuously until burial.

8   *80th Anniversary*, p. 43.

9   *Toledo Blade*, April 24, 1955, clipping, n.p. The newspaper gives the title as the Hebrew Burying Ground and Cemetery Association," but uses the same year.

10   Photocopies of cemetery documents provided by Marshall Isenberg.

11   Marshall N. Isenberg, president, Toledo Hebrew Cemetery Association, in a letter dated January 1997.

12   *80th Anniversary*, p. 34.

13   *80th Anniversary*, p. 43.

14   Photocopies of cemetery documents provided by Marshall Isenberg.

15   Online at www.historic-woodlawn.com/specethnic.html and accessed October 29, 2005.

16   *80th Anniversary*, p. 34.

17   This sum would be nearly $120,000 in 2004 dollars, based on comparable Consumer Price Index models. The computation for this comparison comes from Samuel H. Williamson, "What is the Relative Value?" in Economic History Services, December 14, 2005 as presented on the website www.eh.net and accessed April 11, 2006.

18   *80th Anniversary*, p. 34.

19   All these contribution records are from the *80th Anniversary*, p. 34.

20   *80th Anniversary*, p. 34.

21   *80th Anniversary*, p. 36.

22   Lerner is quoted in *History of Jewish Family Service of Toledo* by Sid Levine, c. 2003, p. 1.

23   Levine, p. 1.

24   Levine, p. 1.

25   Levine, p. 1.

26   Telushkin, pp. 464 – 466.

27   Meyer Straus, in a telephone interview with Alice Applebaum, December, 2004. He noted that his classmate Meyer Kripke subsequently also graduated from Scott H. S., became a rabbi with a congregation in Omaha, Nebraska and was a neighbor to Warren Buffet, whose investing prowess Straus took advantage of by investing early in Buffet's Berkshire Hathaway Fund and which later enabled Kripke to donate $15 million to the Jewish Theological Seminary.

28   *80th Anniversary*, p. 40.

29   Lerner, p. 1. However, he gives no documentation for this statement and no corroborative evidence has been found yet.

30   *The Toledo Blade*, February 23, 1907, no page.

31   *The Toledo Blade*, March 18, 1956, no page.

32   *The Toledo Blade*, February 23, 1907, no page. The article includes a photograph of the Council House. She was inducted into the Toledo Civic Hall of Fame in 2004. Her motto was "Building boys is better than mending men."

33   *80ᵗʰ Anniversary*, pp. 34-35.

34   *Fiftieth Anniversary of the Jewish Community Center*, quoted in Hughes, p. 2.

35   The J. C. C.'s *60 Years 'in pursuit of excellence;' a commemorative pictorial of the Jewish Community Center of Toledo* has two pages listing youth clubs affiliated with the Council House, when they met, the names of the members, and, usually, their addresses.

36   *80ᵗʰ Anniversary*, pp. 34-35.

37   *80ᵗʰ Anniversary*, p. 34. On this page, the text uses 1907 as the completion date; a photo caption for the building uses 1906.

38   *80ᵗʰ Anniversary*, p. 35.

39   *80ᵗʰ Anniversary*, p. 35. The J. C. C.'s *60 Years 'in pursuit of excellence;' a commemorative pictorial of the Jewish Community Center of Toledo* has six pages of photographs of J.E.L. activities and reproduces a list of contributors to the building's construction fund and the sums donated, taken from the cornerstone. The $20,000 sum would be nearly $400,000 in 2004 dollars, based on comparable Consumer Price Index models. The $10 membership equivalent would be $200 based on the same standard. The computations for these comparisons come from Samuel H. Williamson, "What is the Relative Value?" in Economic History Services, December 14, 2005 as presented on the website www.eh.net and accessed on April 11, 2006.

40   *80ᵗʰ Anniversary*, p. 35.

41   Anna Berkowitz was quoted in *80ᵗʰ Anniversary*, 35 and the story is mentioned in Hughes' history of the J. C. C. as well, p. 4.

42   *80ᵗʰ Anniversary*, p. 36. No details provided regarding the Sunday School.

43   *80ᵗʰ Anniversary*, p. 36.

44   Levine, p. 1.

45   *Toledo Times*, April 1, 1923, (clipping) n.p.

46   *Toledo Times*, April 1, 1923, (clipping) n.p.

47   Dedication booklet for the Collingwood Boulevard J. C. C., 1953, p. 6.

48   *Toledo Times*, April 1, 1923, (clipping) n.p.

49   *80ᵗʰ Anniversary*, 36. According to the J. C. C.'s *60 Years 'in pursuit*

of excellence;' a commemorative pictorial of the Jewish Community Center of Toledo, p. 2, the new name was the Federation Building since 1920.

50   Dedication booklet for the Collingwood Boulevard J. C. C., 1953, p. 7.

51   *80th Anniversary,* pp. 36-37.

52   *The Blade,* January 14, 1994, clipping, n.p.

53   *80th Anniversary,* p. 37.

54   Dedication booklet for the Collingwood Boulevard J. C. C., 1953, p. 7.

55   This delay and its cause are corroborated in the Federation's *80th Anniversary* booklet, p. 37, the J. C. C.'s *60 Years 'in pursuit of excellence;' a commemorative pictorial of the Jewish Community Center of Toledo,* p. 2 and the dedication booklet for the Collingwood Boulevard J. C. C., 1953, p. 7.

56   United Jewish Council archives, box 18. Among those attending the June meeting were both Rabbi Feuer and Rabbi Katz, according to Marvin G. Lerner, Jewish Welfare Federation's *Leaders' Manual,* p. 6.

57   According to a signed copy of the constitution of the new Community Council in the U. J. C. archives, box 18, the charter members are listed as "B'nai B'rith, the Toledo Jewish Federation, the Collingwood Avenue Temple, B'nai Israel, B'nai Jacob, Zionist Organization, Hadassah [sic]."

58   Lerner, p. 6.

59   *80th Anniversary,* p. 36.

60   Report of the Committee on Organization of the Jewish Community Council of Toledo, United Jewish Cocuncil archives, box 18.

61   Morris Horowitz, *A Brief Look into the Past,* Toledo Bureau of Jewish Education, [1962 or 1963],
U. J.C. archives, box 24.

62   Newspaper clipping in the Local History Department, n.d., but probably 1929 or 1930.

63   Morris Horowitz, *A Brief Look into the Past,* Toledo Bureau of Jewish Education, [1962 or 1963],
U. J.C. archives, box 24.

64   Morris Horowitz, *A Brief Look into the Past,* Toledo Bureau of Jewish Education, [1962 or 1963],
U. J.C. archives, box 24.

65   *80th Anniversary,* p. 40.

66   *80th Anniversary,* 37. The J. C. C.'s *60 Years* says the year was 1947, p. 2.

67   Dedication booklet for the Collingwood Boulevard J. C. C., 1953, p. 8.

68   Dedication booklet for the Collingwood Boulevard J. C. C., 1953, p.

8.

69   *The Toledo Blade*, March 18, 1956, n. p.

70   *Toledo Jewish News*, September 1968, pp. 1-2.

71   *Study for the Jewish Community Center of Toledo*, cited in Hughes, p. 15.

72   *80ᵗʰ Anniversary*, p. 39

73   *The Blade*, November 13, 1975, clipping, n.p.

74   *80ᵗʰ Anniversary*, p. 39

75   *80ᵗʰ Anniversary*, p. 39

76   *1994 Greater Toledo Jewish Community Population Survey*, p. 4.

77   *The Blade*, April 7, 2001, clipping, n.p.

78   *80ᵗʰ Anniversary*, p. 39

79   *80ᵗʰ Anniversary*, p. 38.

80   Lerner, pp. 7-8.

81   Levine, p. 1.

82   Levine, p. 1.

83   Levine, p. 1.

84   Levine, p. 2.

85   Levine, p. 2.

86   Levine. p. 2.

87   Levine, p. 2.

88   Levine, p. 2.

89   Levine, p. 3.

90   Levine, pp. 2-3.

91   Levine, pp. 3-4.

92   Levine, p. 3.

93   *Toledo Jewish News*, October 2006, p. 1 and insert.

94   *80ᵗʰ Anniversary*, p. 37.

95   *1994 Greater Toledo Jewish Community Population Survey*, p. 3.

96   *80ᵗʰ Anniversary*, p. 38.

97   *The Blade*, July 13, 1960, clipping, n.p. The Edward N. Davis Post, American Legion and the Goldstein-Goodman Post, Veterans of Foreign Wars were agencies represented on the board of the new Federation organization, according to *Toledo Jewish News*, August 1960, p. 1.

98   *80ᵗʰ Anniversary*, p. 39.

99   *The Blade*, April 7, 2001, clipping, n.p.

100   Community Relations Committee, Jewish Community Council, U. J. C. archives, box 23.

101   *80ᵗʰ Anniversary*, pp. 43-44.

102   *80ᵗʰ Anniversary*, pp. 41-42. The stamps were artifacts of the Ohio sales tax process for several decades in the 20ᵗʰ century. Otherwise

unredeemed stamps could be submitted to state government for a payment of face value. Individual stamp value varied greatly, but in the aggregate, the stamps provided a worthwhile income for the ladies support group to use at Darlington House.

103   The United Jewish Fund made its first grant to the Home in 1949, for $6,000. The next year, the grant doubled. Lerner, p. 8.

104   *Toledo Times*, July 14, 1946, (clipping) n.p.

105   *80ᵗʰ Anniversary*, pp. 41-42.

106   *Toledo Jewish News*, November 1961, p. 1.

107   *Toledo Jewish News*, December 1968, p. 1.

108   *West Toledo Herald*, October 3, 1984, clipping, n.p.

109   *80ᵗʰ Anniversary*, p. 43.

110   Yaffe, Shirley in an interview with Alice Applebaum, July 23, 2003.

111   Treuhaft, Roy in an interview with Alice Applebaum, May 19, 2003.

112   *Toledo Jewish News*, October 1980, p. 1.

113   *80ᵗʰ Anniversary*, p. 42.

114   Treuhaft, Roy in interview with Alice Applebaum, May 19, 2003.

115   Information for the preceding four paragraphs provided by Abby Suckow, Interim CEO of the United Jewish Council of Greater Council in an e-mail to the author dated June 23, 2008.

116   Morris Horowitz, Toledo Bureau of Jewish Education, [1962 or 1963], U. J. C. archives, box 24.

117   Dr. Judah Pilch, Toledo Report, Jewish Education Study (Draft), October 27, 1963, U. J. C. archives, box 24.

118   *80ᵗʰ Anniversary*, p. 41.

119   *80ᵗʰ Anniversary*, p. 40 and *The Blade*, January 6, 1964, clipping, n.p.

120   *Toledo Jewish News*, September 1966, p. 1.

121   Minutes, Board of Trustees of the Toledo Board of Jewish Education, March 19, 1969, U. J. C. archives, box 6.

122   *The Blade*, May 23, 1971, clipping, n.p.

123   Hebrew Academy of Toledo, *Annual Report*, May 8, 1996.

124   *The Blade*, August 25, 1999, n.p. online archive

125   *Celebrating 25, 1980 – 2005, the Toledo Jewish Community Foundation* booklet, pp. 1, 4.

126   *Celebrating 25, 1980 – 2005, the Toledo Jewish Community Foundation* booklet, p. 7.

127   *Celebrating 25, 1980 – 2005, the Toledo Jewish Community Foundation* booklet, pp. 11-12.

128   *Celebrating 25, 1980 – 2005, the Toledo Jewish Community Foundation* booklet, p. 14. Names of foundation board chairmen, first part-time director and 2006 assets provided by Arleen R. Levine, Director, Toledo

Jewish Community Foundation in e-mail to the author June 24, 2008.

129   www.en.wikipedia.org/wiki/B'nai_B'rith, accessed May 21, 2008.

130   *History of Jewish Community Organization in Toledo (With special reference to the Jewish Community Center)*, prepared by Albert Brown, Executive Director of the J. C. C., U. J. C. archives, box 18.

131   www.hadassah.org/about/home.html, accessed April 27, 2006.

132   *Four Score and Henrietta Szold Ago*, [a history of Hadassah in Toledo, 1924-2000], copy loaned by Rosemary Bramson to the author. This is the best single source of local information on the topic and is well done. It provided much of the information for this section.

133   *Toledo Blade*, May 18, 1931, clipping, n. d. An interesting artifact of Toledo's Junior Hadassah is a program from the group's presentation of *Love Pirate*, a self-described "merry musical comedy" staged at the State Theater on May 28, 1928.

134   *The Blade*, December 9, 1945, clipping, n.p.

135   *The Blade*, September 9, 1960, clipping, n.p.

136   *The Blade*, October 15, 1965, clipping, n.p.

137   *The Blade*, October 5, 1978, p. 28

138   Information about the Chabad movement in Toledo comes from Rabbi Shemtov in a document sent to the author by Sharon Rainwasser, September 30, 2005.

139   United Jewish Council archives, box 10.

Chapter 4
Other Threads

Introduction

Life is more than worship on Sabbath days and taking care of our fellow man and woman. Life is a day-by-day process, during which each individual copes with minute and grand issues as they affect him or her – and sometimes as he or she hopes to affect them. This history began in chapter one with examining the Jewish immigration to Toledo and the development of neighborhoods and businesses, where daily life is mostly lived. In chapters two and three the important roles of congregations and community organizations were covered.

This chapter has a change of view. For virtually the entire history thus far, we have been "looking at the forest instead of the trees." That is, the larger building blocks of the community: its business types, its settlement patterns, its shuls, synagogues and temples and its supportive organizations. Individuals were mentioned only to give human faces and human scale to these larger developments. The latter portion of chapter four presents very brief biographical sketches of representative Toledo Jewish personalities. These relatively few "trees" represent the thousands of "trees" that actually have built the community and sustain it today. Some may feel errors of inclusion or omission have occurred; such is the selection process and a person's right to have their personal list of "favorite trees." The goal was to conclude the history with examples of how the achievements of Toledo's Jewish community have all come thorough the efforts, firstly, of people and then organizations that people have used to leverage the power of individual efforts.

Athletics/Recreation

Many, many individuals from Toledo's Jewish community have demonstrated extraordinary talent in athletic endeavors over the years. To recognize especially outstanding examples and to symbolically acknowledge all these amateur and professional athletes, the Jewish Community Center of Toledo Sports Hall of Fame was created in 1995. The current inductees are cited below and the inscriptions on their respective plaques quoted *verbatim*:

Jack Gallon (*Photo 80, page 121*)
• Undefeated Big Ten Champion Wrestling Champion at the University of Michigan – 1951

• 3rd Place at the Big Ten Conference Wrestling Tournament – 1952
• Gold Medal in Collegiate Style Wrestling and 3rd Place in Grecco-Roman Style Wrestling at The 1961 World Maccabiah Games in Israel
• Served on numerous committees within the Toledo Jewish Community including The J. C. C. Board of Trustees, Jewish Federation Board of Trustees and The Jewish Federation's Community Relations Committee.
• Chairman of The Jewish National Fund Committee. Recipient of The J. N. F. Tree of Life Award. Charter Member of the Labor Advisory Board of Israel Bonds and a Member of the National Jewish Labor Committee.
• Past President and Current President Emeritus/Vice President of The Toledo Area Metro Parks Board. Active Board member within the O. P. R. A. and N. R. P. A.

Sidney Goldberg
• Brought professional basketball to Toledo, starting in 1931 with the bookings of the Harlem Globetrotters into Toledo and in Ohio, Michigan and Indiana.
• Between 1938 and 1949, founded and managed three Toledo franchises in the National Basketball League, forerunner of today's National Basketball Association – the Toledo White Huts, Toledo Jim White Chevrolets and the Toledo Jeeps.
• Was the first General Manager in modern professional basketball to sign African-American players to play on the same team as whites.
• Business Manager of the Globetrotters throughout the 1950s and owned and coached the Toledo Mercurys, one of the teams that toured with the barn-storming legends.
• Promoted boxing in Toledo nearly 50 years, bringing more than a dozen world champions to the city, including Jack Dempsey and Joe Louis. Brought nationally televised boxing to the nation from Toledo 12 times.
• Managed Toledo Olympic middleweight champion Wilbert (Skeeter) McClure.

Murray Guttman
• Captain of the University of Toledo basketball and baseball teams, All MAC selection 1956-1957 in both sports. The University of Toledo basketball record holder.
• Selected to the second team all-regional NCAA Basketball Team in 1957.
• Selected as National Athlete of the Year in 1957 by Alpha Epsilon Pi fraternity.
• Signed professional baseball contract as a pitcher with the Cincinnati Reds organization in 1957.

• Served as Health and Physical Educational Director at the Jewish Community Center of Toledo for 32 years.

Dr. Alexander Klein
• Played baseball and basketball at Ohio State University 1922-23.
• Played football at Ohio State University 1922, 1923, 1925 and 1926, selected First Team Coach's All American in 1926.
• Drafted by the Green Bay Packers in 1927 (declined).
• Played for the semi-pro football team, The Canton Bulldogs, 1922-27.
• Assistant football coach at Ohio State University, 1927. Assistant football coach at Scott High School between 1928-1940.
• Member of the National Jewish Welfare Board and served on the National Organization's Health & Physical Education Committees.
• Chairman of Midwest Health & Physical Education Committee in 1956.

Victor Isenstein
• First string point guard for Woodward High School basketball, leading his team in assists and to the City League Championship in 1931, 1932 and 1933.
• Led the J. C. C. of Toledo's Junior Varsity basketball team to a City League Championship in 1935.
• Coached J. C. C. youth basketball for ten years.
• Co-Chairman of the J. C. C. Health Club Board of Governors for eight years and member of the Health and Physical Education Committee for nine years.

Elsie Liber
• Well-known athlete before the advent of organized women's sports.
• First place in regional Senior Olympics in Akron, Ohio in softball throw, discus, shotput, Frisbee and tennis singles and doubles in 1983, 1991, 1992, 1993 and 1994.
• Represented the U. S. in doubles tennis at the Maccabiah Games in Israel in 1993. Won the bronze medal.
• U. S. T. A. tennis Senior Champion in 1996.
• Raised five children.
• J. C. C. Board Member and President of Temple B'nai Israel Sisterhood 1972-74.

Sam Rogolsky
• Played varsity football at Northern Arizona University for 3 years.
• Member of Woodward High School Hall of Fame and Ohio Basketball Officials Hall of Fame.

• Served as Director of Jewish Educational League for 5 years.
• Professional basketball referee (pre-NBA) and football official for 28 years.
• Teacher in Sylvania and Toledo Public Schools for 39 years.

Seymour Rothman
• Graduated from the University of Toledo, 1936.
• Feature writer and columnist for The Blade, 1936 – 1991.
• Received a Bronze Star during World War II for his efforts in creating , writing and editing weekly news reports.
• Covered University of Toledo athletic programs for 17 years.
• Wrote weekly sports TV column.
• One of the best known sports writers in the area.
• Memberships include: B'nai B'rith, Temple B'nai Israel, J. C. C., honorary lifetime member of U. T. Varsity T. Club and Old Newsboys Association.
• Chaired publicity for Matzo Ball Revue.
• Produced camp brochure for the J. C. C. Resident Campe Ma-Hi-Ya.
• Interviewed nationally-known celebrities.

Emily Sack
• Emily Sack was a member of the gold medal winning Women's Fast Pitch Softball team at the 17th World Maccabia games in Israel.
• The World Maccabia games are help every four years, drawing over 5000 Jewish athletes from around the world.
• The World Maccabia games are recognized by the International Olympic.
• Emily played college softball at Dennison University in Grandville, Ohio and was a four-year starter on the Sylvania Southview High School Varsity Women's Fast Pitch team.
• A native Toledoan, Emily is the daughter of Richard and Sandy Sack.

Ben Schall
• Played varsity basketball for the University of Toledo from 1936 – 1938.
• Served 4 years in U. S. Army, where he was leading scorer for the Ft. Warren basketball team.
• Lettered in baseball at the University of Toledo in 1936.
• Played on 5 State Championships Fast Pitch Softball Teams.
• Played for the National Basketball League teams: the Toledo Jeeps and the Detroit Gems.
• Successful local businessman.

Sam Schuster
• Award-winning gymnast in the German National Gymnastic Federation

in the parallel bars and the pommel horse.
• Wrestled as the United States freestyle wrestling champion in Europe during World War I, becoming the Allied – European wrestling champion.
• Volunteer coach in Gymnastics, Wrestling and basketball for the Jewish Education League.
• Athletic Director and Social Worker for the Jewish Educational League for 18 years.
• Commander of the Disabled American Veterans Parade and Memorial Day parade for twenty-five years.
• Director of the Toledo Veteran's Day Parade and Memorial Day parade for twenty-five years.
• For twenty years was responsible for the placement of American flags on all Toledo veterans' graves for Memorial Day.

Leo Shible
• 1975 Jewish Community Center volunteer of the year award.
• 30 years J. C. C. volunteer basketball coach.
• Served as Scoutmaster of Troop 91 at Temple B'nai Israel.
• Served as Scoutmaster of Troop 11 at the Jewish Community Center.
• Member of the Toledo Area Council, Boy Scouts of America.
• 38 years as manager and salesman for the Metropolitan Life Insurance Company.
• Member of B'nai B'rith Organization.
• U. S. Army Veteran.

Judd Silverman
• Golf individual medalist in the State High School Championship in 1973.
• Toledo District Junior Golf Champion in 1974.
• Winner of the Frank Stranahan Player of the Year Award in 1975.
• Recipient of golf scholarship to University of South Florida in Tampa, Florida.
• Member of the 1977 U. S. Golf Team at the Maccabi Games in Tel Aviv, Israel.
• Founder and Tournament Director of the Annual Jamie Farr Owens-Corning Classic presented by Kroger LPGA Tour.
• Championship Director of the 2003 U. S. Open at Inverness Country Club.

Abe Steinberg
• Lettered three years in basketball at Scott High School and was the leading scorer and play maker.

- Member of Scott High School Hall of Fame.
- Played basketball at the University of Toledo for two years.
- Won City championships in squash and basketball.
- Initiated the building of Darlington House and was President of Darlington House for six years.
- Community philanthropist.

Don Steinberg
- Played first string End for Ohio State University on their 1942 National Championship Football Team, coached by Paul Brown.
- Received Most Outstanding Student Athlete Award in the Big Ten in 1945.
- Wrote and published the book *Expanding Your Horizons*, based on Paul Brown and the 1942 Ohio State University National Championship Football Team.
- Member of Scott High School Hall of Fame and Toledo City League Hall of Fame.
- Served as President of Congregation Etz Chayim for ten years.
- Accomplished General Surgeon for 46 years, with outstanding contributions in clinical and laboratory research.

Nemo Wexler
- Combination of 73 years of fast pitch & slow pitch in many softball leagues.
- Past President, Organizer, Manager and Player of B'nai B'rith Softball Leagues.
- Past President in 1949 of the B'nai B'rith Bowling League.
- Owned and operated the Bowl-O-Drome for 18 years.
- Basketball player in the Class A City League playing for LIbbey Glass and the American Legion.
- General Chairman and past organizer of the Fraternal Order of Raggedies.
- Past Mayor of the Newsboys Organization.
- Active member of Congregation B'nai Israel.

Mark Wexler
- Mark Wexler is the Past President and Treasurer of the B'nai Brith Men's Bowling League. He won the All Events Scratch Division at the B'nai Brith International Bowling Tournament held in Las Vegas, NV and he represented the United States at the 17th World Maccabiah Games (2005) in Israel in the sport of bowling.
- He also played B'nai Brith softball.

• Mark was a member of the United States Air Force Varsity Bowling Team. He retired form the USAF in 2003 after 22 years of service.
• Mark has bowled two perfect "300" games.

For all those other members of the Jewish community who personally enjoyed recreation and athletics, the J. C. C., described extensively elsewhere in this history, was a very popular and important part of their lives, and the J. C. C./Y. M. C. A. continues to be a vital institution today. Complementing the J. C. C. through the years were several other well-used facilities.

Glengarry Country Club was formally presented to its 150 members on July 26, 1924. The *Toledo Times* reported that the new golf facility included 243 acres and represented a $200,000 investment at the corner of Hill Avenue and Crissey Road. Nationally-known Toledo golfer Sylvanus P. Jermain designed the course. Original officers were President M. H. Lempert, Vice President Irving Krank, Treasurer Lylvin Basch and Secretary King Baer. The two-story clubhouse included a dining room with dance floor, kitchen, locker rooms and several other club rooms. Tennis courts, a children's play area, practice greens and a juvenile course were also to be installed, according to the story.[1] Reviewing the membership list for 1926, Roy Treuhaft described it as a "Who's Who of the local Jewish business and professional sectors. Temple members seemed to have composed a predominant portion of the early club clientele.[2]

In 1930 Glengarry merged with the Progress Club, which dated back to 1889 and in 1930 owned a building at 2360 Monroe Street. Members of each organization gained full use of both facilities. The merger gave the new club a membership of two hundred.[3]

Also in the early 1930s a swimming pool was added, designed and built to resemble more of a pond than a formal pool. Its grand opening was to feature a diving exhibition by Joe Bloom. Because the regulation diving board had not arrived, the contractor installed a 2 by 10 inch plank atop the diving platform to use. Intending to do a swan dive, Bloom made his approach along the plank, jumped into the air, came down on the tip of plank as intended for take off . . . and the plank broke, dumping Bloom into the pool with no grace at all.[4]

The clubhouse burned to the foundation in a fire of undetermined origin in December 1939, while the building was closed for the season. By May 1940 plans were approved for a new, brick clubhouse on the site of the old one. The plans also include rebuilding the adjacent outdoor swimming pool.[5] Until the new clubhouse was ready, longtime member Dr. Jerome Jacobson recalled that a small building with lockers was built on the site and that golfers often brought picnic lunches or used portable grills to cook refreshments.[6]

Fire destroyed a large portion of the new clubhouse in the early hours of July 13, 1987, just days after the club had hosted the Ladies Professional Golf Association's Jamie Farr Classic tournament. Several men were charged with arson. At the time, club membership was estimated to be about 300.[7]

Later that year, plans were announced for a new, $3,375,000 clubhouse, to be built south of the burned one. Implementation of the proposal depended upon financial support from the membership, said club president Richard Gross at the time.[8]

Rebuilding was a tough commitment, largely due to costs. It would have required an investment of $10,000 by each member.[9] Another factor was the club's loss of members after the 1987 fire, according to club president Harry Nistel.[10] Another reason for fewer members, in the opinion of one member, was that other Toledo area country clubs were now admitting Jews.[11]

Because the cost of rebuilding was too great, Glengarry was sold to the Cavalear Corporation in 1988, according to club president Harry Nistel.[12] Some of the members stayed with the club under new ownership, while others moved to Sylvania Country Club or the Inverness Club.[13]

Only about 150 acres of the club's total 320 acres were developed at the time, said purchaser Robert Cavalear. The former club's property will be joined with other adjoining Cavalear properties to form a "low-density residential housing community," according to a newspaper story at the time and the golf facility will be re-named Stone Oak Country Club.[14]

The **Twins Oaks Swim Club**, 5700 W. Bancroft, half a mile west of McCord Road was a very popular family destination during the summer.[15] A story in the *Toledo Blade* in 1955 was probably bad news for the swimmers just waiting to take a plunge: "Work is progressing on the construction of the clubhouse and pool . . . Original plans called for completion by early June, but the $125,000 project is somewhat behind." The club's steel pool was fabricated in Cleveland and then shipped to the club site where it was welded together, said to be the first of its kind in the area to use that technique. Pool size was 42 by 90 feet, with depths from 3 to 10 ½ feet. The club also had a 60x60 foot clubhouse, a shallow pool for youngsters, tennis courts, softball diamonds and play areas with sand boxes and swings, as well as a paved parking lot for 150 cars. The club site included 8 ½ acres, allowing for future expansion.

Joel Beren recalled many family outings there, including the common practice of bringing a grill along for outdoor cooking. The fireworks shows were pretty great too.[16]After several decades of fun, the club was sold and is the basis for today's St. James' Club on the same site.[17]

Some persons interviewed for this project referred to **Sunningdale Country Club** as "the third Jewish country club." A review of information at the public library sheds some light on this description, but hardly verifies it to the same degree as Glengarry. The earliest mention is a *Toledo Times* story in 1930 that announced work was beginning on the Sunningdale club house, on property Harold Weber and H. W. Kline were developing at 2162 Alexis Road. The clubhouse was to be in the style of an English manor house and set amid a rolling 18-hole golf course.[18]

The club stayed out of the newspapers until 1960 when Norman Cohen, a Toledo attorney, was named receiver of the club after a suit seeking foreclosure on a $226,666 mortgage on the club was filed in Common Pleas Court. By then a Mr. Miller was the owner. Interestingly, the day before Toledo city council had approved an ordinance declaring the city's intention to purchase the club from Mr. Miller and turn it into a public course.[19] Nine months later the city approved the sale price of $486,000.

Such was not to be. A taxpayer law suit was filed to prevent the city's purchase, alledging that gambling had gone on at the club and that the city lacked the legal power to act without a public vote. Things got worse by January of 1961. The newspaper reported that an impasse had been reached: a closer examination of the property found serious access problems for expected traffic and part of one fairway was discovered to be off club property.[20] All these problems prevented the city from making its down payment.

With the deal apparently cold, the club was put up for public auction in March 1961. The city did not bid and the winning bid came from the Pleasant View County Club, an organization of twenty-two persons who have second mortgages totaling $226,000 against the property.

The club apparently operated as a public club until 1968 when Norman Cohen, now president of Pleasant View Country Club, Inc., proposed informally to the city that the municipality buy the club for $700,000. Mr. Cohen cited his failing health as the reason he wanted to sell. Toledo Mayor William Ensign and Vice Mayor Robert Savage were opposed to the deal, thinking the price was too high, it did not fit into city priorities and needed more study. A second law suit concerning the club was also still in the courts. Six days later, Mr. Cohen sent the city a one-sentence letter withdrawing the club from sale.[21]

The country club moved out of our orbit when on February 1, 1972 Charles A. Fuhrman and Joseph Mast bought it and re-named it the Tamaron Country Club. The agreed upon price as $700,000. The last law suit had been dismissed in July 1969.[22]

If one defines "recreation" broadly, then the **Toledo Bath House** probably deserves to be mentioned. Before it closed Christmas Eve of 1979, "it has been a meeting place of sorts since it was built in 1913 as a community endeavor by European immigrants." Abraham 'Shorty' Greenberg, 84, was "director" for 41 years, ever since he arrived in Toledo from New York City, drawn here by "the Depression blues." His nickname "Shorty" came from his 5-foot height. In New York City he had owned an apparel shop on 42nd Street, but went out of business as the Depression worsened.

The bath house was as well-known for its salads and steaks as for its steam baths. Shorty recalled that he got into salads first by making them for 50 cents each from vegetables that customers brought themselves, soon he decided that he could profit more by buying the vegetables himself and selling the complete salad. Customers soon asked him to provide steaks also. During WW II he had a hard time providing the steaks, usually purchased at Villhauer's on Bancroft Street, due to rationing. The government was not issuing him enough meat stamps. The problem was resolved when a customer sold Shorty 100,000 stamps for $70. (*Photo 81, page 121, Toledo Bath House*)

Prior to 1951 there was one ladies' day a week and he had two masseuses for them. However, "I quit that in 1951. The customers would bring in chicken salad or salmon sandwiches and the masseuses would fight all the time. I just quit Ladies Day all together. Besides, I ordered six dozen large bath towels for them with 'Shorty's Bath House" written on them, and every towel disappeared," he said. Massages for men were given up in about 1974, it was "too tough to get a good European masseur anymore." Decorations were sparse, the walls baby blue. When the building was scheduled to be razed for urban renewal, Shorty decided it was time to retire.[23]

Raggedy Ass Cadets

Certainly "the Cadets" are one of the most distinctive threads in this history. Former Lucas County Sheriff William Hirsch told his version of how the group got its name: By far the most common job of this group of youngsters was selling newspapers, mainly in the central business district. One day they decided to follow a parade that made its way through downtown, thinking that the parade would attract a crowd and a crowd usually meant good newspaper sales. The young entrepreneurs, dressed as usual in worn, patched and ragged clothes, attached themselves to the end of the parade and acted like they were another marching unit. In place of horns and drums, the youngsters used their voices, long honed for volume and stamina by yelling to sell papers and they attracted quite a bit of attention. Someone on the sidelines yelled, "There go the Raggedy Ass Cadets!" and, as Sherriff Hirsch said, ". . . the name has been ours for over fifty years."[24]

The group began taking informal shape in the early years of the 20th century on the north edge of downtown. The streets of Canton, Bancroft, Yates, Mulberry, Franklin, Southard and Woodruff roughly outlined the home neighborhood. The most commonly attended schools were B'nai Israel, Fulton, Scott, Sherman and Woodward. While predominantly comprised of Jewish boys, a 1997 commemorative video tape about the Raggedies described the membership as also including youths with Polish, Irish, Black, Italian, Greek and Arabic heritages.[25] They all shared the characteristic of being the children of first generation immigrants to Toledo and spoke a common language – according to the video tape – "survival."

In 1958 Moe Okun and Izzy Mitchell mustered the remaining original cadets and formally established the Raggedy Ass Cadets. The organization was simple: one annual meeting orchestrated by a few organizers, no dues, no on-going functions. By that time each of the original cadets had grown into living examples of the Horatio Alger dream of becoming an American success story. A *Blade* article in 1998 quoted Sanford Stein, nephew of original cadet Harry Nistel, saying "They had economic success combined with strength of character and a concern for humanity."[26]

The sole objective was to meet once a year "to remember where we came from" and to preserve a "feeling of roots and camaraderie." As Dr. Marvin Sharpiro, a charter member and longtime local podiatrist said, "We're here to appreciate how lucky we are. The greatest thing that ever happened to us was our parents didn't miss the boat over here."[27] Subsequent generations (sons and grandsons of earlier cadets) have joined with the remaining charter members to maintain that original spirit and commitment to each other to the present day. Some two hundred members still attend the banquets. One of the few formalities is the annual presentation of the Isadore Mitchell Memorial Mensch Award, whose first recipient was Martin Janis.

Goldstein-Goodman VFW Post

Even though a number of local Jewish war veterans belonged to the American Legion, soon after World War II there was interest in starting a Jewish post. After considering organizing a post under the auspices of either the Jewish War Veterans of the United States of America or the Veterans of Foreign Wars, a majority of interested veterans favored the V. F. W. Consequently, Post 6909 of the V. F. W. officially began on May 2, 1946 in ceremonies at the Jewish Community Center with fifty-two charter members. The original officers were Commander Louis Baum, Senior Vice Commander Arthur Faudman, Junior Vice Commander Manuel Tarschis, Quartermaster Louis Sharfman, Chaplain Philip Black, Adjutant Louis Dolgin and Post Advocate Hyman D. Garrison. The members continued to meet at the J. E. L. for some years.

The post name memorialized two local Jewish service men who died in World War II. Morris Goldstein was a Toledo native, born in 1923 and a graduate of Scott High School. He enlisted in the U. S. Navy on January 31, 1941, served on the battleship U. S. S. Maryland with "gallantry and valor" and received many decorations while serving in the Pacific Theater. Seaman 1st Class Goldstein was killed November 1, 1944 in the battle of Leyte. Barnett H. Goodman was born in London, England on July 9, 1911 and immigrated to the United Stated in 1926 to live with his Toledo uncle and aunt, Mr. and Mrs. Albert Bellman. He enlisted in the Army Air Force in February 1942 and rose to the rank of Technical Sergeant in the 338th Squadron of the 96th Bomber Group, based in England. A post history noted that as his plane flew over the Toledo area on its way to Europe, he dropped a parachute made from a handkerchief, on which he had written "Dear folks: I'm taking a last look at the finest town in the U. S. A. I wish I could land and stay awhile, but that's impossible. Hope to see you real soon. Regards from the entire crew and love from me. Barney." The hand-made parachute was recovered on a farm by Swanton. He died in action during a bombing run over Germany on July 29, 1943.

A history of the post recorded that the members turned the post's motto, "Dedicated to Community Service," into their credo, undertaking many activities to help various needy groups, including parties for patients at the Toledo State Hospital, toys for blind children, participation in blood drives and a fund raising campaign for Sunshine Children's Home. The post also became a Life Member of the VFW's National Children's Home in Eaton Rapids, Michigan. Such efforts of the post were recognized nationally when the national VFW organization granted the post a Perpetual Charter in 1958, only the nineteenth such post to receive that distinction in sixty years.[28]

The post relocated from the J. E. L. most likely in the early 1950s when the Collingwood Boulevard Community Center opened. Staying on the north side of downtown, the post used space at 309 Lagrange Street, which the 1961 City Directory identified as the Three Hundred & Nine Hotel, at the corner of N. Summit Street. The next listing locates the post at 2224 Monroe Street, just east of Collingwood and across the street from Burling's Brass Rail restaurant. Sponsorship of bingo games was a successful fund raiser for a number of years, helping to finance the post's good works. Eventually, however, traffic regulations for that busy area prohibited on-street parking, which cut down on the number of bingo players and the games were soon curtailed. Sometime later the post moved its meetings to Etz Chayim synagogue, which opened at its Woodley Road site in 1973. Due largely to a declining membership, a condition experienced nationwide among veterans' organizations, the post merged with V. F. W. Post 606 on Laskey Road in about 2004.[29]

Scouts

Until around World War II, Toledo Jewish scouting consisted of four troops. Troop 11 was the senior troop, established in 1914 (only four years after the Boy Scouts of America were incorporated). Bernard Lempert was the first scoutmaster and the local B'nai B'rith chapter sponsored it.[30] Thirty-three scouts of Troop 11, the entire membership, headed the 231 member Toledo scout contingent to the 1957 Valley Forge Jamboree. *The Toledo Blade* reported it was the only troop to attend *en masse*. Scouts from six other local troops also attended, according to the newspaper.[31] The troop eventually drifted into inactivity and unofficial dissolution in the 1950s.[32]

Troop 37 became the second troop with its formation in April 1918. An early scoutmaster was Louis Hausman, who would continue for nineteen years. The Men's Club of the Collingwood Temple sponsored the troop. A major part of the Troop's crack reputation was its record in the competitive field meets among local scouts, usually held at school stadiums.[33]

Troop 91, formed in January 1921, became the third Jewish troop in Toledo. Adult leaders were: Scoutmaster – Sam W. Sherman, who served until 1929; Assistant scoutmaster – Martin Miller; Troop committeemen – Joe Reingold, A. B. Bame and Morris Kobacker. B'nai B'rith sponsored the troop.[34] In the depth of the Depression, Joseph J. Feldstein, field commissioner for the Toledo Area Boy Scouts, reported that the troop was unable to find a meeting site or adult leadership for the group. In 1939 the local Scout Council authorized the expiration of the troop.[35]

Troop 9 completed the quartet of Jewish troops with its establishment in March 1926. The first leader was Scoutmaster Louis R. Schwab, who served until 1930; The B'nai Israel Men's Club sponsored the troop.[36] There were fifteen charter members in 1926, including Joseph Feldstein, Seymour Rothman and Joseph Stein. Most of the Troop's meetings were in the B'nai Israel annex, 12th and Bancroft streets, with some musters at the Rosenthal cabin.[37] Within two years, the total fell to 11 Scouts in 1939 and 1940, with a rebound to 17 in 1941. The last records date from 1941 or 1942.[38] One account said that Troop 9 merged with Troop 11 at some point, but this is unconfirmed.[39] (*Photo 82, page 121, Boy Scout Planning Committee*)

From 1914 to1926, Jewish Girl Scout troops also existed in Toledo. A *Toledo Times* newspaper article dated April 1, 1923 reported on two troops being established at the Jewish Education League building. Troop 4 was described as the "oldest in the city" and composed of older girls, while Troop 6's members were younger girls. The account also spoke of a Brownie Troop for girls under the age of 10 and a "Citizens' Troop" of young women over 21 who were training as leaders in scouting, with a special interest in intensive training and First Aid.[40] A Troop 27 also formed in the 1920s, sponsored by the Collingwood Temple, where it met. Mrs. Eugene (Lucille) Farber was scoutmistress from the 1920s to the 1940s, with Assistant Scoutmistresses Helen Davis and Eve Mostov.[41]

Fraternities and Sororities

During the period of this history, fraternities and sororities composed of Jewish members existed on both high school and college levels and were a common feature in urban areas with Jewish communities.

In interviewing former members of local high school fraternities and sororities it is very clear that they enjoyed their days in those organizations and still believe that membership was – on balance – a very positive experience for themselves and for all other members. Their recollections provide the basis for this section as few formal or tangible records of the fraternities and sororities were discovered in research.[42]

The one non-local option for local teens regarding fraternity and sorority membership was the B'nai B'rith Youth Organization. B'nai B'rith offered AZA (The International Order of Aleph Zadik Aleph) for boys and BBG (B'nai B'rith Girls) for girls. The Toledo members met at the J.E.L., as did so many groups. (*Photo 83, page 122, Iota Phi Kappa founding members*)

Membership in either A.Z.A. or B.B.G. did not rule out also belonging to one of the local fraternities or sororities. Such overlapping memberships were not uncommon, according to my interviews. Compared to the local fraternities and sororities, A.Z.A. and B.B.G. seemed a bit more "open," operated "less like one of fraternities," and undertook more "civic activities."[43] One of the activities mentioned in Jewish Welfare Federation records was when ". . . a work party of volunteers provided by the two chapters of AZA and the two chapters of BBG in the city spent three days at the camp [Ma-Hi-Ya] helping to put it in shape."[44]

The history of "Aleph Zadik Aleph began in 1923 as a high school fraternity in Omaha, Nebraska and was founded originally as primarily a social group. A local group of 14 young men in Omaha began the group. According to the organization, the group was founded as a protest against the local Greek high school fraternity which did not allow Jews to become members. By April 1925, the order had expanded to include seven groups around Omaha. Sam Beber went to the national convention of B'nai B'rith, to see if they would sponsor the organization. Although there was strong opposition to the proposal at first, Henry Monsky delivered a stirring speech which led to the approval and adoption of AZA to become a part of B'nai B'rith.[45] (*Photo 84, page 122, Sorority Fun*)

"In 1944, B'nai B'rith Girls became recognized by B'nai B'rith, and BBYO as it is today was born. Anita Perlman is credited with the development of BBG as Sam Beber is credited with the AZA. BBYO as it is today was born. In 2002, BBYO changed its name to BBYO Inc., becoming a legally independent organization in the process. . ."[46]

Currently, The BBYO spans 40+ regions with 500+ chapters, roughly 45% BBG, 40% AZA, and 15% BBYO (coed). There are approximately 18,000 members internationally. In addition to the United States, BBYO also exists in Australia, Bulgaria, Canada, England, France, Ireland and Israel.[47]

The purpose of both orders was to ". . . provide Jewish youth opportunities to form leadership skills and to commit to their own personal development."[48] Programming for both orders is to reflect the Five Folds: Social, Athletic, Community Service/Social Action, Education and Judaic. Any given program should include at least three of the folds, but can concentrate on one.[49] Locally, both groups primarily had social activities, although the boys did also participate in intramural sports, according the recollections of former members. One local fraternity brother recalled dances at the Naval Armory and another believed that there was some reciprocity with non-Jewish frats in terms of attending dances. The *Toledo Jewish Times* carried a story about the A.Z.A. Chanukah dance and bingo party on December 8 at the Jewish Federation Building in 1938, for example.[50]

For Toledo Jewish male teens, the choice of local fraternities was among three that existed for most of the period : I.A. (the "Independent Asses"), Iota Phi Kappa and Kappi Phi Sigma.

The interviewees shared some common perceptions as they compared the three fraternities. Kappi Phi Sigma members were generally students at DeVilbiss High School or Ottawa Hills High School. There might have been a few members from Scott High School. One person thought the membership was mainly guys from The Temple. Iota Phi Kappas included more Scott people, while one former Iota Phi Kappa member recalled the group was pretty well mixed and a third member believed it included a few Woodward and DeVilbiss guys also. The I. A. men were largely Old West End residents (which meant Scott and Woodward high schools) and some DeVilbiss students. The inference is sensed that the IAs prided themselves on not being in either of the other fraternities.

This degree of mixture was generally advantageous, it seemed to the former members. Having some friends from your school, neighborhood or congregation made it comfortable, but the fraternities also included members from other schools and congregations, so one got to know peers from outside one's own immediate circle. One former fraternity member mentioned that membership was also good to combat shyness or introversion, at least it helped him. There was a consensus that each fraternity and sorority had roughly two or three dozen members at any given time and that a majority of Jewish youths belonged to some one of the groups.

Another benefit occurred to one former S.R.T. sister as she looked back. The sorority experience was so positive and helped the girls make so many friends, including male friends, that they married locally and remained in the community to raise their families, at least to a greater degree than later.

Toledo Jewish females could choose among three local sororities: Sigma Rho Tau, Gamma Sigma Chi and Alpha Beta Gamma.

The perceptions that were shared about these three organizations were similar to the fraternities. Sigma Rho Tau was the oldest of the three and included mainly Temple members and "girls from more money" in the words of one interviewer. Gamma Sigma Chi was established soon after S.R.T. and the members were a mix of DeVilbiss and Scott high schools girls, as well as B'nai Israel and B'nai Jacob synagogues. Alpha Beta Gamma began about 1941 and some girls who belonged to one of the other sororities saw it as a refuge for "all the girls not in the other two sororities."

Membership seemed to begin with one's freshman year in high school and followed the conventional pattern of "rush activities" so that candidates could be appraised and then desired individuals received bids from the groups that wanted them. One former sorority member believed that in this process some girls "found out" that being Jewish played a bigger influence than earlier in their growing up. Once a sorority member, she believed that some were not included in gentile activities or invited to attend non-Jewish events as much. Even with the possibility of some disappointments along the way, she thought that the majority of Jewish girls did join a sorority, or at least tried to. "Once a member, I quit two or three times for some reason, but then always rejoined," joked one former sorority member. Likewise, former fraternity members had the sense that most of their peers wanted to belong and did so. Overall, the impression is that most Jewish youths belonged, but some were pointedly not asked to join. Understandably, one tended to gravitate to a group if he or she had older friends who were already members in that frat or sorority. None of the interviewees recalled that dues were any problem to pay out of their available funds.

Both fraternities and sororities focused on a variety of social activities, from just meetings to dances, some pretty formal. Many of the meetings were at the J.E.L., as were some of the basketball games. One former brother said dances were sometimes at the Commodore Perry or Secor hotels or the Women's Club building. A member of Sigma Rho Tau fondly remembered the spring party every year at the Hillcrest Hotel as a chance to get really dressed up. Several interviewees recalled that members of other fraternities and sororities, even some non-Jewish ones, also attended some of the dances.

Nationally and locally high school fraternities and sororities declined somewhat in membership and standing as the United States became more involved in World War II. This decline was hastened by a change in Ohio Revised Code in 1948 or 1949 which declared high school fraternities and sororities illegal.[51] In the following years, the Toledo Public Schools administration successfully pressured the groups to convert into "clubs." This change was perhaps not drastically felt, however, as one former Iota Phi Kappa member who graduated in 1951 and was president did not recall any difference in school policy during his time.

In the post-war years, a similar pattern of waxing and waning afflicted college-level fraternities and sororities as well, growing in the 1950s and weakening in members and chapters in the 1960s.

At Toledo University (as it was called until it became part of the state system) the two Jewish fraternities were Lambda Chi and Kappa Iota Xi, which subsequently merged into Alpha Epsilon Pi in the mid-1950s. George Glasser, later to serve as judge on three benches in Toledo, was the first president of the merged fraternity. Another AEPi from the late 1950s, Stanford Odesky, continued his activity and was International President and received the fraternity's highest award, "The Order of the Lion."

Alpha Epsilon Pi had no fraternity house until the later 1950s so meetings were at members' homes or at the old Student Union, which was near the old Field House, according to one member.

Sigma Alpha Mu was also on campus for many years, a TU chapter of the fraternity that also had local men belonging at The Ohio State University.

The Ohio State University and the University of Michigan were two other institutions which attracted numbers of Jewish men from Toledo and the area. One Findlay High School graduate remembered that O. S. U. had three Jewish fraternities on campus: Sigma Alpha Mu (to which he belonged, as did a "plurality" of Toledoans attending O. S. U.), Zeta Beta Tau (which also had a chapter at the University of Michigan) and Alpha Epsilon Pi. One former S. A. M. brother said fraternity membership was "extremely important" because it provided camaraderie and leadership opportunities. Quite literally, it also enabled him to attend college by providing him with a paying job.[52]

Jewish newspapers

Three publications have served the news and advertising needs of the Toledo Jewish community during the time period of this history. First came the *Israelite*, published from sometime in the 1920s to the early 1930s. The editor was Elsie Gould. One account of local Jewish journalism described it as consisting ". . . mainly of social activities and social events."[53]

Around 1936 - 1938 the *Toledo Jewish Times* appeared. David Alter published it, along with similar Jewish monthly newspapers for other U. S. cities, out of his editorial office in Pittsburgh. Irvin Edelstein, a young aspiring journalist in Toledo at the time, wrote a column for the paper to give it more local interest and sometimes served as news editor of the Toledo edition. He estimated that the official circulation was between 500 and 900 copies per issue. A major source of income was advertising in the two issues of the paper during the local Jewish fund raising campaign every year.[54]

In 1950 *The Toledo Jewish News* began publication as the local monthly. A letter to the Internal Affairs Committee in 1952 from "Irvin L. Edelstein, editor and publisher" presented his argument that the Jewish Community Council should provide more financial support than just a small subsidy based on the number of local Jewish households. This author is grateful that all these papers have played an important role in preserving the local scene for later researchers.[55] (*Photo 85, page 123, Toledo Times*)

Anti-Semitism and the Holocaust

A 1994 survey of Toledo's Jewish community found that 83% of the people polled believed it was "very important" to oppose anti-Semitism.[56] The likelihood of anti-Semitism existing in Toledo to some degree is equaled by the probability that formal or substantive evidence of it is generally lacking. In researching this history, local anecdotal evidence was certainly encountered: A Jewish-owned store was believed to be burned out by a neighboring dentist who was a Ku Klux Klan member; one Jewish football player encountered it on the field and after the game; a researcher was told there was "nothing in the files" about a once-prominent local Jewish Boy Scout leader; Jewish buildings and tombstones have been defaced and/or damaged; "a gentile-owned department store did not hire Jews in the 1950s" was said in a meeting; and, Glengarry Country Club was said to be founded because Jews were not allowed to join other existing clubs at the time.

As one reads Dr. Elaine Anderson's history of Toledo Jews from 1845 to 1895, some incidents show such animosity being implied, inferred, sensed, or occasionally carried out. But similarly, such an attitude probably can not be proven in except a few cases or even strongly asserted. The same is true for this account of Jewish Toledo from 1895 to the present.

More importantly, the occasional incidents of blatant anti-Semitism or the existence of low level latent hostility have not prevented the Toledo Jewish community from prospering, providing an improving life style for each succeeding generation and making major contributions to many facets of the greater Toledo community.

The degree of local anti-Semitism nearly disappears, however, when compared to the persecutions in Hitler's Germany, collectively commemorated as the Holocaust. Like many Jewish communities around the world, Toledo's Jews include several victims who personally experienced – and survived – the Holocaust. The stories of three of them illustrate the varied nature of that horrific ordeal.

Phil Markowicz was born in a small town near Lodz, Poland, where his father was a rabbi. After Poland surrendered to the Germans in 1939, he was among the thousands of Jews consolidated into the Lodz ghetto. He remained there until 1944, when he and his brother were transferred to Birkenau (also known as Auschwitz II), an extension of the original Auschwitz concentration camp. The youths were selected to be workers and were forced to construct roads and tunnels, sometimes hundreds of miles from the camp.

As the Allies closed in on German-held Polish territory, the concentration camp prisoners were marched into Germany. Markowicz' last camp was in the area of Regensburg. To keep the prisoners from the advancing Americans, Germans began another "death march," away from Regensburg. The column of prisoners and guards moved by night and took cover during daylight, seeking shelter in barns and other buildings. During one such stop, Markowitz and a few others hid in a barn, but were ultimately discovered and guards lined them up in a farmyard, preparing to execute them. Deciding they had nothing further to lose, the prisoners began yelling for help and their cries brought out a German mother and her daughter from a house. The woman argued with the guards, insisting they not execute the men in her farmyard. The condemned men took advantage of the controversy to run away and mix in with other Jews in the nearby column. The Germans did not come to find them again and the march resumed. On the following day's march, the column unexpectedly halted; some of the guards stripped off their equipment and uniforms and just walked away; other guards fired at random into the prisoners and then left. Phil and his brother rolled into a roadside ditch and played dead until the guards had departed. Once it was safe to move, cold and exhausted, they hid under stairs at a nearby farmhouse. One of the German residing there discovered them and informed them that the war was over and American troops were in the area. They made contact with the soldiers and were housed with other refugees first in a former woman's prison and then in a Displaced Persons Camp.

Phil Markowicz spent the next five years in camp, marrying and having a son during that period. In 1950 the family of three immigrated to Toledo because his wife had cousins in Toledo who served as sponsors and guaranteed him a job. One of the cousins worked in a local garment factory and the union there also assisted in the settlement of his family and one other.[57]

Phillip Masters survived the Holocaust as well, but due to far different circumstances. He was born in Poland to Jewish parents. After the war broke out, his parents and others hid their children in a cabin in nearby woods to protect them from anticipated reprisals. The youngsters, mostly older and about fifteen in number, grew restless at this confinement and subsequently broke out of the cabin and for the next several years lived on the run. They stole food and improvised shelter in the forest. Phil imagines they must have covered hundreds of miles during their trek. Some youngsters left the group and others joined. After the war, his mother searched for him and miraculously found him, calling him by name when she recognized him.

Together again, the family returned to their pre-war home, but encountered local pogroms and eventually obtained refuge in a Displaced Persons Camp in Germany. With the help of a distant cousin, he and his family were able to immigrate to Canada in December 1948. They settled in Toronto and lived there for the next thirty-five years, Phil becoming an accountant. Looking for a change in business in the 1970s, he relocated to Toledo and became active in commercial real estate development and sales.[58]

Mary Neufeld preferred not to publicize her specific Holocaust experience. Suffice it to note that she was residing in her native Poland when the Germans invaded from the north and west in September1939, followed sixteen days later by a Russian incursion from the east. As the sole survivor of her immediate family, she joined many other displaced persons in a camp in Austria as the war ended. By 1948 she had married Dr. Oscar Neufeld and immigrated to the United States. Following his medical residency in Denver, the young couple moved to Toledo so that he could assume position at the former William Roche Memorial Hospital in south Toledo. Dr. Neufeld later served as director of the pulmonary function at Mercy Hospital, was a faculty member at the Medical College of Ohio prior to its merger with the University of Toledo and dedicated many hours to local union health clinics.[59]

Worldwide, survivors of the Holocaust persevered to continue with their lives, but they retained indelible memories of that horrific period. As a survivor, Mary Neufeld was a logical person to propose a local memorial, as she did in 1975 at a meeting of the Women's Board of the Jewish Welfare Federation. She believed that such a memorial was "[a] matter of community need and responsibility" and that the memorial itself is "an important testimonial to the survival of the Jewish people."[60]

Later that same year the Jewish Federation commissioned Lois Dorfman to sculpt a memorial to the victims of the Holocaust. The well-respected artist conceived of a series of individual statues, saying "This rendering of individuals is the only way I can try to comprehend the immenseness of this tragedy." Boris Nelson, art critic for *The Blade*, described the memorial thusly: "Its 13 bronze relief figures of men, women, children – afraid, surprised, resigned, questioning – rise from a brick-scattered base as if frozen at the instant." The title of the Holocaust Memorial is taken from the last line of Jeremiah 4:23-28: "For this the earth mourns." The very impressive memorial was dedicated April 13, 1980 at the community's Yom Hashoah observance; Mary Neufeld delivered the dedicatory remarks. A plaque at the site reads "Erected in Memory of the Victims of the Holocaust by the Jewish Welfare Federation of Toledo." The art work is the centerpiece of the Toledo Holocaust Memorial Park, which was made possible by the David S. Stone Fund in memory of David S. Stone, on the J. C. C. campus.[61] (*Photo 86, page 123, Holocaust Memorial*)

A Holocaust Center was established in 1980 with a collection of materials that could be used to study that horrific episode. Irma Scheon was the first director. In 1997 it was renamed the Ruth Fajerman Markowicz Holocaust Resource Center of Greater Toledo, following her family's endowment in support of the Center. Housed in the Hebrew Academy on the Jewish Community Center campus, the collection has grown as a "working library" with multi-media materials, including curriculum guides for teachers. The current director is Hindea Markowicz.[62]

The Rackets

One explanation of the nickname "Holy Toledo" is plausibly straightforward and is based on the supposedly large number of houses of worship found in the city. Another explanation is that the sobriquet is meant to be hyperbole, that the city was, in fact, very un-Holy. Toledo native Harry Illman's book, *Unholy Toledo*, makes that point in its very title and then the author proceeds to use the next 361 pages to prove it.[63] Opinions on Illman's recollection range widely from "80% fiction" to "filled with errors" to "a payback" to all who he felt had done him wrong. I commend the book as interesting reading which includes some undeniable facts, regardless of what final verdict you reach.

A second, more recent, account worthy to be consulted is Kenneth R. Dickson's book, *. . . nothing personal just business. . .*, which is sub-titled *Prohibition and Murder on Toledo's Mean Streets*. The book describes the evolution of the local rackets and their operation in the early decades of the 20th century.

For this history, it is stipulated that crime, particularly in the form of "the rackets" (numbers running, bootlegging during Prohibition, prostitution, protection shakedowns, slot machines and gambling in general) existed in Toledo and there was a Jewish presence. Its extent and its intensity, not to mention its colorful incidents and characters, simply is too great a topic to be more fully accommodated in this history.

Biographical Sketches

The selection of names for inclusion in such a history is fraught with multiple possibilities for giving offense. The primary purpose of this section is to give only a representative impression of the impact that the local Jewish community has had, through individuals, among the many facets of the greater Toledo community. That impact stretches over virtually a century, through the appointment of Sheila Odesky as a trustee of the Toledo-Lucas County Public Library in September 2007 and carries forward as many of the persons cited continue to work for the benefit of their community.

Louise Brunner, *The Blade* art editor, described him as the "Dean of Toledo Artists" and many other critics on two continents agreed on his great talent, so **Israel** (Abe) **Abramofsky** seems a likely representative for local Jewish artists. He was born in a village near Kiev, Russia, much like the one in "Fiddler on the Roof," according to him. While attending a meeting in the village with other Jewish teens, the police arrested them all and sent them to Siberia. At age nineteen he received permission to leave the country. Once he was in Toledo, Mayor Brand Whitlock and Municipal Court Judge Aaron Cohn befriended him. Eventually they got him hired as a radiator welder at Willys-Overland at $12 a week. Other than the $6 a week for room and board, he spent all his money for art studies. He saved up $300 to finance a trip to Paris, but a necessary operation ate up that sum. He saved up again and made it to Paris, staying for many months. He also briefly studied at the Royal Academy in London. He returned to Toledo in 1929, made one more trip to Europe in 1934 and then lived the balance of his life in Toledo, for many years in the 800 block of Madison Avenue.

His works have been displayed at the Art Institute of Chicago, the Corcoran Gallery in Washington, D. C., the Library of Congress and the Weyhe and Charles Morgan galleries in New York. Locally, his paintings have been exhibited in the Toledo Museum of Art, the Toledo-Lucas County Public Library and the Jewish Community Center. He generally painted persons and places around him, from Parisian markets and the shores of Brittany to the Anthony Wayne Bridge and Madison Avenue in Toledo.

Following his death, there was a public display of his work at the Temple Shomer Emunim. Funeral services were held in The Temple. Abramofsky named the Temple as custodian of more than 3,000 works left in his estate. Sale of these items was to fund the Abramofsky Art Fund to help worthy art students through grants and scholarships. Since he had received help as a young artist, he wanted to do likewise. The probate court appraised the collected works at $175,000.[64]

Ira Bame was a native Toledoan, born of Russian immigrant parents, a graduate of Woodward High School and the University of Toledo and, in 1926, a graduate of The Ohio State University law school. He served six terms as a Toledo City Councilman, and as such, was chairman of a committee which achieved a 20% reduction of domestic electrical rates, an accomplishment unrivalled in more recent times. Subsequently he served two six-year terms as a Toledo Municipal Judge, retiring in 1975. He died at Darlington House in 1995, age 94.[65]

Joel Beren received his B.B.A. from Franklin University in 1979. He held several management positions in the family firm of A. Edelstein & Son, Inc., culminating as president in 1992. Professional involvement included serving on the board of directors of the Cleveland-based Northern Ohio Chapter of the Institute of Scrap Recycling Industries, a trade association, and on the board of Mid-Am Bank & Trust Company. In 1996 he was one of twenty community leaders under the age of forty recognized by the Toledo Area JayCees for their community commitment and career attainments. He is a past president of Temple B'nai Israel, a former trustee of the Jewish Federation of Toledo and served as C.E.O. of its successor, the United Jewish Council of Greater Toledo, from 2003 until 2008. He has also a member of the executive committee of the Young Leadership Cabinet of the United Jewish Appeal and was chairman of that cabinet 1994-95.[66]

Dr. **Sol Boyk** was a Toledo chemist, inventor, founder of the former Ottawa Chemical Company and a trustee of the Medical College of Ohio. Born in Pinchow, then part of Russian Poland, by 1944 he had immigrated to the United States and received a doctorate in chemistry from Purdue University. He subsequently joined the Purdue faculty as assistant professor of chemistry. In 1948 he began the Ottawa Chemical Company, wishing to do more research. He led the development and production of several different hormones, germicides, pigments and ferrite powders. Dr. Boyk served as a vice-president of the Jewish Welfare Federation and was the first president of a new board of Jewish education in 1971-1972.[67]

Aaron Cohen was born in Hungary in 1883. He was a 1903 graduate of Toledo High School. He next went to The Ohio State University and graduated from its law school in 1910. Upon return to Toledo, he became a teacher in law at St. John's College. Then he moved to the University of Toledo and was law school dean for 11 years. During that time, he was also Toledo commissioner for the Boy Scouts of America and he helped draft the Toledo Municipal Court Act. Elected Municipal Court judge in 1917, he held that post until 1926, when he ran unsuccessfully for Common Pleas Court judgeship. While on the municipal bench, his courtroom, as well as police HQ and a jail, were in a "vermin-infested building" in the 100 block of Superior Street. His campaign for a new building was successful when voters approved a bond issue for construction of the current Safety Building. His obituary said "He had long been given credit for the being the person most responsible for the construction of the present Safety Building, and he always considered that as the high mark of his long career in municipal and state affairs." He was elected to city council in 1936, from which he fought for the city manager form of government. He did not seek re-election in 1941, but later held posts regarding workmen's compensation and labor claims for Ohio. His two favorite hobbies were muskellunge fishing with Bernie Lempert and outboard boating. The two started outboard boat racing at Toledo Beach. He died at the age of 77. [68]

Harry Friberg, although a native of London, England, he lived most of his adult life in Toledo. He graduated from the University of Toledo and The Ohio State University Law School (1926). After being first in private practice, Lucas County Prosecutor Frazier Reams appointed him assistant county prosecutor in 1933, a position he held for twenty years. In 1952 he won the first of ultimately six terms as Lucas County Prosecutor, serving a total of forty-three years in the prosecutor's office. He retired from office in 1976. The Ohio Prosecuting Attorneys Association named him Outstanding Prosecuting Attorney for 1972, commending him for his handling of cases involving the Licavoli gang and fraudulent bank claims, among others, over the years. While county prosecutor, he was a prime mover in the merger of the three public library systems in the county into the current Toledo-Lucas County Public Library system. [69]

Leon Frankel (1910-1998), born in New York, attended college there and received his law degree from St. John's University. After serving in WW II, he relocated to Toledo, and worked for his brother David, a founder of the Toledo Hosiery and Underwear Company. As his obituary noted, Mr. Frankel returned to the law in the mid-1960s, successfully passed the Ohio bar exam and was appointed as a referee in the local domestic relations division of the Court of Common Pleas, from which he retired as chief referee in 1980s. In a newspaper interview, he said he had heard more that 5,000 divorce and other family-law cases in his career. All during his life he enjoyed athletics, especially tennis, and played in a B'nai B'rith baseball league for many years. In retirement he, and his wife Tillie, participated in the Senior Olympics, placing highly in the 1987 national championships. His top events were tennis, track and field and baseball throw. [70]

Marcus Friedman was described in his May 13, 1990 obituary as ". . . a scrappy and active lawyer for 62 years." Appeals Court Judge George Glasser agreed, characterizing him as ". . . a very scrappy lawyer [and] one well-respected by his peers." He graduated from the College of Law of Ohio

Northern University in 1928 and also attended the University of Toledo. In 1942 he was named an Assistant United States Attorney and served until 1953. He was a founding partner in the law firm of Friedman, Adler and Goldberg, later Friedman, Adler, Goldberg and Rosen. An active member of the American Trial Lawyers Association, he became a friend of nationally-known lawyer Melvin Belli, whom he once represented in Toledo in a fraud case. Friedman was a past president of the former Anshai Sfard Congregation and Darlington House and a member of both Congregation Etz Chayim and Temple B'nai Israel.[71]

George Glasser, born in Pittsburgh, graduated from Scott High School, the University of Toledo and UT's College of Law. Following a successful law practice, he was appointed to Toledo Municipal Court in 1963 and subsequently voters returned him to office from 1965 to 1970. That year he was appointed as a judge of the Lucas County Common Pleas Court and served there until his 1986 election to Ohio's 6th District Court of Appeals. At the time of his pending retirement, he noted with pride that many of the Appeals Court's decisions are not predictable, saying "We consider the cases and discuss them applying law." Judge Peter Handwork, administrative judge of the court, described Judge Glasser as ". . .patient and steady and focused." The judge's one acknowledged frustration has been ". . . the public's lack of understanding how the court system works."[72]

Alix Greenblatt has been a particularly committed member of her Sylvania community, residing in Sylvania Township for more than 20 years. She has been a longtime member of the Sylvania Rotary and a former past president. She has also served on the Sylvania Board of Education, the Sylvania Area Joint Recreation District board and the Sylvania Community Arts Commission. She has been chair of the Sylvania Area Family Services Board, chair of the Grants Committee of the Flower Hospital Foundation Board and chair for the Susan D. Komen Northwest Ohio Race for the Cure. She is a former executive director of the United Jewish Council of Greater Toledo.[73]

Toledo's second Jewish sheriff was **William Hirsch** (1892 – 1979). He was born in Bucharest, Romania and came to Toledo with his family in 1905. They lived in the 1900 block of Spielbusch Avenue and operated a newsstand at the corner of Madison and St. Clair. From 1910 to 1933 he worked in circulation operations for the *News-Bee* newspaper. He left the paper when newly-elected Toledo Mayor Solon Klotz appointed him Superintendent of the Toledo Workhouse. For the next two decades he managed the workhouse so that it became self-sufficient and sometimes even turned a profit for the county, all the time treating the inmates with humanity, which was his trademark. In 1953 he ran for Lucas County sheriff and won on the first try and continued to be re-elected until he declined to run again in

1969. In 1964 he published *Treat Them Human*, which recounted his life and extolled his philosophy.[74]

Sandy Isenberg is a DeVilbiss High School graduate and member of the school's Hall of Fame. She began her political involvement lobbying for a traffic light on Secor Road. She progressed to being a Democratic Ward Chairman 1970-76 and a State Central Committeewoman 1973-79. In 1977 she won election to Toledo City Council (being the only woman on council at the time). In 1980 she was appointed as Lucas County Recorder (the first woman in the office) and in 1985 was appointed a Lucas County Commissioner (again the first woman in that office). Re-elected to multiple terms, she served as president of the commissioners from 1985 until 2002. The Jewish National Fund presented her with the Tree of Life Award in 1990.[75]

Marvin Jacobs, a Toledo native, received his B.A. degree from the University of Toledo in 1950 and his J.D. from the University of Michigan in 1953. Following U. S. Army service, he entered private practice in 1955. In addition to memberships in several professional organizations, he served on the Sylvania Board of Education 1973-77 (president 1976). In 2007 he received a Toledoan of the Year Award, being the honoree in the Toledo Pride category. The award recognized his fund-raising for the centennial celebration of the Lucas County Courthouse, where he has given student tours, as well as his service as a volunteer Ohio Reads mentor with elementary school students. He was also one of The Temple-Congregation Shomer Emunim members who worked with *sofer* Neil Yerman in 2007 to write a new copy of the Torah for the congregation.[76]

David Katz earned his B.S. degree from The Ohio State University in 1955 and his J.D. *summa cum laude* from O.S.U. in 1957. He also worked on the *Ohio State Law Journal* 1956-57. Following law school, he began private practice with the Toledo firm of Spengler Nathanson. Leaving the firm in 1994, he accepted a federal judgeship, moving to the U. S. District Court for the Northern District of Ohio. In 2005 he assumed senior judge status at the District Court. Besides membership and offices in many professional organizations, Judge Katz has been a member of St. Vincent Medical Center Foundation (Chairman of the Board of Trustees, 1990-92; Honorary Trustee for Life), Toledo Zoo Foundation, Toledo Symphony Board of Trustees (Executive Committee) and Mercy Health Partners Board (Executive Committee). He is also a past president of the Jewish Federation of Toledo (1976-79) and Temple B'nai Israel (1970-73).[77]

Sara Kaufman (1868 – 1941) was inducted into the Toledo Civic Hall of Fame in 2004. Her motto was "Building boys is better than mending men." She had a 30-plus year career as a Lucas County courts juvenile probation officer and domestic relations counselor. While a young woman, Kaufman attended the Chicago School of Social Work and worked with Jane Addams, the first American woman to win the Nobel Peace Prize. Miss Kaufman helped establish several organizations: the J. E. L., the Banner Boys Club, the local Hadassah chapter and the Florence Crittenden Home. Hadassah inscribed her name on the Golden Book in Jerusalem's Hebrew University in 1942. She is also a major character in the historical novel *O'Brien's Desk* by Ona Russell, published in 2004.[78]

For twenty-four years **Marvin Kobacker** (1911 – 1993) was president of the former Tiedtke's Department Store, whose family bought the Toledo business in 1925. In 1956 he was also the co-founder of Epko Shoes (operating as Pic-Way Shoes). Following the sale of the store several decades later, he devoted much time to local philanthropic interests. Perhaps his most prominent role was as a board member of the Toledo Museum of Art, including being president in the 1970s. He was also a major donor to the Medical University of Ohio's center for emotionally-troubled children. He was inducted into Toledo's Civic Hall of Fame in 2001 and his plaque notes his ". . . unyielding commitment to the community."[79]

Susan Hartman Muska is a third-generation Toledoan, daughter of Henry L. and Eve Hartman. Her father relocated from Bridgeport, Connecticut for the practice of psychiatry following WW II. He was a forensic psychiatrist and clinical professor of psychiatry at the Medical College of Ohio (now University of Toledo, Health Science Campus) from 1967 to 1980. An annual conference in forensic psychiatry is named in his honor at the University of Toledo. Susan Hartman Muska received her law degree from the University of Toledo College of Law in 1977. She worked in Landlord-Tennant Legal Services from 1978 to 1981. She began her private legal practice in 1982. She was subsequently appointed as a Magistrate in the Toledo Municipal Court, Housing Division and served in that capacity for eighteen years, retiring in 2005. She has also been a member of the Community Relations Committee.

Joseph Nathanson (*Photo 87, page 123*) was "one of the key figures in leading Toledo government out of the depths of the depression in the 1930s and 1940s." He was born in Pittsburgh but moved to Toledo at age 10, later graduating from Woodward Technical High School and the University of Toledo. One of his first paying jobs as a lawyer was devising and implementing a plan to collect delinquent taxes for the Lucas County Treasurer's Office. It succeeded very well. As a consequence, he was hired as assistant city law director in 1936. In 1941 he was named city finance director. While in city government, he introduced the payroll income tax idea as one solution to the city's money problems. Voters approved the income tax proposal in 1946, 37,985 to 21,682. He also fought the Ohio

Fuel Gas Co. in the courts to achieve a larger supply of natural gas at lower rates. He won plaudits from many as he worked on the plan that solved the problem of redeeming the city-issued script during the Depression to pay its employees. He retired from the city in 1945 and formed a law partnership with Bert Hebenstreit, Joseph Heyman and Otto Spengler. Walter Brown was an associate counsel. He also served on the boards of the Toledo Public Library, the Toledo Zoological Society and the J. C. C. He was a member of Etz Chayim. He died April 2, 1992 in Darlington House, after living there more than six years. He was 85. His obituary described him as "Armed with a disarming smile, an open face, and a devastating sense of logic, Mr. Nathanson was good at reducing problems to the simplest terms and then going after the solution."[80]

Stanford Odesky graduated from Scott High School and received a B.B.A.(1959) and a M.B.A. (1960) from the University of Toledo. After short stints as field secretary for Alpha Epsilon Pi Fraternity and assistant program director at the Jewish Community Center, he began a twenty-five year career with National Family Opinion, Inc. and its successor firms. He fulfilled several different managerial and vice presidential positions, responsible for a variety of market research and data interpretation. In 1985 he founded his own firm, Stanford H. Odesky & Associates. His firm provided a full range of quantitative and qualitative marketing research services to local, regional and national organizations involved in industrial, consumer service, scholastic and nonprofit sectors. He became well-known for his pre-election political polling and some forty years of election night analysis for TV stations WTOL and WTVG. Among his community involvement roles have been a charter volunteer for the Jamie Farr LPGA Toledo Classic; board member of WGTE Public Broadcasting; past president of the Jewish Community Center, president of the Toledo Board of Jewish Education, the Toledo Opera Association, Alpha Epsilon Pi International Fraternity and the University of Toledo Alumni Foundation; Board of Trustees, Etz Chayim Synagogue; Executive Committee, Ohio Jewish Communities, Inc.; treasurer, United Jewish Council of Greater Toledo; and board member of Jewish Family Service.[81]

Melvin Resnick is a 1945 graduate of DeVilbiss High School, the University of Toledo and The Ohio State University Law School. He is a U.S. Navy veteran. He was admitted to the bar in 1952 and after private practice, he was appointed as an assistant Lucas County prosecutor in 1961 and served to 1974, when he became chief prosecutor, 1975-76. Subsequently he was elected as a judge to the Lucas County Court of Common Pleas and climaxed his judicial career by serving on the bench of the Sixth Ohio District Court of Appeals. He retired from that court in 2003.[82]

Toledo's third Jewish mayor was **Cornell Schreiber** (1881 – 1945). Born in Budapest, Hungary, he was in Toledo by age ten. As a youth, he worked as a "book boy" at the Toledo Public Library and from 1901 to 1914 was secretary to the library board. He gained degrees from the University of Toledo and the University of Michigan law school and began practicing law. In 1908 he served as a Democratic member of the Ohio General Assembly, but resigned from that office when he won election as an Independent to serve as Toledo city solicitor during Mayor Brand Whitlock's tenure. He was re-elected to that office and then in 1917 was elected as Toledo's last Independent Party mayor. He served a second term and then returned to his law practice.[83]

Alfred Samborn, a Toledo native, showed an interest in engineering while at Woodward High School, where he belonged to the Woodward Engineering Society. He then earned his engineering degree from the University of Toledo (1939) and did graduate work at Case School of Applied Science in Cleveland. Following WW II service as a lieutenant in the U.S. Navy Seabees, he returned to Toledo and started his own engineering firm. Jack Steketee soon joined as a partner and their momentum of success and growth ultimately resulted in the formation of Samborn, Steketee, Otis and Evans (later shortened to SSOE), a company which has acquired an international reputation for its architecture and engineering expertise. He retired in 1984, but continued to devote himself to many community endeavors. His accomplishments were recognized in 2007 when he was named as a Toledoan of the Year for his innovation and leadership as a founder of the international engineering and architectural firm of SSOE. In the midst of a busy professional life, he was a leader in the B'nai Jacob congregation, including being president during the merger phase with two other Orthodox congregations. He was also a committed Boy Scout, from his membership in one of Toledo's Jewish troops to his recent chairmanship of a sub-committee which oversaw the writing of the story of Jewish scouting in Toledo as part of this history.[84]

Eva Epstein Shaw (1891 – 1951) was one of Toledo's early women lawyers, and sister of two brothers who were also lawyers, Morris and Jacob. She was a graduate of the University of Toledo and St. John Law School. She began her practice in 1918; in 1919 became a partner of Ben W. Johnson and Associates[85]; then in 1922 went into practice with her brother Jacob. In 1922, she was nationally recognized for drafting the bill that created the Domestic Relations Court of Lucas County. She was also instrumental in getting the five-day waiting period between the marriage license application and the marriage. She belonged to Congregation B'nai Israel and was the first president of Toledo's Hadassah chapter, serving from 1925 to 1927.[86]

Peter Silverman, a Toledo native, earned his B.A. degree at George

Washington University in 1977 and his J.D. degree from the University of Michigan in 1981. He has passed the bar exams of Michigan, New York and Ohio. Following law school, he was an associate at Debevoise & Plimpton (New York City) 1981-84 and has been at Shumaker, Loop & Kendrick (Toledo) since 1984. He served two terms each on Toledo City Council and the Toledo Board of Education. For four years he was on the National Jewish Democratic Council; for six years he was a member of the Executive Committee, Young Leadership Council, United Jewish; and he served on the Executive Committee of the International Hillel Organization. He was a trustee for Darlington House, 1985-92.[87]

Arlene Singer received her B.A. from the University of Toledo in 1972 and her J.D. from its College of Law in 1976, after which she went into practice. She was an assistant Lucas County prosecutor from 1989 to 1990 and served in the 117th Ohio General Assembly. She began her twelve years of service on the Toledo Municipal Court bench in 1990 and in 2002 she was elected to the Sixth District Court of Appeals, where she still serves. She is a member of the Toledo Bar Association, Toledo Women's Bar Association, Ohio Judicial Conference and the Court of Appeals Association. In 2003 she was appointed to the Board of Commissioners on Grievances and Discipline of the Ohio Supreme Court and was elected a Vice-chair for 2007.[88]

Pauline Perlmutter Steinem (1863 - 1940) was aptly characterized in her *Toledo Blade* obituary as a ". . . remarkable woman who helped to shape the feminist movement in this country and was an influential force in educational, philanthropic and cultural endeavors. . ."[89] Born in the Polish region of the Russian Empire, she received her higher education in Bavaria, Germany, married her husband Joseph there in 1884 and then they came to in Toledo in 1887. She was a member of Temple Shomer Emunim and served as president of its sisterhood. Her first club office in Toledo was secretary of the Hebrew Ladies' Benevolent Association; she was also an early president of the Jewish Associated Charities and Free Loan Association. She founded the Toledo Council of Jewish Women around 1900. After working to change state law so women could vote for local school boards, she was elected to the Toledo School Board as the first woman member in 1904 and served five years. She subsequently served as a trustee as of the Toledo Public Library from 1910 to 1914. Woman suffrage was always a major cause for her and among her efforts was leading the Ohio Woman Suffrage Association (forerunner of the League of Women Voters) from 1908 to 1911. Her granddaughter is the feminist activist Gloria Steinem.[90]

Lawrence Steinberg looms large in the history of local Teamsters. Long affiliated with the Teamsters, it was his efforts that convinced the members of two large locals to merge in 1953. He further successfully advocated for all locals in northwest Ohio to move their offices into a new Joint Council headquarters on S. Hawley Street in Toledo. In addition to being president of Local 20 and Joint Council 44, Steinberg was the personal representative of International Brotherhood of Teamsters Presidents Beck and Hoffa. His obituary suggested that his greatest legacy was the concept of a Stewards Council as the highest governing body of the local union. He also worked hard to have the local union provide a variety of services to its members, such as a credit union, a blood bank, a religious counselor and a monthly newsletter. Upon his retirement, he was voted President Emeritus of Local 20. As a well-known labor leader, he was a charter member of the Labor-Management-Citizens Committee and the first union representative on the University of Toledo's board of trustees. He died at the age of 85.

Norman Thal, Jr. served his local community via two terms on the Sylvania Board of Education (1970-1978), including holding all offices of the Board during his tenure. He also served on the Board of The Temple-Congregation Shomer Emunim. His involvement with The Temple took special form when he served as co-chairman, along with Charles Stockstiel, of the committee which did much of the planning for the current Temple. Among the many facets of this planning responsibility, he drew on the expertise of his wife Marguerite, a professional musician, regarding the design and installation of the two musical organs included in the new structure.

Charles Wittenberg received a B.A. degree from the University of Toledo in 1969 and graduated *cum laude* from the UT College of Law in 1973, having been a member of the school's Law Review. He then served as an Ohio assistant attorney general in the state's Transportation Department. In 1975 he and his brother Joseph opened a law office, Wittenberg and Wittenberg, in Toledo, practicing general law. He was appointed a part-time magistrate in Toledo Municipal Court in 1991. Elected as a judge of the Lucas County Common Pleas Court in 1996, he was re-elected in 2000. He retired from the bench in 2006. Besides his professional affiliation, he has served multiple terms on the Sylvania School Board, twice being president of the body, and has also boards of the Sylvania Community Services and the Sylvania Community Improvement Corporation.[91]

Sol Wittenberg was described in his obituary as ". . . the archetypical politician, tireless campaigner, quick wit, frequent winner, graceful loser, skilled administrator, and a quick recoverer." by Seymour Rothman. This native Toledoan was a graduate of Scott High School and the University of Toledo and, while in school, helped his father Sam with the family produce business. His career in Democratic politics began with appointment as deputy county recorder in 1930. In 1955 he became Toledo City Water Commissioner. He moved on to defeat Andy Douglas for a County Commissioner's chair in 1964, holding office for a total of ten years. He was twice Citizen of the Year for the local B'nai B'rith chapter (1964 and 1967) and served in WW II.[92]

Connie Zemmelman received her bachelor's degree from Bowling Green State University in 1976 and her J.D. from the University of Toledo College of Law in 1981.. She has been a partner in the firm of Britz and Zemmelman and a staff attorney for the UT College of Law Legal Clinic. From 1994 to 1997 she was a magistrate for the Lucas County Probate Court, with special responsibilities for adoption cases. From 1998 to 2007 she was in private practice, concentrating on adoption, juvenile and probate law. In May 2007 Ohio Governor Ted Strickland appointed her to the Lucas County Court of Common Pleas bench, succeeding retiring Judge James Ray. She was chosen by her colleagues for a listing in *The Best Lawyers in America* for her work in family-related areas of law.[93]

Norman Zemmelman received his J.D. degree from the University of Toledo College of Law in 1969. He was in private practice as a partner in Britz and Zemmelman for many years. In 1996 he was elected as a judge of the Lucas County Court of Common Pleas, serving on the bench of the Domestic Relations Division and currently serves in that capacity.[94]

Joseph Zimmerman (1889 – 1983) was the earliest identifiably Jewish Lucas County Sheriff. He served as sheriff from 1929 to 1932. A printer by trade, he joined the International Typographical Union in 1905 and was later recognized as the union's sixth most senior member in terms of length of membership. He was a WW I veteran. He served three terms on Toledo City Council before becoming sheriff in 1929.[95]

References

1   *Toledo Times*, July 27, 1924, clipping, n.p.
2   Treuhaft, Roy. E-mail to the author, March 5, 2005.
3   *Toledo Blade*, April 17, 1930, clipping, n .p.
4   Treuhaft, Roy. E-mail to the author, March 5, 2005.
5   *Toledo Times*, May 8, 1940, clipping, n.p.
6   *The Blade*, July 13, 1987, clipping, n.p.
7   *The Blade*, July 13, 1987, clipping, n.p.
8   *The Blade*, December 1, 1987, clipping, n.p.
9   Treuhaft, Roy. E-mail to the author, March 5, 2005.
10 *The Blade*, March 22, 1988, clipping, n.p.

11 Treuhaft, Roy. E-mail to the author, March 5, 2005.

12 *The Blade*, March 22, 1988, clipping, n.p.

13 Treuhaft, Roy. E-mail to the author, March 5, 2005.

14 *The Blade*, May 11, 1988, clipping, n.p.

15 One interviewee said that the impetus for Twin Oaks grew from a "clash of personalities" at Glengarry Country Club and led some people to leave Glengarry and establish Twin Oaks.

16 Interview with the author, April 21, 2006.

17 *The Toledo Blade*, June 7, 1955, clipping, n.p.

18 *Toledo Times*, April 25, 1930, clipping, n.p. and *The Blade*, January 8, 1956, clipping, n.p.

19 *The Blade*, March 15, 1960, clipping, n.p.

20 *The Blade*, January 26, 1961, clipping, n.p.

21 *The Blade*, September 3, 1968, clipping, n.p. and *The Blade*, September 9, 1968, clipping, n.p.

22 *The Blade*, February 1, 1972, clipping, n.p.

23 *The Blade*, Nov. 11, 1979, clipping, n.p.

24 Hirsch, William, *Treat Them Human*, pp. 34 – 39.

25 *The Raggedy Ass Cadets*, Rerucha Video Productions, video tape, 1997.

26 *Blade*, June 13, 1998, p. 11

27 *Blade*, June 13, 1998, p. 11

28 *15 Years, Goldstein – Goodman Post 6909, Veterans of Foreign Wars of the United States.* [Copy in UJC archives.]

29 Telephone interviews with Jay Glassman on August 17, 2007 and Harry Schulman (last Post Commander) on July 19, 2007.

30 Samborn, [typescript of Troop 11 info], p. 1.

31 *Toledo Blade*, "Scouts to Valley Forge Jamboree," n.d.

32 Samborn, interview May 14, 2001. Of the four local Jewish troops, only Troop 91 officially disbanded.

33 Samborn, [notes re Troop 37], 2001, p. 2 and Samborn, Jewish Scouting in Toledo, Ohio--An Outline, 2001, pp. 2-3

34 Samborn, Research notes from Camp Miakonda records re Troop 91, p. 2 and Samborn, Jewish Scouting in Toledo, Ohio--An Outline, 2001, p. 1

35 Samborn, Jewish Scouting in Toledo, Ohio--An Outline, 2001, p. 1

36 Samborn, Research notes from Camp Miakonda records, p. 3 and Samborn,, Jewish Scouting in Toledo, Ohio--An Outline, 2001, p. 2

37 Samborn, Research notes from Camp Miakonda records, p. 1

38 Samborn, Research notes from Camp Miakonda records, p. 2

39 Applebaum, Alice, in speaking with the author.

40 Samborn, Al, Jewish Scouting in Toledo, Ohio--An Outline, 2001, p.

3 and Applebaum, Alice, p. 1

41   Samborn, Al, Jewish Scouting in Toledo, Ohio--An Outline, 2001, p. 3

42   My thanks go the following persons who were interviewed for this section: Gary Beren, David Katz, Arnold Remer, Marlene Remer, Marvin Odesky, Stanford Odesky, Joanne Stocksteil, and Roy Treuhaft.

43   Marvin Odesky, interview with the author, April 18, 2006.

44   *Toledo Jewish News*, September 1968, p. 1-2. This was during the time that the Federation was buying it.

45   www.answers.com "Aleph Zadik Aleph" accessed 4-5-2006

46   www.answers.com "B'nai B'rith Youth Organization" accessed 4-5-2006

47   www.answers.com "B'nai B'rith Youth Organization" accessed 4-5-2006

48   www.answers.com "Aleph Zadik Aleph" accessed 4-5-2006

49   www.answers.com "Aleph Zadik Aleph" accessed 4-5-2006

50   *Toledo Jewish Times*, December 2, 1938, p. 10.

51   www.chuh.org/CHHS/CHHS1901-1966/page09.html accessed April 11, 2006.

52   The *Toledo Jewish Times* mentioned a Kappa Iota Xi fraternity and an Alpha Mu Epsilon sorority at Toledo University in 1938 and 1939 also.

53   Information for this section comes primarily from a short report on the topic by Irwin Edelstein in "Jewish Community Council, Internal Affairs Committee," U. J. C. archives, box 24.

54   One Nat Charnas may have been involved also. There is a weekly issue, dated October 14, 1938, by the Toledo Jewish Publishing Company, Charnas listed as publilsher and Earle Edward Rosenblum as managing editor. U. J. C. archives, box 24

55   The issue of *Toledo Jewish News* for August 1967 stated the paper was starting its seventeenth year of publication.

56   *1994 Greater Toledo Jewish Community Population Survey*, p. 3.

57   Telephone interview with Phil Markowicz on August 15, 2007.

58   Telephone interview with Phil Masters on August 15, 2007.

59   Interview with Mary Neufeld on August 20 and September 11, 2007.

60   *Toledo Jewish News*, [date needed]

61   *The Blade*, April 14, 1980, clipping, n.p.

62   *The Blade*, May 5, 1997 online archive and March 30, 1998 online archive; Hindea Markowicz, telephone interview with the author, May 21, 2008.

63   Illman, Harry, *Unholy Toledo*, San Francisco: Polemic Press Publications, Inc., 1985.

64 *The Blade*, January 17, 1975, clipping, n.p. *Toledo Times*, 4-28-1929, clipping, n.p. *The Blade*, March 15, 1976, clipping, n.p.

65 *The Blade*, October 16, 1995, clipping, n. p.

66 http://search.marquiswhoswho.com/executable/popupprint.aspx, accessed May 22, 2008 and *Blade*, October 10, 1996 online archive, accessed May 20, 2008

67 *The Blade*, November 1, 1974, p. 12.

68 *The Blade*, January 5, 1961, clipping, n.p.

69 *The Blade*, May 5, 1968, clipping, n.p., December 12, 1972, clipping, n.p., April 6, 1976, clipping, n.p.

70 *The Blade*, November 1, 1998, n.p. online archive, accessed May 21, 2008.

71 *The Blade*, May 12, 1990, n.p. and May 13, 1990, p. 18

72 *The Blade*, November 16, 1998, online archive, n.p.

73 http://onesylvania.com/main/?page_id=2, accessed May 21, 2008

74 He told his life's story in *Treat Them Human*.

75 Source: *The Blade*, December 29, 2002, online archive, n.p. and *Toledo City Paper*, September 23 – 29, 2004, clipping, n.p.

76 http://0-search.marquiswhoswho.com.catalog.toledolibrary.org/executable/SearchResults.aspx?db=E, accessed May 28, 2008, *Blade*, May 3, 2007, n.p. online archive, accessed May 21, 2008 and *Blade*, February 24, 2007, n.p. online archive, accessed May 21, 2008

77 http://www.ca6.uscourts.gov/lib_hist/Courts/district%20court/OH/NDOH/judges/dak-bio.html, accessed July 19, 2007

78 See biographical materials in the Local History and Genealogy Department, Toledo-Lucas County Public Library.

79 *The Blade*, February 1, 2001, clipping, n.p.

80 *The Blade,*, April 3, 1992, clipping, n.p.

81 http://0-search.marquiswhoswho.com.catalog.toledolibrary.org/executable/SearchResults.aspx?db=E, accessed May 28, 2008 and e-mail correspondence with the author

82 Toledo-Lucas County Public Library, Local History and Genealogy Department scrapbooks and clippings.

83 *The Toledo Blade*, June 12, 1959, clipping, n.p. Toledo had two 19th century Jewish mayors: Guido Marx (Republican, newspaper editor and businessman, mayor 1875 - 1877) and William Kraus (Democrat, banker, mayor 1869 - 1871

84 http://www.ssoe.com/history_print.htm, accessed May 21, 2008 and numerous conversations with the author

85 Holly Taft Sydlow, *In Search of Our Past; Women of Northwest Ohio*, Vol I, pp. 39-40.

86   See biographical materials in the Local History and Genealogy Department, Toledo-Lucas County Public Library; also *Four Score and Henrietta Szold Ago*, [a history of Hadassah in Toledo, 1924-2000], copy loaned by Rosemary Bramson to the author.

87   http://0-search.marquiswhoswho.com.catalog.toledolibrary.org/executable/SearchResults.aspx?db=E, accessed May 28, 2008 and telephone interview with the author, July 26, 2007

88   www.co.lucas.oh.us/Appeals/JUdgeBiographies.asp, accessed May 21, 2008

89   *Toledo Blade*, January 6, 1940, clipping, n.p.

90   See biographical materials in the Local History and Genealogy Department, Toledo-Lucas County Public Library.

91   http://www.zoominfo.com/Search/PersonDetail.aspx?PersonID=17030273, accessed May 21, 2008

92   *The Blade*, March 22, 1989, clipping, n.p.

93   http://www.sconet.state.oh.us/Communications_Office/Press_Releases/2007/zemmelmanAppt_051407.asp, accessed May 21, 2008

94   See biographical materials in the Local History and Genealogy Department, Toledo-Lucas County Public Library.

95   *The Blade*, March 14, 1983, clipping, n.p.

Senior or Chief Rabbis of Toledo Congregations

B'nai Israel
This list is reproduced from Congregation B'nai Israel's *Service of Dedication; Our Rabbis*, prepared for the dedication of the new B'nai Israel synagogue in 2007.

Abraham Goldberg, 1873-77
Abraham Cohen, 1878-79
Abram Goldberg, 1887-88
Joseph Goldberg, 1888-89
Joseph Lavin, 1889-1890
Abraham Cohen 1890-1891
Alfred Arndt, 1891-1892
Joseph Levin, 1892-1900
Brachia Mayerovitz, 1900-01
Herz Benowitz, 1902-1904
E. Hirschowitz, 1905-06
Simon Glazer, 1906-07
Jacob Silverman, 1907-1909
Isaac M. Silverman, 1910-1918
Elias Bachman, 1919-20
Charles L. Cohen, 1920-21
Herz Benowitz, 1921-22
Michael Lichtenstein, 1922-36
Dr. Morton Goldberg, 1937-72
Fishel Pearlmutter, 1972-82
Herbert Yoskowitz, 1982-84
Arnold Bienstock, 1984-97
Michael Ungar, 1997-2002
Sylvan Kamens, 2002-04
Barry Leff, 2004-07
Moshe Saks, 2007-present

B'nai Jacob
Louis Radion, c. 1879- c.1898
Isaac Shapiro, 1898-c.1900
Abraham Hirschowitz, c.1900-06
Isaac Silberman, 1906-34

Nehemiah Katz, 1935-73

Sharei Zedeck
B'nai Jacob Rabbis Isaac Silberman and Nehemiah Katz provided
rabbinical services, as did Rabbi Lazer Schacter, a member of the
congregation.

Anshai Sfard (later Meadowbrook Court)
Isaac Silberman, 1906-34
Nehemiah Katz, 1935-73
Shaiall Zachariash, 1962-64
Ephraim Zimand, 1964-73

Etz Chayim
The lists for Etz Chayim and for the earlier congregations that merged
to form Etz Chayim – B'nai Jacob, Sharei Zedeck and Anshai Sfard
(Meadowbrook Court) – were completed with the assistance of Rabbi
Edward Garsek and Elsa Leveton of Etz Chayim.

Nehemiah Katz, 1973-81
Edward Garsek, 1981- present

Vermont Avenue
Edward Benjamin Browne, 1905-06
David H. Wittenberg, 1906-07

Shomer Emunim
This list is based on the archives of The Temple-Congregation Shomer
Emunim and was completed with the assistance of volunteer archivist/
librarian Alice Applebaum.

Benjamin Eger, 1875-80
Tobias Schanfarber, 1885-87
Clifton H. Levy, 1887-89
Edward Benjamin Morris
    Browne, 1890-91
Emanuel Schreiber, 1892-1897
Julius Meyer, 1898-1900
Charles Freund, 1900-05
David Alexander,1905-19
Rudolph Coffee, 1919-21

Samuel Harris, 1921-24
Joseph Kornfeld, 1924-34
Leon Israel Feuer, 1935-75
Alan Sokobin, 1972-92
Samuel Weinstein, 1992- present

Tobias Schanfarber,
1885-87

Charles Freund, 1900-05

Edward Benjamin Morris
Browne, 1890-91

Samuel Harris, 1921-24

Julius Meyer, 1898-1900

Joseph Kornfeld, 1924-34

Toledo Jewish Federation Leaders

Organization name	Time period	President	Time period	Executive Director
Toledo Federation of Jewish Charities				
	1907-10	Nathan Kaufman		
	1910-13	Charles K. Friedman		
	1913-15	Henry Streetman		
	1916-17	Morris Rosenberg		
	1917-19	Isidore Silverman		
Jewish Federation of Toledo				
	1920-26	Harry Levison	1920-26	Maurice Sievers
	1926-36	Joe H. Ringold	1926-35	Joseph Wolff
	1936-40	J. Eugene Farber	1936-43	Elmer Louis
	1940-42	Dr. Lester J. Kobacker		
	1942	Eliot L. Kaplan		
	1942-46	Earl M. Rosengarten		
Jewish Community Service Association				
	1946-47	Earl M. Rosengarten		
	1947-51	Joseph H. Nathanson		

1948-52   Julian Stone
1951   Sidney Tuschman
1951-52   Jules D. Lippman

Jewish Community Council

1943-44   Harry Levison
1944-46   J. Eugene Farber
1946-47   Dr. Morton Goldberg
1947-48   Eliot Kaplan
1948-50   Lester D. Alexander
1950-51   Rabbi Melbourne Harris
1951-52   Marvin Kobacker
1952-54   Sydney Mostov
1954-55   Harvey Fain
1955-57   George S. Davidson
1957-60   Burton Silverman

Jewish Welfare Federation

1960-61   Arthur H. Edelstein
1961-64   Stanley K. Levison
1964-66   Milton F. Silverman
1966-67   Sydney Mostov
1967-70   Stanford E. Thal
1970-73   Richard L. Kasle

1969-84   Alvin Levinson

Toledo Jewish Federation Leaders continued

Organization name	Time period	President	Time period	Executive Director
	1973-75	Lawrence B. Raskin		
	1975-77	William Osterman		
	1977-79	David Katz		
	1979-81	Marilyn Steinberg		
	1981-83	John Bloomfield		
	1983-85	Joel Levine	1984-94	Steve Edelstein
Jewish Federation of Greater Toledo				
	1985-87	Robert Gersten		
	1987-89	Marla Levine		
	1989-91	James J. Akers		
	1991-93	Michael Berebitsky	1994-97	Judah Segal
	1995-96	Michael Rosenberg		
	1997-2000	Joel Beren	1997-2001	Alix Greenblatt
United Jewish Council of Greater Toledo				
	2000-02	Jon M. Levine	2001-2002	Marvin Goldberg
	2002-04	Dr. Brent Rubin	2002-2008	Joel Beren
	2004-05	Cyndi J. Rosenthal	2008	Abby Suckow
	2005-08	Stephen A. Rothschild		

Jewish Community Center Presidents

Morris Lampert	1912-20
Harvey Levinson	1920-26
Joe Ringold	1926-36
Eugene Farber	1936-40
Lester Kobacker	1940-42
Elliot Kaplan	1942
Earl Rosengarten	1942-47
Joseph Nathanson	1947-51
Sidney Tuschman	1951
Jules Lippman	1951-54
Lester Alexander	1954-57
Abe Levine	1957-59
I. R. Miller	1959-60
Milton Starsky	1960-62
Rubin Cohen	1962-64
Elliot Davis	1964-68
James Fox	1968-70
Gordon Levine	1970-72
Joel Levine	1972-73
Melvin Nusbaum	1973-75
Gary Beren	1975-77
Robert Gersten	1977-79
Charles Kaminsky	1979-81
Michael Powder	1981-83
Jeffrey Cohen	1983-85
Dr. Michael Zalob	1985-87
Jerome Phillips	1987-89
Daniel Steinberg	1989-93
Andrew Klumb	1993-95
Dr. Michael Cooper	1995-97
Robert Kripke	1997-99
Stanford Odesky	1999-2001
Richard Greenblatt	2001-2003
Jay Margolies	2003-2005

Darlington House Presidents

Joseph Ringold	1963
Dr.A.H. Steinberg	1964
Mort Goldman	
Dr. Francis Epstein	1964-65
Allen Adler	
George Glasser	
Sam Webne	1981
Roy Treuhaft	1982-83
Steve Weiner	1984-86
Marvin Jacobs	1986-88
Sandy Schafer	1989-92
Steve Dolgin	1992-93
Arnold Gottlieb	
Alan Wagner	
Michael Kadens	

Toledo Board of Jewish Education

Executive Directors:	Assistant Principals/Principals:
Morris Horwitz	Susan Dunn
Otto Baruch Rand	Tony Gerber
Arnold Carmel	Marjorie Siegel
Harvey Raben	Ken Newbury
Ed Frim	Marjorie Siegel
Garson Herzfeld	Karen Knoppow
Aviva Panush	LeeAnne Bohleke

Presidents:

Norman Rubinoff	Majorie Romanoff	Eugene Simon
Marla Levine	Howard Friedman	Linda Beren
Stanford Odesky	Carol Simon	Ricki Rubin
Frances Perlmutter	Allen Markowicz	Daniel Steinberg
Marci Klumb	Barbara Straus	Andrea Delman
Bennett Romanoff		

Jewish Family Service of Toledo

Past Presidents

Lewis R. Basch, 1950 – 52, 1956 – 60
Burt Silverman, 1952 – 53
Dr. Henry L. Hartman, 1953 – 56
Louise Greenson 1960 – 63
Myron Edelstein, 1964 – 66
Morris Fruchtman, 1966 – 68
Elliott L. Miller, 1968 – 70
Richard Gross, 1971 – 74
Edna Rosen, 1974 – 76
Leonard Simon, 1976- 77
Harold Steinberg, 1978 – 79
Gilbert Linver, 1980 – 81
Richard Greenblatt, 1981 – 83
Barry Himmel, 1983 – 85
Richard Friedmar, 1986 – 87
Gerald Resnick, 1988
Donna Greenfield, 1989 – 90
Barry Nistel, 1991 – 92
Pam Korn, 1993 – 94
Mark Jacobs, 1995 – 1996
Beverly Gottlieb, 1997 – 98
Dr. Ken Brochin, 1998 – 2000
Elliot Feit, 2000 – 03
Matt Kripke, 2003-05
Nate Segall, 2005-07

Toledo Jewish Community Foundation

Chairmen

Marvin Kobacker
Gordon Levine
Harley Kripke
Frederick Treuhaft
Donald L. Solomon

The Jewish Community of Toledo

gratefully honors these men for their service in

World War 1

LOUIS ABRAMS
SAUL ABRAMS
SAMUEL ACKERMAN
LOUIS AFTERGOOD
HARRY APPLEBAUM
WILLIAM ARENSON
SIDNEY AUSLANDER
FELIX BAER
ABE BAME
BERNARD BARCLAY
MAX BARKAN
DAVID BARRY JR.
MORRIS M. BECKER
HARRY BENDEROFF
JULIUS BENWAY
EARL BERMAN
HERSH BERMAN
LOUIS BERMAN
SAM BERNSTEIN
DR. EDWARD BINZER
ROYAL B. BINZER
MORRIS BIRMAN
MAX E. BLANK
HARRY BLANKENSTEIN
JULIUS BLOOM
ISADORE B. BLUM
ABE BOOKMAN
HERMAN BOOKMAN
JACOB B. BRACKER
ELMER CALISCH
NORMAN CALISCH
JACK CALLIF
DAVID CAPLAN
JACOB CIRALSKY
MAX CIRALSKY
MORRIS CIRALSKY
NATHAN CIRALSKY
A. NAT. COHEN
BARNEY COHEN
BENJAMIN COHEN
GEORGE COHEN
HARRY M. COHEN
HARRY S. COHEN
JOSEPH A. COHEN
MAURICE COHEN
MELVIN M. COHEN
CARL M. COHN
DR. I. R. COHN
ISADORE COHN
MORT B. COHN
RUBY COHN
HAROLD COUSINS
MAX COWEN
WILLIAM CUTLER
MORRIS DAMRAUER
DAVID D. DAVIS
EDWARD N. DAVIS
IRA I. DAVIS
MAURICE DAVIS
HARRY DOCTOR
LOUIS M. DORF
FRANK DREYFUS
MORRIS DREYFUS
HARRY EPSTEIN
JOSEPH EPSTEIN
MORRIS AARON EPSTEIN
PAUL EPSTEIN
GEORGE I. ETIGSON
ARTHUR P. FEINBERG
JULIUS F. FELDSTEIN
NATHAN FINE
LOUIS FINK
SOLOMON C. FISHER
JACOB FORASTER
HARRY FRANK
JACOB FRANK
AARON A. FREED
SIDNEY FRIEDENTHAL
BENJAMIN FRIEDMAN
BERNIE FRIEDMAN
EMANUEL FRIEDMAN

JOE FRIEDMAN
SAM FRIEDMAN
STANLEY M. FRIEDMAN
CHARLES FRUCHTMAN
LOUIS GILL
ALEX GINSBURG
OSCAR GINSBURG
JOSEPH I. GLICKMEN
JOSEPH GOEBLE
ABE GOLDBERG
JOSEPH GOLDBERG
MILTON S. GOLDBERG
LEO GOLDING
LOUIS L. GOLDING
FRED GOLDMAN
NATHAN GOLDMAN
HARRY GOLDSTEIN
IRA H. GOLDSTEIN
LOUIS GOLDSTEIN
MORRIS GOLDSTEIN
MORTON C. GOLDSTEIN
MORRIS GOODMAN
J. JAY GOULD
HERBERT GREENBERG
SOLOMAN GREENBERG
GEORGE J. GROSS
ISADORE L. HARRIS
ABE HENING
PHIL HENING
OSCAR B. HERMAN
SAM HERMAN
DR. J. B. HIRSCH
JACOB S. HOFFMAN
LOUIS HOFFMAN
JOE HOROVITZ
JAY ISAACSON
LEO KAHN
BENJAMIN KALISHER
JACOB KANDER
SAMUEL Z. KAPLAN
ADOLPH KATZ
HYMAN KATZ
PHILIP KATZ
SAMUEL A. KATZ
DAVE KAUFMAN
ISADORE KAUFMAN
MAX KLINE
J. LESTER KOBACKER
NATHAN H. KOBACKER
JACK KOZMAN
LEO KRAWETZ
HERMAN KROSNER
SAM LADERMAN
MAX S. LEITNER
DR. HENRY LESSER
PHIL LEVEY
RUBY LEVEY
ABRAHAM LEVINE
SIMON LEVINE
WM. A. LEVINE
HARRY LEVINSON
DR. L. A. LEVISON
EDWARD LEVY
HARRY G. LEVY
ROBERT LEVY
MITCHEL LIBERMAN
SAMUEL LICHTENSTEIN
WILLIAM LIEBERMAN
SAM MAERSON
LOUIS MANDEL
WILLIAM MANOFF
BEN MARGOLIS
EMIL MARKS
MORRIS MAY
A. LINCOLN MEYERS
HARRY MICHAEL
LEO MICHAEL
PHILLIP J. MONHEIT
HERMAN C. MOSS
SAMUEL NATHANSON
AARON NEWMAH

ED NEWMARK
RALPH OBERLIN
TRACY L. OPPENHEIN
LOUIS OSTERMAN
PHILIP PALEY
PHIL M. PARIS
CARL PEARLMAN
ABE PLOTKIN
MAX POPKIN
SAUL POWDER
NATHAN RAINWASSER
LOUIS H. RAPPAPORT
LOUIS A. RAYMAN
LOUIS A. RAYMAN
NATHAN RAYMAN
SAMUEL O. REMER
MORRIS RICHMAN
HARRY P. RICKLES
WILLIAM ROMANOFF
BENJAMIN L. ROSEN
NATHAN ROSEN
HENRY ROSENBAUM
EDWARD H. ROSENBERG
IRVING L. ROSENBERG
JACK ROSENBLUM
BERNIE ROSENCRANTZ
HARRY ROSENZWEIG
WILLIAM ROSUCK
WILLIAM ROTH
LEO ROTHSCHILD
PHILIP RUBEN
SAMUEL L. RUBIN
GILBERT RUDIC
ELIAS RUSSELL
BENNY SABESKY
JOSEPH SACKS
LEON SAVE
LOUIS SCHRAM
JACOB SCHULMAN
SAMUEL SCHUSTER
HENRY SCHWARTZ
WM. SCHWARTZBERG
BEN SELIGMAN
HARRY SELIGMAN
CHARLES SELKER
DAVID SHAPIRO
WILLIAM M. SHAPIRO
SAMUEL SHOEN
HYMAN SHOPNECK
ABE SIEGEL
SAM SILVER
SANDER SIMON
ROBERT J. SKOLWICK
MITCHEL A. SLESH
SIDNEY SMILACK
OSCAR J. SMITH
ARCHIE STONE
NATHAN J. STONE
JACOB SULKIN
LOUIS SUPERIOR
MAX TAVEL
MORRIS THAL
THEODORE E. THAL
DAVID TOPPER
JACK S. TREUHAFT
HENRY B. UNGAR
SAM WASSERSTROM
JOE WEINER
LOUIS WEINER
SAM WEINSTEIN
CHARLES WINEMAN
HARRY YAFFE
SAM YOUNGHEART
JACOB ZAFT
JOHN J. ZAFT
JACOB ZIATZ
MARTIN ZIEGLER
HARRY ZIMMERMAN
JOSEPH ZIMMERMAN
PHILIP H. ZIMMERMAN
ABRAHAM ZOHN
JULIUS ZOHN
MAX ZOLLER

Presented by

THE GOLDSTEIN-GOODMAN POST 6909, VETERANS OF FOREIGN WARS
and THE EDWARD N. DAVIS POST 546, AMERICAN LEGION

JEWISH COMMUNITY CENTER - NOVEMBER 13, 1966

The Jewish Community of Toledo

gratefully honors these men for their service in

World War II

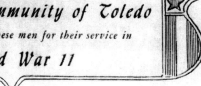

IRVING ABRAMS
ROBERT ABRAMS
SIMON ABRAMS
HAROLD ABRAMSON
CECIL ABRAMOVITZ
EARL ACK
JEROME ACK
KURT ACKERMAN
MILTON ACKERMAN
MARVIN D. ADLER
NORMAN AFTERGOOD
MELVIN ALBERT
WALTER S. ALPERT
IRVING ALLOY
SEYMOUR ALLOY
CHARLES ALPERT
WALTER ALPERT
WILLIAM ALPERT
MORRIS ALTMAN
JOSEPH ALTSCHULLER
DAVID APPLEBAUM
MYRON APPLEBAUM
EDWARD ARENSON
MITCHELL ARNSEN
SOL ARNOVITZ
LAWRENCE ARONOFF
ALICE ARONSON
HERMAN ASHNER
ABE AXONOWITZ
LOUIS AXONOWITZ
HARRY BAER, JR.
MASON BAER
SIDNEY BAIM
ISADORE BAKER
JACK BAKER
LEWIS BAKER
L. V. BAKER
HARRY BAME
MARK BARKAN
ROBERT BARON
SIDNEY BARON
LEWIS BASCH
RICHARD BASCH
ROBERT BASCH
BENJAMIN BASMAN
JOHN BATAVIA
ABRAHAM BAUER
FRANK BAUER
SIDNEY BAUER
LOUIS BAUM
MILTON BAYGELL
ROBERT BECK
PAUL BELKIN
ARTHUR A. BELLMAN
IRWIN BELLMAN
JEROME BELLMAN
BARTON L. BENDEROFF
MERVIN BERENSON
SAM BERG
GERALD BERKMAN
ISAAC BERKMAN
ALFRED BERKOWITZ
PHILIP BERKOWITZ
LOUIS BERMAN
MARVIN BERMAN
PAUL BERMAN
SHELDON BERMAN
WILLIAM H. BERMAN
DAVID BERNSTEIN
DONALD BERNSTEIN
JOSEPH J. BERNSTEIN
ALBERT BERSHON
BURT BERSHON
ROBERT BILLSTEIN
HERMAN BINZER
ISADORE BINZER
PHILIP BLACK
WARREN L. BLANK
WILLIAM BLANKENSTEIN
MEYER BLATT
JACK BLETTERMAN
DAVID BLITZ
SAMUEL H. BLITZ
SIDNEY BLITZ
PHILIP BLITZER
STANFORD BLITZER
WILLIAM BLOCK
HARRY BLOOM
JOE BLOOM
FRANK BLUM

HERBERT BLUMBERG
ALFRED BLUMENTHAL
ARTHUR BOOCHEROFF
SAM BORMAN
BERNARD BOTSCH
JULIUS BOXENBAUM
RALPH BOXENBAUM
DAVE BOXMAN
HARRY A. BOYK
HARRY BRACKER
ABE BRANDMAN
JACK BRANDMAN
MELVIN BRODSKY
ROBERT BRODSKY
SAMUEL BRODY
ALBERT BROOKENTHAL
GERALD BROOKENTHAL
RUTH BROTER
LOUIS BROWARSKY
HARRY BROWN
JEROME SAMUEL BROWN
HENRY BURSTEIN
JACK BUSTOW
MERRIL CALISCH, JR.
NORMAN CALISCH
WILLIAM A. CAMP
JOSEPH CANNON
IRVIN CARR
SAM CARTIN
BENJAMIN CHASIN
MORRIS CHASIN
BETTY CHEYFITZ
EDWARD CHEYFITZ
JACOB CLOSE
SAMUEL CLOSE
AARON YALE COHEN
HOMER COHEN
ISADORE COHEN
ALLEN COHN
MILTON COHN
MORTON R. COHN
HARRY CONN
LIONEL CONN
MELVIN CONN
STEVE CONTIS
IRVING COOPERMAN
JACK COOPERMAN
MURRAY COOPERMAN
SIDNEY COUSINS
JERRY COWEN
MAX CRADEN
DAVID CRONBERGER
ERNEST DAMRAUER
MARVIN SEEMAN DAMRAUER
BERNARD A. DAVIS
DANIEL DAVIS
DAVID DAVIS
ELLIOT DAVIS
MAX DAVIS
MEYER DAVIS
NATHAN DAVIS
ROI C. DAVIS
FRED FALK DEFRANCE
EDWIN DELON
ROBERT DIAMOND
WILLIAM DIAMOND
BERNARD DOCTOR
SEYMOUR DOCTOR
IRVING DOLGIN
LOUIS DOLGIN
NORMAN DOLGIN
NORMAN R. DOLGIN
STANLEY DOLGIN
FRANK DOOMCHIN
IRWIN DORF
SAMUEL DRESSER
ALBERT DRUBE
MARVIN DRUBE
LOUIS DWORKIN
DONALD ECKBER
PETER EDELMAN
IRVING EDELSTEIN
JAMES EDELSTEIN
JOSEPH EDELSTEIN
DANIEL EGET
JOSEPH EISER
MENDEL EISER
MILTON EISER
J. NATHAN EISER
JOE EISLER

ALEXANDER ELLISON
JACK ELLISON
EDWARD J. EPPSTEIN
JAMES EPPSTEIN
JULIUS EPPSTEIN
RICHARD EPPSTEIN
ROBERT EPPSTEIN
FRANCIS EPSTEIN
ISADORE EPSTEIN
MARVIN EPSTEIN
ROBERT EPSTEIN
WILLIAM EPSTEIN
HOWARD L. ESCH
DAVID ESSAK
DAVID ESSICK
IRVING ESSICK
MAURICE ESSICK
RAPHAEL ETIGSON
ARTHUR FAUDMAN
MAURICE BERNARD FEDER
SYLVAN FEDER
GEORGE FELDMAN
ABE N. FELDSTEIN
ABIE FELDSTEIN
ALEXANDER FELDSTEIN
BERNIE FELDSTEIN
GERALD FELDSTEIN
LEO FELDSTEIN
MORRIS FELDSTEIN
PHILIP FELDSTEIN
ARNOLD FELLMAN
FRANK FELSTEIN
HARRY FELSTEIN
JOE FELSTEIN
JULES FELSTEIN
MARTIN YALE FENIGER
NATHAN FERBER
ABRAHAM FIELDS
JOSEPH FIELDS
EDWARD FINE
TED FINE
BENNIE FINGERHUT
DAVE FINGERHUT
FRANK FINGERHUT
HERBERT FINGERHUT
ISADORE FINGERHUT
JACK FINGERHUT
WILLIAM FINGERHUT
AL FINK
ALBERT FINK
JEROME FINK
JOSEPH L. FINK
MYRON FINK
SOL FINKELSTEIN
ALEX FISHBEIN
HARVEY FISHER
HERBERT FISHER
EMANUEL FISHLER
JOSEPH FISHLER
LEONARD FISHMAN
LOUIS FISHMAN
WILLIAM FLAUM
LOUIS FORMAN
SAM FORMAN
SEYMOUR FORMAN
DAVID FRANK
DONALD FRANK
IRVING FRANK, JR.
JACK FRANK
ARTHUR FRANKEL
SHELDON FRANKEL
GILBERT FRAZEN
MELVIN FREECORN
ARTHUR FREEDMAN
BERNARD FREEDMAN
JACK FREEDMAN
EUGENE FRESHMAN
GILBERT FRESHMAN
WALTER FREY
JOSEPH MORRY FRIEDLANDER
DAVID FRIEDMAN
JOEL FRIEDMAN
MURRAY FRIEDMAN
PHIL A. FRIEDMAN
SAM FRIEDMAR
IRWIN FRUCHTMAN
LEONARD FRUCHTMAN
HARRY GADEL
JACK GADEL
ELTON GALLON

SAMUEL GANDEN
HYMAN GANIELS
DAN GARDER
DAVE GARDER
JESSE GARDER
BERNARD GARFINKEL
HYMAN D. GARRISON
ELMER GERSON
SAM GERSON, JR
ARTHUR L. GINSBURG
CHARLES GINSBURG
HYMAN GINSBURG
MATTHEW GINSBURG
ROBERT GINSBURG
ROLAND GINSBURG
ROY GINSBURG
HARRY GLASSMAN
IRVING GLASSMAN
JAY S. GLASSMAN
ALFRED GLICK
DANIEL CLUCK
LEONARD GLUCK
ABE GOLDBERG
ALEX GOLDBERG
EUGENE GOLDBERG
HAROLD GOLDBERG
HARRY L. GOLDBERG
HARRY A. GOLDBERG
LOUIS GOLDBERG
MELVIN GOLDBERG
MORRIS GOLDBERG
WALTER GOLDBERG
WILLIAM GOLDBERG
RUVIN GOLDFARB
ALFRED W. GOLDMAN
BERYL GOLDMAN
ELMER GOLDMAN
JOSEPH GOLDMAN
NAT C. GOLDMAN
NORMAN GOLDMAN
SAUL GOLDMAN
STANFORD GOLDMAN
EDWARD GOLDMANN
HARRY FRANCIS GOLDMANN
LEO GOLDNER
BEDFORD I. GOLDSTEIN
HOWARD GOLDSTEIN
MAURICE GOLDSTEIN
MORRIS GOLDSTEIN
MORRIS GOLDSTEIN
NORTON GOLDSTEIN
SEYMOUR GOLDSTEIN
SHELDON GOLDSTEIN
SHERMAN GOLDSTEIN
MORRIS GOLPER
KOLMAN GOODMAN
MORRIS GOODLEMAN
SAM GOODLEMAN
ALBERT GOODMAN
BARNEY GOODMAN
GILBERT GOODMAN
HARRY GOODMAN
MORRIS GOODMAN
NATHAN GOODMAN
NORMAN GOODMAN
DAVE GOTTHELF
FRANK GOTTLIEB
ARTHUR GOULD
BERNARD GOULD
FRED GOULD
J. I. GOULD
LEO GOULD
RICHARD GOULD
ROBERT GOULD
ROBERT GOULD
STANLEY GOULD
BEN GREEN
BEN GREEN
JOSEPH GREEN
MANUEL GREEN
MERVIN GREEN
WILLIAM GREEN
WILLIAM GREEN
DAVID GREENBAUM
JACK GREENBAUM
MEYER GREENBAUM
BERNARD GREENBERG
EARL GREENBERG
JONNARD GREENBERG
MEYER GREENBERG

Presented by

THE GOLDSTEIN-GOODMAN POST 6909, VETERANS OF FOREIGN WARS
and THE EDWARD N. DAVIS POST 546, AMERICAN LEGION

JEWISH COMMUNITY CENTER - NOVEMBER 13, 1966

The Jewish Community of Toledo

gratefully honors these men for their service in

World War II

NATHAN GREENBERG
SIDNEY GREENBERG
MEYER GREENBURG
WALTER I. GREENSON
IRVING GREENSPOON
ARMAND GROSS
RICHARD GROSS
ROBERT GROSS
SANFORD GROSS
ERNEST GROSSMAN
JOSEPH GRUBSTEIN
BERNARD GURALNICK
DONALD GUTOWITZ
LOUIS GUTOWITZ
NORTON GUTOWITZ
ALEX HAMBERG
JEROME HAMMERMAN
MELVIN HARRIS
SAMUEL R. HARRIS
SEYMOUR HARRIS
WILLIAM HARRIS, JR.
BERNARD HARRISON
MERRILL HARRISON
JOE HASCAL
MARVIN HASCAL
JACK HATTNER
LOUIS HATTNER
BENJAMIN HAUSMAN
FREDERICK HAUSMAN
JAMES HAUSMAN
WILLIAM HAUSMAN
LOUIS HEILBRUN
MAURICE HELBRANT
PHIL HELD
SOL M. HELD
MORTON HENICK
MAURICE HERMAN
CLARENCE HERTZ
JOSEPH HERTZBERG
MARTIN HERTZBERG
EDWARD S. HERZOG
JESSE S. HESLIP
WILLIAM FRANCIS HETHERINGTON
ARNOLD MORTON HEYMAN
GEOFFREY H. HIMELHOCK, JR.
JULIUS HIMELHOCK
HERMAN J. HIRSCH
LOUIS HIRSCH
STEWART HIRSHBERG
LOUIS HIRSHKOWITZ
CHRIS L. HOAK
ROBERT HOFBAUER
BEN HOFFMAN
IRWIN HOFFMAN
JACK HOFFMAN
JULIUS R. HOFFMAN
MAX HOFFMAN
OSCAR HOFFMAN
PETER HOFFMAN
MORRIS HOLTS
ABE HORWITZ
EMMANUEL HORWITZ
STANFORD HORWITZ
TOLLY HORWITZ
JULES HOUSMAN
FRANK HUBER
JEROME HYAMS
HAROLD B. IGDALOFF
HAROLD BURTON IGDALOFF
IRVING IGDALOFF
SANFORD IGDALOFF
BEN ILLMAN
IRWIN INSELMAN
SAMUEL M. ISAACS
ROBERT ISAACSON
RALPH ISENSTEIN
VICTOR ISENSTEIN
CARL JACOB
DR. ALBERT JACOBS
MARSHALL JACOBS
ALVIN LOUIS JACOBSON
HOWARD JACOBSON
JEROME JACOBSON
LOUIS JACOBSON
SIDNEY JACOBSON
HAROLD JAFFE
MAX JAFFE
MONROE JAFFEE
PHYLIS JOELSON
HOWARD JOFFA

NORMAN B. JOHNS
ALBERT JUDIS
JOSEPH JUDIS
SAM JUDIS
JACK KALE
JACOB KALISH
BERNARD KALNIZ
ALBERT KAMINSKY
JACK KAMINSKY
HERMAN KANDER
IRVING KANDER
SEYMOUR KANDER
SIDNEY KANDER
BERTON KAPLAN
DAVID KAPLAN
ELIOT L. KAPLAN
LEONARD KAPLAN
LOUIS L. KAPLAN
REUBEN KAPLAN
SAM KAPLAN
JULIAN KAPLIN
MAURY KAPLIN
RICHARD KAPLIN
THOMAS KAPLIN, JR.
HOWARD N. KARP
ALVIN B. KASLE
DAN KASLE
IRWIN KASLE
SHIRREL KASLE
TRAVIS KASLE
KENDEL KATCHER
ARTHUR KATZ
CALVIN KATZ
PHILIP KATZ
SOL KATZ
BARNEY KAUFMAN
DONALD CARL KAUFMAN
HOWARD KAUFMAN
MARVIN KAUFMAN
MARVIN L. KAUFMAN
VIRGINIA KAUFMAN
LAWRENCE KEIDAN
SAM KERKEN
EDWARD KEZUR
JEROME KIMMELMAN
WILLIAM KLATZEL
ARTHUR KLEIN
RUTH HELEN KLEIN
WILLIAM KLEIN
BERNARD KLIVANS
J. LESTER KOBACKER
MARVIN KOBACKER
NATHAN KOHLER
OSCAR KOHN
FAYE KOHN
MARTIN KOHN
ROBERT KOHN
ARTHUR IRVING KONTROVITZ
ARTHUR KOZMAN
MYRON KOZMAN
ISRAEL KREAMER
JEROME KREINBERG
KENNETH NORMAN KRIPKE
SHERWIN E. KRIPKE
DANIEL G. KROSNER
DAVID KROSNER
DONALD KROSNER
CHARLES M. KUGELMAN
SAMUEL KUPERMAN
HEINZ T. KUSNITZKY
SHELDON KUTCHER
DAVID LADERMAN
DAVID LADERMAN
EUGENE LAMPERT
PHIL LANG
NORBERT LASUS
ELIOT LATEZ
ISADORE E. LATEZ
ERICH LAUTER
WOLFGANG LAUTER
SAMUEL LEEDYN
LOUIS LEIBER
MORRIS LEIBOVICH
ABE LEIBOVITCH
BERNARD LEIBOVITZ
ISADORE LEIBOVITZ
JAMES VICTOR LENAVITT
HARRY LEOPOLD
HERMAN H. LERNER
JULIUS LERNER

GORDON LESS
LINCOLN LESS
CHARLES LESSER
EUGENE LESSER
RUTH CLAIR LESSER
SARAH LESSER
JEROME LEVETON
PHILIP LEVETON
MARK L. LEVEY
MERVIN N. LEVEY
NATHAN LEVEY
NORMAN J. LEVEY
PHIL LEVEY
DAVID K. LEVIN
SAMUEL S. LEVIN
LOUIS LEVINE
LOUIS LEVINE
SAM LEVINE
SIDNEY LEVINE
SIDNEY LEVINE
STANLEY LEVINE
EMANUEL LEVINSON
SIDNEY LEVINSON
RICHARD LEVISON
ROBERT LEVISON
STANLEY K. LEVISON
MYRON LEVISTEIN
NORMAN LEVITN
JEROME LEVITON
BERNARD N. LEVITT
EDGAR LEVITT
HARRY J. LEVY
HARRY G. LEVY
ISADORE LEVY
MERVIN N. LEVY
PHILIP LEVY
RUBY LEVY
WINSTON D. LEVY
WILLIAM LEWAND
VICTOR LEWIS
CHARLES LIBER
MITCHELL LIBERMAN
ISADORE LICHTENSTEIN
MARVIN LICHTENSTEIN
LOUIS LIEBER
HAROLD LIEBERMAN
ROBERT LIEBERMAN
JAMES LIGHT
CHARLES LINVER
IRVIN J. LINVER
JOE LINVER
RAYMOND LIPPMANN
WILLIAM LIPPMANN
LOUIS LITTLE
MAURICE LOBERT
HYMAN LONDON
J. C. LORE
LYN B. LUBELL
HARRY LUBLIN
LOUIS LUBLIN
BARNEY LUPU
NATHAN LUPU
HERMAN MAINWOLD
SAM MAINWOLD
HAROLD B. MALKIN
LEWIS MALKIN
SADIE MALKIN
WILLIAM MALKIN
BEN MANDELBAUM
EDWARD MANN
NATHAN MANN
SOLLIE MANN
ROBERT MANOFF
ISADORE MARENBERG
LEONARD MARENBERG
LOUIS MARENBERG
LOUIS MARENBERG
MARVIN MARKOWITZ
EVAN LEE MARKS
ARCHIE MARMAR
JOSEPH MARMAR
IRVING A. MATHEWS
JERRY MAY
JOSEPH MENDELSON
MILFORD MEYERS
ARTHUR P. MILLER
CARL I. MILLER
ELLIOTT MILLER
HADLEY MILLER
HAROLD MILLER

IRVIN MILLER
MURRAY MILLER
PHILIP MILLER
SIMON MILLER
WADE N. MILLER
FRANK MILLMAN
ARTHUR MILSTEIN
MORTON MILSTEIN
IRVIN MINDEL
MARVIN LEE MITCHELL
SAM MOLLE
WILLIAM MOLLE
JAMES MOHETTA
DAVID MORGAN
JOHN MORGAN
LISBETH A. MORGAN
RUBE MORTZ
STEPHEN MOSBACKER
CHARLES MOSKOWITZ
MARTIN MOSKOWITZ
ALBERT MOSS
DAVID MOSS
DAVID MOSTOV
HASCAL MUNTZ
ROBERT MUNTZ
ARTHUR E. NAGLER
WILLIAM NAPERSTICK
ALVIN NATHANSON
STANLEY NATHANSON
DONALD NAVIS
EDWIN G. NAVIS
LEONARD NEWMAN
SEYMOUR ZALE NEWMAN
ABRAHAM NEWMARK
BEN NISTEL
HARRY NISTEL
ALLEN NUSBAUM
HAROLD NUSBAUM
LOUIS J. NUSBAUM
STANLEY OBERLIN
KURT ODENHEIMER
ALEX ODESKY
DONALD OKUN
JOSEPH J. OLSON
PHILIP OLSON
SAM OLSON
LEWIS N. OSTERMAN, JR.
EDWARD PALASH
MARVIN PAPURT
PHILIP PAPURT
MARTIN PARCEL
MORRIS PARCELL
BYRON PARIS
MORRIS PARIS
BERNARD PARISKY
WILLIAM PART
JACOB PATLIN
DAVID PENN
DONALD PENN
HERBERT PERLIS
ABE PERLMAN
SHIMON PERLMUTTER
BEN PERTCHECK
RALPH PERTCHECK
MAURY PERVIN
RICHARD PERVIN
SEYMOUR PERVIN
DR. CHARLES A. PHILLIPS
DR. WILLIAM A. PHILLIPS
FRED W. PIKER
NATHAN PINE
GEORGE PINKUS
HANS POLLAK
FRIEDA POLLENS
HAROLD POHEMAN
MEYER POHEMAN
SAMUEL POPKIN
HERBERT POWDER
IRVING POWDER
BERNARD PRAGER
HAROLD PRAGER
MARVIN J. PRAGER
IRVING PRICE
HOWARD PUGH
MAURICE RABINOWITZ
JOE RACHLIN
HAROLD RAINWASSER
SAM RAINWASSER
HARRY RAISNER
SAM RAISNER

Presented by

THE GOLDSTEIN-GOODMAN POST 6909, VETERANS OF FOREIGN WARS
and THE EDWARD N. DAVIS POST 546, AMERICAN LEGION

JEWISH COMMUNITY CENTER · NOVEMBER 13, 1966

The Jewish Community of Toledo

gratefully honors these men for their service in

World War II

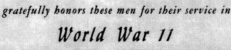

ROBERT P. RAND
LOUIS RAPPAPORT
MONROE RAPPAPORT
MORRIS RAPPAPORT
SOLOMON RAPPAPORT
ALEXANDER RAYMAN
ALVIN RAYMAN
JONAS B. RAYMAN
LAWRENCE RAYMAN
WARREN RAYMAN
ISADORE REICHLIN
ZALE M. REINSTEIN
LOUIS REMER
MELVIN L. RESNICK
ZALE REUBEN
NORMAN RICHMAN
RAYMOND RICHMAN
WILLIAM RIMAN
LOUIS ROBBINS
MORRIS ROBBINS
LOUIS ROGOLSKY
HAROLD ROMANOFF
MILFORD ROMANOFF
RICHARD ROMANOFF
MAX ROSE
WILLIAM ROSE
TONY ROSEN
HENRY ROSENBAUM
MARVIN ROSENBAUM
ALFRED ROSENBERG
DAVID ROSENBERG
ISADORE ROSENBERG
JOE ROSENBERG
WILLIAM ROSENBERG
ROBERT ROSENBERGER
HOWARD ROSENBLATT
H. JAMES ROSENTHAL
SIGMUND ROTENSTEIN
HERBERT ROTH
WILLIAM ROTH
MYRON ROTHMAN
SEYMOUR ROTHMAN
DONALD ROTHSCHILD
ALEXANDER ROTSTEIN
ARCHIE RUBIN
EVA RUBIN
SIDNEY RUBIN
MERLE R. RUBINS
ZALE R. RUBINS
GILBERT RUDICK
JAMES S. RUDOLPH
HARMON J. RUSGO
IRVING SACK
SIMON SACK
DAVE SAKA
ISAAC SAKA
JOE SAKA
LEWIS SAKS
BEN N. SALZMAN
ALFRED SAMBORN
MELVIN SANDLER
ALVIN SANGER
ALEX SATLER
BERNARD SATTINGER
SIDNEY SATTINGER
BERNARD SAXON
MINNA SAXON
BENJAMIN SCHALL
HARRY SCHALL
SAMUEL SCHALL
SIDNEY SCHALL
IRWIN SCHARF
LOUIS SCHARF
GEORGE SCHASBERGER
DAVID SCHEER
HAROLD SCHEER
IRVING SCHEINBACH
MORRIS SCHINDLER
MILT SCHNIEDERMAN
MELVIN SCHNOLL
NATHAN SCHOEN
ARNOLD SCHONBRUN
LEON SCHONBRUN
WALTER SCHONBRUN
ROBERT SCHRAGENHEIM
WALTER SCHRAGENHEIM
WILLIAM SCHULLER
ALBERT SCHULMAN
HAROLD SCHUSTER
HOWARD SCHWAB

CARL SCHWARTZ
CLARENCE SCHWARTZ
JACK SCHWARTZ
JACK L. SCHWARTZ
JOE SCHWARTZ
MAURICE A. SCHWARTZ
NATHAN SCHWARTZ
SAM SCHWARTZ
SANFORD SCHWARTZ
JOE SEGAL
ROBERT SEGAL
BENJAMIN SEGALL
CHARLES SEGALL
RICHARD SEITNEF
BERT SELIGMAN
EUGENE SELIGMAN
HYMAN SELIGMAN
IRVING SELIGMAN
MARSHALL SELIGMAN
PHILIP SELIGMAN
WILLIAM SELIGMAN
ARNOLD SELLS
SAM SELLS
MORRIS SELMAN
ABRAHAM SELRENIK
DAVID SERETSKY
BEN SHALL
MORRIS SHALL
ALBERT SHAPIRO
ALLEN SHAPIRO
EDWARD SHAPIRO
IRVING SHAPIRO
MARVIN SHAPIRO
WILLIAM M. SHAPIRO
LOUIS SHARFE
SOL SHARFE
LOUIS SHARFMAN
ROBERT SHARFMAN
BENJAMIN SHAVINSKY
BETTY SHAW
HAROLD SHAW
BEN SHENOFSKY
HARRY SHERMAN
LEONARD SHERMAN
CARL SHIFF
JAY SHIFF
JAKE SHINBACH
AL SHINIDER
NORMAN SHOFFER
GEORGE SHOPNECK
SAM SHOPNECK
FRANKLIN SHORE
IRVING E. SHORE
JACOB SHORE
BERNARD SHUER
JAY SHUER
DONALD F. SHUGARMAN
JOSEPH D. SHUGARMAN
IRVING SHYAVITZ
BERNIE G. SIEGEL
FRED SIEGEL
JOSEPH A. SIEGEL
MAJOR A. SIEGEL
ARTHUR SIGMAN
D. SILVER
JERFY SILVERBLATT
ALBERT SILVERMAN
ALEX SILVERMAN
ARTHUR SILVERMAN
ARTHUR I. SILVERMAN
BURT SILVERMAN
HENRY R. SILVERMAN, JR.
ROBERT SILVERMAN
SAMUEL SILVERMAN
WM. I. SILVERMAN
MURRAY KARL SIMON
BURTON SINGER
GERALD SINGER
MELVIN SINGER
DR. A. H. SIRAK
H. MARTIN SITZMANN
NED SKOLNICK
LAWRENCE SKUTCH
WILLIAM G. SKUTCH, JR.
DAVID SLOTNICK
HARRY SLOTNICK
BERNARD SMILACK
HARLAN SMILACK
SHELDON SMILACK
SAMUEL SMIRIN

JOS. B. SMITH
BENJAMIN SNAPP
JAY SNYDER
REUBEN SOLDINGER
ABE SOLOMON
ERNEST SOLOMON
HAROLD SOLOMON
HYMAN J. SOLOMON
SAM SOLOMON
MAX SPANGLET
WILFRED SPEVAK
MOLLY SPIRO
ROBERT STADLER
ALFRED J. STARK
STANFORD STARK
GENE STAUBER
ALFRED STEIN
NATHAN STEIN
ABE H. STEINBERG
DONALD STEINBERG
MORTON STEINBERG
NATHAN STEINBERG
RAYMOND STEINBERG
ALBERT STEINGROOT
DANIEL STEINGROOT
MORRIS STEINGROOT
ABRAHAM STEINMAN
SAMUEL J. STEINMAN
THEODORE STEPHENS
RUDOLPH STERN
DR. ERNST STERNFELD
JACK STEUER
CHARLES B. STOCKSTIEL
SAM STOHL
DAVID STONE
KENNETH STONE
MARTIN STONE
LESTER STRAM
MEYER STRAM
CLIFFORD A. STRAUS
LOUIS R. STRONG
MYRON BERNARD SUSMAN
RUBIN SUSMAN
SEYMOUR SWARTZ
ARTHUR SWEET
HAROLD SWEET
ROBERT M. SWEET
JAMES C. SYLVAN
MILTON TARLOFF
DONALD TARSCHIS
HARRY TARSCHIS
MANUEL TARSCHIS
MEYER TEITLEBAUM
DONALD TELLER
BERNARD TEMAN
MARTIN TEMAN
PHIL TEMAN
MARTIN H. THAL
STANFORD THAL
ARTHUR TOFFLER
HERMAN TOFFLER
IRVING TOPPER
MARVIN TRATTNER
RICHARD KEITH TRATTNER
JACK J. TREUHAFT
PHILIP L. TREUHAFT
ROY TREUHAFT
NORMAN B. TURE
HARRY ULLER
VICTOR ULLMAN
ALBERT USHER
OSCAR USHER
LAWRENCE VENIG
HARRY WAGNER
EDWARD WALDMAN
ISADORE WALKER
JOHN R. WALKER
LOUIS WALKER
LEONARD WARREN
EUGENE WASSERMAN
MAURICE WASSERMAN
HAROLD WASSERSTROM
PHILIP WASSERSTROM
CHARLES WATSON
MORRIS WEBNE
SAM WEBNE
HARLEY M. WEIDE
WILLIAM WEIDE
MORRIS WEINBLATT
HENRY WEINMAN

MELVIN WEINMAN
ALVIN WEINSTEIN
MARVIN WEINSTEIN
MILTON WEINSTEIN
GERALD WEINTRAUB
JULIUS WEISBERG
IRA WEISMAN
ALLEN WEISS
DAVID WEISS
LEO WEISS
SAM WEISS
NATE WELCH
ROY WENCROW
DAVE WEXLER
FRED WEXLER
GUSTAVE WEXLER
HARRY WEXLER
JOE N. WEXLER
MAX WEXLER
MORRIS WEXLER
MORRIS H. WEXLER
OSCAR WEXLER
RALPH WEXLER
ERNEST L. WHITEMAN
EDMUND WILE
ABE WILENSKY
JACK WILK
MORRIS WILK
LYNN WILLIS
ANDREW A. WINTER
WILLIAM WIRICK
MANUEL WISHNEWITZ
HYMAN WITTENBERG
MEYER G. WITTENBERG
MILTON S. WITTENBERG
SOL WITTENBERG
VALDEMIR DAVID WITTENBERG
JACK WOHLSTADTER
JACOB WOHLSTADTER
AUER F. WOLF
DR. FREDERICK WOLF
SAMUEL B. WOLFF
FRED WOLIN
GEORGE ROBERT WOLK
HARRY WOLK
ROBERT WOLK
HARRY H. WOLMAN
BERNARD B. WOLSON
MAX WOLSON
HAROLD WOODRUFF
CHARLES K. WOOLNER
RALPH WORSHTIL
HOWARD YAFFE
LEON BERNARD YAFFE
LEON H. YAFFE
SANFORD YAFFE
SEYMOUR YAFFE
STANLEY YAFFE
DAVID YERZY
EDWARD YONOVITZ
FRANK YOURIST
ISADORE YOURIST
LEO YOURIST
MORRIS YOURIST
SOL YOURIST
MILTON YURO
ABE ZAFT
ADRIAN ZAFT
ALFRED ZAFT
MORTON ZAFT
SANFORD ARTHUR ZAFT
HENRY ZANVILLE
ISADORE ZANVILLE
MARVIN N. ZANVILLE
PHILIP ZANVILLE
ROBERT ZANVILLE
FRANK ZELDEN
HENRY ZELDEN
MAX ZELDEN
FRANK ZELDON
CARL ZERNER
IVAN ZETOMER
MILTON ZIMMERMAN
MORRIS ZIMMERMAN
ROBERT ZIMMERMAN
SANFORD J. ZIMMERMAN
MAX ZISMAN
ALVIN ZOHN
LEON ZOTKOW
CARLTON ZUCKER
RALPH L. ZUCKER

Presented by

THE GOLDSTEIN-GOODMAN POST 6909, VETERANS OF FOREIGN WARS
and THE EDWARD N. DAVIS POST 546, AMERICAN LEGION

JEWISH COMMUNITY CENTER · NOVEMBER 13, 1966

The Jewish Community of Toledo

gratefully honors these men for their service in

Korean Conflict

MERLE ACK	RICHARD GROSSMAN	RAPHAEL SACHER
ARNOLD ARONOFF	RONALD HARRIS	HARRY SCHULMAN
JACK BARKAN	RICHARD HELBURN	DANIEL SHAPIRO
ROBERT BERKOWITZ	KLAUS HESS	BERNARD H. SHOCKED
JERALD BROOKENTHAL	JACK HIRSCH	LEO SHIBLE
LEONARD COHAN	WILLIAM KALB	IRWIN SILVERMAN
STANFORD CONN	ROBERT KAPLAN	RICHARD SILVERMAN
ROI DAVIS, JR.	ERWIN KATZ	DONALD SOLOMON
CHARLES DERSHER	MELVIN MANOFF	JACK STONE
SANFORD FELDSTEIN	HAROLD C. MARKS, JR.	THEODORE STONE
LEON FEUER, JR.	RICHARD METZGER	BERNARD TERMAN
MORRIS FRUCHTMAN	LOUIS MILLMAN	EDWARD THAL
BRYAN BRUCE GOEBLE	LOUIS O'DESKY	HARRY THAL
SANFORD GOLDING	FREDERIC OKUN	IRWIN R. THAL
JOSEPH GOODMAN	ALAN PORUS	NORMAN THAL, JR.
MARVYN GREENBERG	GARY PORUS	WILLIAM R. TREUHAFT
PHILIP GREENBERG	LAWRENCE RALPH RESNICK	LAWRENCE WITTENBERG
	DAVID RUBIN	MARVIN J. YAFFE

Presented by

THE GOLDSTEIN-GOODMAN POST 6909, VETERANS OF FOREIGN WARS

and THE EDWARD N. DAVIS POST 546, AMERICAN LEGION

JEWISH COMMUNITY CENTER - NOVEMBER 13, 1966